GIRLS WHO LIKE BOYS
WHO LIKE BOYS

GIRLS WHO LIKE BOYS WHO LIKE BOYS

True Tales of Love, Lust, and Friendship
Between Straight Women and Gay Men

• • • • • • • • • • • • • • • • • •

EDITED BY

Melissa de la Cruz & Tom Dolby

DUTTON

DUTTON
Published by Penguin Group (USA) Inc.
375 Hudson Street, New York, New York 10014, U.S.A.
Penguin Group (Canada), 90 Eglinton Avenue East, Suite 700, Toronto, Ontario M4P, 2Y3, Canada (a division of
Pearson Penguin Canada Inc.); Penguin Books Ltd, 80 Strand, London WC2R 0RL, England; Penguin Ireland,
25 St. Stephen's Green, Dublin 2, Ireland (a division of Penguin Books Ltd); Penguin Group (Australia), 250
Camberwell Road, Camberwell, Victoria 3124, Australia (a division of Pearson Australia Group Pty Ltd); Penguin
Books India Pvt Ltd, 11 Community Centre, Panchsheel Park, New Delhi – 110 017, India; Penguin Group (NZ),
67 Apollo Drive, Rosedale, North Shore 0745, Auckland, New Zealand (a division of Pearson New Zealand Ltd);
Penguin Books (South Africa) (Pty) Ltd, 24 Sturdee Avenue, Rosebank, Johannesburg 2196, South Africa
Penguin Books Ltd, Registered Offices: 80 Strand, London WC2R 0RL, England

Published by Dutton, a member of Penguin Group (USA) Inc.

First Printing, May 2007
10   9   8   7   6   5   4   3   2   1

Compilation © 2007 by Melissa de la Cruz and Tom Dolby

Foreword © 2007 by Armistead Maupin; Introduction © 2007 by Melissa de la Cruz and Tom Dolby; "That Unset-
tling Feeling" © 2007 by Mike Albo; "The Long Trip Home" © 2007 by Zakiyyah Alexander; "Everything I Always
Wanted to Know About Sex (and Life) I Learned from Gay Men" © 2007 by Stacey Ballis; "My Fairy Godfathers" ©
2007 by Cecil Castellucci; "Get This" © 2007 by Cindy Chupack; "Love in Other Lifetimes" © 2007 by Anna David;
"A Manhattan Love Story" © 2007 by Melissa de la Cruz; "Future Perfect" © 2007 by Tom Dolby; "Fag Hags: The
Laughter, the Tears, the Marabou" © 2007 by Simon Doonan; "Man's Best Friend" © 2007 by David Ebershoff; "Like
Father, Like Daughter" © 2007 by Abigail Garner; "My Dinners with Tom" © 2007 by Gigi Levangie Grazer; "Fam-
ily Albums" © 2007 by Philip Himberg; "A Harvard (Fag) Hag-iography" © 2007 by Alexandra Jacobs; "My Best
Girlfriend" © 2007 by James Lecesne; "The Good Girls" © 2007 by David Levithan; "Super Couple" © 2007 by Sarah
Kate Levy; "Shutterspeed" © 2007 by Bennett Madison; "Marriage Material" © 2007 by Wendy Mass; "Welcome to My
Dollhouse" © 2007 by Michael Musto; "Shop Girls" © 2007 by Karen Robinovitz; "Donny and Marie Don't Get Mar-
ried" © 2007 by Brian Sloan; "The Collectors" © 2007 by K. M. Soehnlein; "In Praise of Women" © 2007 by Andrew
Solomon; "Life Before Gays" © 2007 by Elizabeth Spiers; "Sitting in the Dark with My Mother" © 2007 by Zach Udko;
"Darling, I Like You That Way" © 2007 by Ayelet Waldman; "Lay It All Down" © 2007 by Edwin John Wintle

LIBRARY OF CONGRESS CATALOGING-IN-PUBLICATION DATA

Girls who like boys who like boys : true tales of love, lust, and friendship between straight women and gay men /
edited by Melissa de la Cruz and Tom Dolby.
p. cm.
ISBN 978-0-525-95017-2 (hardcover)
1. Gay men—Relations with heterosexual women—Anecdotes. 2. Friendships—Anecdotes. I. De la Cruz, Melissa,
1971– II. Dolby, Tom.

HQ76.G55 2007
306.76'62090511—dc22   2007004583

Printed in the United States of America
Set in Granjon
Designed by Leonard Telesca

To gay men everywhere
and the straight women who love them

CONTENTS

MY DINNERS WITH TOM
Gigi Levangie Grazer

MAN'S BEST FRIEND
David Ebershoff

MARRIAGE MATERIAL
Wendy Mass

III. A Fine Romance

EVERYTHING I ALWAYS WANTED TO KNOW ABOUT
SEX (AND LIFE) I LEARNED FROM GAY MEN
Stacey Ballis

LOVE IN OTHER LIFETIMES
Anna David

FUTURE PERFECT
Tom Dolby

A MANHATTAN LOVE STORY
Melissa de la Cruz

SUPER COUPLE
Sarah Kate Levy

GET THIS
Cindy Chupack

IV. Growing Up, Coming Out

THE GOOD GIRLS
David Levithan

WELCOME TO MY DOLLHOUSE
Michael Musto

V. Fathers and Daughters, Mothers and Sons

FOREWORD

Armistead Maupin

I was seventeen when I first saw *Breakfast at Tiffany's* at a movie house in Raleigh, North Carolina. Looking back, it's easy enough to see why a fledgling queer would fall for it. There was Audrey Hepburn, to begin with, so delicate and witty and spritelike that she seemed somehow . . . beyond sex. Here was a girl you could talk to all night without being expected to put out. I loved her apartment, too. That half-bathtub sofa, and the common fire escape, and the way that Audrey, when depressed, would climb through George Peppard's window and sleep with her head planted chastely on his well-muscled chest. What I loved, in effect, was a gay boy and his girlfriend.

Peppard, after all, is playing the writer character from the novella—the Truman Capote character, for heaven's sake—so despite the film's heterosexual intentions, the easy intimacy and candor and (yes) love between Holly Golightly and Paul Varjak somehow suggest two people who aren't out to fuck each other. I melt over that final wet-cat-in-the-rain kiss as much as the next person; I just can't imagine what comes next. More shopping on Fifth Avenue, I guess, more breezy banter and true confessions.

A decade later, I recognized the same chemistry between Liza Minnelli and Michael York in *Cabaret*, another story about an urban apartment house and its polyglot residents, though (I'm embarrassed to admit) I was just as ignorant of its queer creator, the great Christopher Isherwood, as I had been of Capote at the dawn of the sixties. Isherwood's writer alter ego in *Goodbye to Berlin*—the 1939 source material for *Cabaret*—remains coy about his own sexuality while tracking his platonic friendship with the quirky Sally Bowles. The film, of course, makes it clear that its handsome hero likes boys and that Sally adores him for it, though this revolutionary concept is eventually blunted by a drunken tryst between Minnelli and York that left me, frankly, a little queasy.

By then, I was already living in San Francisco and had girlfriends of my own. One was a struggling actress like Sally/Holly; another a rusty-haired mother of two who called me Babycakes, and who, upon receiving my quavering confession of homosexuality, snorted "Big fucking deal." With both women I shared everything: my exploits at the baths (largely joyful) and the heartbreak that inevitably followed when I tried to turn playmates into lovers. I was almost thirty by then, but I was braving the masculine wilderness for the first time, so it helped immensely to have women on my side. And since sex and romance were not factors in our relationship, we were free to open our hearts—or spill our guts—when joy or catastrophe demanded it.

Such friendships were rarely celebrated back then, so I knew they would make perfect fodder for *Tales of the City*, the daily serial I launched in the *San Francisco Chronicle* in 1976. In my own variation on the urban apartment house—28 Barbary Lane—a young queer named Michael Tolliver takes devilish glee in scandalizing his friend, Mary Ann Single-ton, a bright young naif fresh out of Cleveland. Inhabiting both these characters came naturally to me, since, if the truth be known, I *was* both of them. I was a wide-eyed newcomer like Mary Ann and a randy gay blade like Michael, though the decadent poses I struck for my straight girlfriends were often a cloak for my own insecurities, making me, I suppose, more akin to Sally and Holly than their more sensible male companions. Michael, therefore, would need someone to call him on his shit, someone older and less blindly sentimental. Enter Mona Ramsey, a world-weary lude-popping lesbian who'd tried a few men and found them decidedly lacking. Both Mary Ann and Mona would hold a mirror to Michael's dreams, just as he would do for them.

That was over three decades ago, so the notion of women bonding with gay men is far less exotic than it used to be. Which is not to say that the experience is any less rewarding or complex or richly amusing as it always was. The essays in this book, as widely varied as life itself, stand in vivid counterpoint to the clichés that popular culture has already codified about gay men and the women in their lives. They remind us once again that neither gender nor sexuality can ever fully dictate the tenants of our hearts.

INTRODUCTION

The two of us are sitting in a banquette in a dimly lit bar down-town. Throughout our friendship, we will meet in many more dark, trendy bars, the type that, as former nightlife reporters, we both favor. We drink Pimm's cups or champagne, vodka highballs or frozen cosmos. We meet at the Hudson Library, Fez, Pastis, and G in New York, the Standard, the Chateau Marmont, and the Formosa in Los Angeles. Our rendezvous have an escapist air—tucked away from the outside world, we can indulge our love of swanky surroundings, stiff cocktails, and gossip. We must look like a couple, our heads leaning in toward each other, quietly laughing. It occurs to us that we embody the quintessential urban marriage—a gay man and his straight female friend.

When we first met, Tom was twenty-four and Melissa was twenty-seven. Our relationship started as editor to writer, but soon deepened into lasting intimacy, thanks to a flurry of e-mails covering everything in our lives from personal triumphs and crises to vacation reading lists to esoteric pop cultural dish. Even as we've lived on different coasts for the past five years, our friendship has intensified, our exchanges marked with an unwavering support for each other's literary ambitions, a rare and unexpected gift between writers. We are colleagues, confidants, kindred spirits, and each other's greatest cheerleaders.

In the summer of 2005, we spent a heavenly week together in Lake Tahoe, California, a relaxing interlude with both of us working on our latest books, talking shop, grilling up fajitas, and lazily sunning on the dock. Melissa had big news for Tom and his family—she and her husband Mike were three months' pregnant. Everyone toasted Mel and Mike and this exciting new chapter in their lives.

A few weeks later, when Mel suffered a miscarriage, Tom was one of the first people she told. His strength and unfailing optimism helped her through one of the toughest times in her life. As she worked through her sadness, it occurred to Mel that she had never encountered a book that documented and explored a friendship like theirs—the deep and loyal bond that exists between straight women and gay men. She proposed that they put together an anthology of personal essays about the subject, and was thrilled when Tom was as enthusiastic about the idea as she was. (We are also happy to report that Mel had a beautiful baby girl just as this book was going to press.)

When we first conceived of this project, we wanted to show the many ways in which this friendship can manifest. Of course there would be stories, the type celebrated in popular fiction, films, and television, of the single girl-about-town and her gay best friend going on shopping sprees and bonding over brunch. But we knew not all relationships fit this mold. While many of our contributors embrace the classic "fag hag" archetype, claiming it and reinventing it as an empowering moniker of their own, others have created new and unusual paradigms of friendship, love, and solidarity.

Girls Who Like Boys Who Like Boys is divided into five sections, each dealing with a different aspect of this special relationship. "Gays and Gals" focuses on group dynamics, whether it's a gaggle of frivolous fashionistas or lifelong friends who have helped each other through infatuation and heartbreak. "Close Confidants" is about those one-on-one relationships that are the bedrock of many a straight woman and gay man's life, whether they're in Hollywood, the New York theater world, or the Ivy League. "A Fine Romance" is filled with stories of love and lust, from mixed signals and comic misunderstandings to well-intentioned advice and tearful resignation. "Growing Up, Coming Out" covers friendships that started in the formative years, with outcast girls and misfit guys banding together. And the final section, "Fathers and Daughters, Mothers and Sons," is about the ties that bind, as friendship and family are redefined, often with hilarious and poignant results.

Girls Who Like Boys Who Like Boys: True Tales of Love, Lust, and Friendship Between Straight Women and Gay Men is a book we have always wanted to read. We hope it makes a powerful statement about alliances between the gay and straight communities at a time when many in our country are striving to be divisive.

We hope you too will find your stories reflected in these pages, though we realize that one book could never cover the plethora of relationships that exist between gays and their gals. It is our wish as well that others will keep writing and talking about this topic, as it's one that's close to our hearts. Come visit us online at www.girlswholikeboys.com, where you can learn about readings, special events, and our online musings on the interplay between gay men and their gals. We can't wait to meet you, either in person or virtually, as you, the real-life gay guys and their gal pals, are the readers for whom this book was created.

—Melissa de la Cruz and Tom Dolby
Los Angeles and New York

1

• • • • • • • • • • • • • • • •

Gays and Gals

*"For a girl with delusions, and a bit of imagination,
becoming a fag hag was the only way to go."*

—from "Fag Hags: The Laughter, the Tears, the Marabou,"
by Simon Doonan

SHOP GIRLS

. . . .

Karen Robinovitz

Save for my husband, I scare men. Straight men, anyway.
They never seem to get me—and I'm not saying this just because
a few of my past boyfriends have actually said, "I don't get you."

But the gays, they're another story.

From the time I was in nursery school, I have been something of a
fag hag. The little boy I told my mother I'd marry when I was five?
Gay. Growing up, my best guy friend, the one I'd sit with on my front
lawn, watching all the neighborhood guys play football as we quietly
provided critical commentary on their choice of wardrobe? Gay. The
first boy I kissed with tongue, the summer before sixth grade? Gay. The
fifteen-year-old Ping-Pong prodigy at Environ, a retirement refuge for
Jewish grandparents in Fort Lauderdale, circa 1985, whom I was hopelessly in love with? Gay, gay, gay! The jury's still out on my junior
year prom date, but I'm going with gay. He was, after all, the one who
picked out my hot pink and black jet beaded ensemble and called it a
"lambada dress."

Today I am happily married and have a fabulous husband, a manly
motorcycle racer from Brooklyn who does get me. He's also not at all

homophobic, which is good since we live near Christopher Street, home of the bridge and tunnel gays who ogle him whenever we walk by. Other than him, every male I gravitate toward is a friend of Dorothy, a Mary, or a queen—with the occasional big lumberjack shirt-wearing muscle bear for good measure.

My friends have mused that my love affair with boys who like boys is out of safety—there's no threat, no fear of rejection. The usual pop psychology tropes.

I wholeheartedly disagree, as does my therapist, who is, for the record, gay.

It's all about fashion. Yes, fashion. My gays and I share a bond that runs deep and often into superficial subject matters such as luxury labels, discussing what celebs wear (we're harsher than any tabloid—eat, Nicole, eat!), and Kate Moss obsessions (like me, they rip tear sheets from magazines and mimic what she's wearing—be it sailor jeans and a tucked-in gray T-shirt or jean shorts and a brown leather bomber jacket, sometimes even her red patent booties—yes, I am talking about the boys wearing those things, even down to the dresses in some cases). We revel in how Nicolas Ghesquierre of Balenciaga's sartorial idealism has changed our lives and who's got the best costumes on *So You Think You Can Dance*, a show that only my gay friends and I can give the excitement it deserves (we try those hip-hop moves while the girls watch in horror as we fall flat—and we have the bruises to prove it). I don't know why, but the girls in my life are not into frivolity to the obsessive level that leads my gays and me to chat rooms, reading up on our favorite contestants, and forwarding one another online photos we find of last year's dance contest runner-up Travis in pink girl's panties.

With girls, it's not the same. They don't let themselves go with the same reckless abandon that gay men do. Of course, not all gay men care about the new collection of limited edition Marc Jacobs T-shirts or channeling Dorothy Draper when doing their apartments, but for the ones I keep in my inner circle, such conversations are serious business akin to giving stock tips to Martha Stewart.

Don't get me wrong: My gays have also been there for me emotionally, for every breakup, failure, and career mishap. (And they are excellent spooners, at that.) We even talk intelligently about the situation in the Middle East (Hezbollah aside, apparently women in Saudi Arabia are obsessed with fragrance and layer it on as a way to assert their personal style under their modest covered-up garb), global warming (we agree: Gore should really lose some weight and eat organically if he's going to walk the walk), and babies (I pray I have at least one boy who likes boys).

It's just that the politics of fashion are different with my girlfriends, even the ones who are, like me, in the industry. With women, there is an underlying competitiveness that doesn't exist with the gays. Whether we're covering the New York fashion shows or hitting our favorite stores in search of yet another chic everyday black coat, I have found that girls either secretly want your ass to look fat or to one-up you. And they always bring their baggage along for the ride. Girls don't just look at the way a dress fits you; they have to deliver a whole analysis about how it will fit into your life.

I took a very good friend of mine—I'll call her Isabella (she needs a fashionista name, even if it's a pseudonym)—to a handbag showroom in order to buy the most luxurious python bags at wholesale, half of what they were at Bergdorf's. We spent hours carefully editing down our favorites, a difficult task considering there were about a dozen bags we were both dying for and our bank accounts could only accommodate one. I managed to get it down to two bags—an oversized hand-painted silver rectangular number and a bright pink and red tie-dyed tote that, while hardly a basic, would make an outfit pop.

The pink and red was a sample, never produced. There was only one in existence; I'm a sucker for having the only one of something, no matter how impractical. "You will wear the silver soooo much more," Isabella urged. "The other is so hot, but you'll get sick of it."

She had a point. Eighty-five percent of what I own are what my husband calls "concert costumes": look-at-me-wear-it-once-only items. These clothes are appropriate for the cocktail and fashion parties I cover, but then I often end up complaining about not having anything to wear for, say, lunch on Sunday afternoon.

Maybe Isabella was right. Silver was really what I needed, so I bought it. But the morning after, I suffered from regret. I was walking out the door in jeans and a white sweater with a hugely dramatic cowl neck and thought, damn, that red-and-pink bag would look sick with this!

I called the designer to trade.

"Oh, I'm sorry. Isabella came back and bought the red and pink, too," she cooed.

She did what? I felt so cheated. When I asked Isabella about it, she made up some story about how her husband got it for her as a Christmas gift. I wasn't buying it—and that was the last time she got an invitation for showroom privilege with me.

Every one of my gays would have told me to get the red bag! The gays have no ulterior motives. They don't want to fuck me. They don't want to be me. All they want is for me to look good. They go through racks for me with the laser focus of a fashion sniper. They will deliver wrath with a mere glance to any salesperson who mistreats me. Most importantly, they never pass judgment when I creatively finance something I have to own by finagling it on three credit cards and a borrowed hundred dollars.

"It's like gambling" was the advice I got from two wise gays once. "Shuffle the credit cards, have a poker face, and look confident when you can't afford something."

Shopping with gays is my prom-queen moment—when we're out together, you'd think we were Marie Antoinette and her court (as played by Kirsten Dunst and a host of handsome actors, of course). As I try on heels, my gays squeeze their size-eleven feet into the same shoes. They hold my handbags more gracefully than I do. A few have been known to roll around the floor of a dressing room swathed in chiffon Oscar de la Renta one minute, and try on the latest skinny jeans in my size the next. They all have perfect size 2 or 4 bodies; the bitches look better than I do! My gays are all about encouraging me to go for the ridiculous big-ticket item just because it's deee-vine. They understand that one piece that makes you feel amazing is better than ten pieces that are "eh."

A certain voluminous Lanvin dress, so overpriced that I asked the salesgirl to throw away the receipt and lie to me about the total, comes to mind. Plus, it was so large it would look big on Andre Leon Talley.

"Giiirrrlll, it's fabulous! You have to have it. You can pull it off. Oh, please! Look at you. You're fierce. You work it better than SJP. It's an iconic piece," was what my pusher Don said when I was in doubt.

"But where will I wear it? It's an occasion piece and I have no occasion."

"Um, the grocery store! Brunch! Occasions are a state of mind," he said.

Now tell me, what straight male or female would say such a thing?

I did get "Big Red," as I affectionately call her, though I have yet to introduce her to an admiring public at large. But she sure does look lovely hanging in my closet, sandwiched between a wildly graphic Gaultier Mexican-inspired blue dress with a built-in petticoat (worn once to a salsa lesson with a gay man who generously loaned me his skills when I needed to practice for my wedding and my fiancé was out of town) and a white, strapless, curly ostrich-feathered number that I wore to the White Party in New York last year. On the night of that gay bacchanal, I found myself on the receiving end of more attention than a postbaptism baby in church.

A big hat? The gays will tell me to bring it on, while my girlfriends tend to think it's too much. Uncomfortable shoes? The gays, like me, believe that there's no other kind, while my girlfriends tend to err on the side of practical. Is it any surprise that my all-time favorite shoe designer, Christian Louboutin, is an openly gay man whom I am obsessed with? Or that I am in love with all things made by Philip Treacy, the very gay milliner known for hats that resemble intricate sculptures of museum quality? I think not.

When I was getting married in April of 2006, I didn't want bridesmaids. I had bridesgays. Why? Well, for one, when I was in three gay weddings last year, none of the brides (some of them call themselves brides, it's true) asked me to traipse down the aisle in a taffeta bridesmaid number so hideous even the Salvation Army wouldn't take it!

One of my gays generously offered to accompany me to go lingerie shopping for my honeymoon, though I ended up spending the day help-ing him pick out a harness for a leather daddy convention in Chicago (I was called to the dressing room for cock ring 911). Another was on call for tablecloth, linen, and floral approval with the event designer. My team of bridesgays never rolled an eye, complained, or pulled any kind of high maintenance routine, cock ring moment notwithstanding. Instead, they were incredibly supportive—even offering free blow job lessons at the bachelorette party! And let's not forget that they gave the best bridal shower and wedding gifts.

My bridesgay-of-honor was in charge of attending my bridal fittings in order to learn how to get me into my complicated, one-of-a-kind, custom-made Zac Posen gown (I realized after the second fitting that there was no way I could attempt such a feat alone). During that year of manic wedding planning, Zac became my fairy godmother of couture.

While I appreciate Vera Wang for what she does, the idea of being in an estrogen-laden bridal salon—no, thanks. I'm a girl's girl all the way: I support my girlfriends unconditionally, lending them everything from my not-yet-worn clothes and a sympathetic ear during breakups and ca-reer dramas to my husband for fix-it emergencies (the man is good with a hammer!) and dating advice if need be. In high school, I always shared my notes. But an all-female bridal frenzy would have been too anxiety provok-ing. (Handling my mother was enough!) I didn't have the strength to take on other women's issues with weddings, marriage, and fertility. After all, as soon as you get the ring, they all start asking about procreation.

I figured that the only person whom I could really trust with my dress would be a gay man. And Zac represented whimsy, fantasy, a beautiful escapism. Only he would understand my need to look like a flamenco queen chic enough for a proper Great Gatsby moment, even if the pet-ticoat would get in the way of every twirl on the dance floor. The dress he made me was a glorious confection that combined twenties refinement with cascading tiers of pleated silk tulle, trimmed in pom-poms, complete with a glamorous cowl back. Heaven! As much as I adored the gown, it wasn't the easiest to walk in, but as my gays say, "When it comes to fashion, walking is overrated, but a little champagne will take care of that."

Since I tend to be a heady neurotic type who could give Woody Allen a run for his Zoloft, my gays have a magical way of bringing light and laughter to my world. While primping in the bridal suite hours before my wedding, my girlfriends (they weren't in the wedding party, but they were on hand to play in the bridal suite) and I relaxed as the team of hair stylists and makeup artists went to work. We were all talking quite seriously about relationships, communication issues, and the self-help book *Getting the Love You Want*.

In a surreal moment, just as I craved some levity, in walked Don and Thom, two beautiful, chiseled gay men who had donned white Gatsby-inspired dinner jackets. They popped the Cristal, put Sheila E.'s "The Glamorous Life" on the stereo, and swiped blush brushes from the makeup artist, handing them to everyone in the room as if they were microphones.

They grabbed my mother, still in her robe, to dance. They threw confetti. They screeched gleefully over the (borrowed) diamonds I was planning to wear. My girlfriends are a fun bunch, but not one got up to dance. They sat, almost self-consciously, nibbling at carrots and taking photos with their camera phones. I begged them to get up and shake it, but I had no such luck. Don and Thom were giving the room life, getting the energy flowing. As they ripped off their shirts, I realized that they were turning my wedding day into the madly blissful party it was supposed to be.

"Girl, you're getting married. Get your ass up and dance! This is your theme song," Don said, before belting out the chorus of the eighties pop song I lived for as an eighth-grader. *"She wants to lead the glamorous life. She don't need, a man's touch!"*

A few hours later, as I walked down the aisle with my nervous dad, getting ready to give myself to my husband, I thought about Don and Thom for a second and turned my slow walk into a supermodel's sashay. I nearly tripped, only saving myself by shouting out, "It's not easy to be graceful in couture!"

Sam, one of my bridesgays, yelled out, "It doesn't matter. You look fabulous!"

All 167 guests burst out in laughter.

That's my love affair with the gays: No matter how often I fall, my crew of boys who like boys will always be on hand to prop me back up in my four-inch heels.

FAG HAGS: THE LAUGHTER, THE TEARS, THE MARABOU

• • • • • • • • • • • • • • • •

Simon Doonan

I once knew a fag hag called Ginger. One day she lost her mind and stuffed her fur coat in the oven. Then she turned the oven on high. It smelled horrible. The fur coat was destroyed, but Ginger wasn't. She eventually recovered.

Fag hags in 1970s London were resilient. They were young and silly and often drunk, just like us fags.

I consider myself fortunate to have been born a happy-go-lucky card-carrying fag. If, for whatever reason, I were to have been denied this privilege, then I would have settled for being the next best thing: a fag hag.

Maxine, Eve, Pamela, Jeanine, Hattie! Where are you now? Where are the great fag hags of yore? And why did they disappear? Like 8-track cassettes and princess phones and Idi Amin, the fag hag, as I knew her, is a thing of the past. She's an obsolete concept. An extinct species. She's very last century, dahling! *Haggus fagulous* ceased roaming the earth about a quarter of a century ago. The 1970s was, in fact, the golden age of the fag hag. I know whereof I speak. I was fag to many a hag.

It all made perfect sense at the time. The smartest, most sensible thing you could do back then, if you were a single working-class girl, was to get a job in a fag-rich environment, be it a hair salon or a department store. Then, with the encouragement and support of your new coterie of fags, you could henna your hair, buy a few Bowie and T. Rex albums and an electric blue jumpsuit, and become a raging, screaming, eyebrow plucking, feather boa totin', fishnet lovin', cocktail quaffing, cigarette holder manipulatin' fag hag.

Fag hags emerged from the working classes. Upper-class gals never became fag hags. Why would they? Their idyllic lives were a montage of privilege, country houses, tweed skirts, hunt balls, and dinner parties with Clarinda and Arabella and Sebastian. No such guaranteed delights awaited a working-class gal—a Sharon, a Sheila, or a Shirley. If she didn't watch out, she could easily find herself pulling entrails out of chickens' bums in a factory for the rest of her life. To avoid this fate, Sharon or Sheila or Shirley had to do something drastic.

Becoming a fag hag was something you did if life handed you a second-class ticket and you had a deep-seated, unshakeable feeling that this was the wrong ticket and that you might be a lot more comfy if you were able to sneak into that tarted-up, squishy, velvet-draped first-class carriage. For a girl with delusions and a bit of imagination, becoming a fag hag was the only way to go. Instead of a nylon chicken-gutting uniform, you could wear a cape made of jet-black, glazed cock-feathers with a spot-veiling fascinator covering your eyes, like Marlene Dietrich in *Shanghai Express*, and you could stare at the world with an amused, heavy-lidded, irony-drenched gaze.

Life as a fag hag was camp and fizzy and fun. You could jump on the sequined coattails of gay boys, gay boys who could cross socioeconomic boundaries. We gay boys could take you places or at least make you feel that you might stand a chance in hell of *going places*! Even if we were standing still, hanging out with us fun-loving perfumed nellies was so much more appealing than dealing with smelly beer-drinking straight blokes—the ones we gay boys often had our eyes on—who just wanted to beat each other up and whose idea of a romantic night out was to shag Shirley, Sheila, or Sharon up against a wall behind the pub.

We 1970s gay boys were insanely more fun to be around, and unlike uncouth straight boys, we got invited to things. We knew about things. We knew about people, people like Yma Sumac and Yves Saint Laurent and La Lupe and Kiki de Montparnasse and the Marchesa Casati and Nancy Cunard, the rebel aristo who had a penchant for black men and wore hundreds of ivory bracelets right up to her armpits. We were common and lowborn but we had a natural instinct for ferreting out fabulous historical tidbits and eccentric personalities from our culture. We smoked colored cocktail cigarettes and found humor in everything and wore outré outfits and did whatever the fuck we wanted to. If skinhead gangs chased us and called us "bloody poofs," we jumped on buses that were going in the wrong direction to get away and then giggled about it.

The fag hag took her cue from the fag: Armed with her faggotry, she side-stepped the grim demands of adult life. She found a way to feel very grown-up and glamorous—her look was often a pastiche of Hollywood grown-up glamour—while simultaneously prolonging the innocence of childhood dress-up.

The fag hags that I knew were all flashy dressers. Jerry Hall, Bianca Jagger, Tina Chow, Paloma Picasso, Loulou de la Falaise, Zandra Rhodes, Marisa Berenson, The Pointer Sisters, Angie Bowie, Amanda Lear, these were the idols and role models for my fag hags. It is possible that there were dowdy, frumpy fag hags with Iris Murdoch–bowl haircuts and flannel skirts and thick underwear and crummy eyewear, but I seriously doubt it. To be a fag hag in seventies London was to wear cat-eye glasses and be in a perpetual state of readiness to be discovered and shot for the cover of the next Roxy Music album. To be a fag hag meant you were out twirling a feather boa, on display, every night of the week.

We—me and my fags and fag hags—hung out at gay pubs like the Vauxhall Tavern and The Black Cap and small groovy clubs like The Masquerade and Chaguaramas. Our fave was a tatty club with a light-up dance floor on Kensington High Street called The Sombrero. It was piss elegant and posey, which perfectly matched the mood of fashion at the time—very art deco, if you know what I mean. When the massive Biba store—one of the largest employers of fag hags in British history—opened across the street, The Sombrero was packed with boys with pomaded hair and Bakelite bracelets and girls in suede platforms and smoky eyes and, for the thinner fag hag, leopard-print belts that were about a foot wide. Fags and fag hags believed in the transformative power of accessories.

Trish wore marabou mules from Frederick's of Hollywood and carried a vintage hatbox instead of a regular purse. It had two pom-poms on the top and was a nightmare to get things in and out of but great for stashing a small bottle of gin. There was a gal called Irene, a hairdresser, who was the first person I knew to adopt a Louise Brooks–Anna Wintour hairdo. She wore men's silk pajamas (very Claudette Colbert), high, vintage, suede stilettos, and Chanel pearls. Paula collected important vintage. She owned an entire outfit—complete with turban and peacock feathers—by Paul Poiret. She could also do the fifties Dior New Look because she was thin. Chubby fag hags like Cherie and Yvonne did the Carmen–YSL–cigarette-girl thing with forgiving but tempestuous off-the-shoulder blouses and red, tiered taffeta skirts and fans.

When she roamed the earth, the fag hag was more than just a fashion poseur: She was formidable, especially after a few drinks.

My fag hags lived for champagne and cocktails. Don't judge them. You too would rely on the tranquilizing effects of alcohol if you were young and excitable and libidinous and had to continually sublimate your sexual feelings for your constant and indifferent gay male companions.

Each of my fag hag friends had a special signature drink, usually something brightly colored and sickly. We're talking drinks with fancy French names in lurid colors like parfait amour and crème de menthe. If, after a few drinks, a fag hag heard another fag hag ordering her signature drink, she would get irate: "Why do you have to order my drink? Get your own. Why don't you have a pint of lager? You butch slag!"

After drinking too much, a fag hag would often vomit. This was not unusual, especially in 1970s England. The food was horrible and rotten, and everyone drank too much. Everyone was vomiting. Along with being the golden age of the fag hag, this was also the golden age of vomit.

I remember a fag hag called Lou. Lou modeled her look on Betty Page—very dominatrix—black bangs and a leopard trench like a fifties stripper. One night, in the back of a taxi, she vomited into her purse, which was a shame since it was a beautiful vintage purse. She had her reasons. She knew that if you threw up in a London taxi, you were immediately driven to the taxi depot and forced to hose and clean the cab for hours until it was spotless. Fag hags were good at weighing their options. Lou chose to ruin her purse over hours of scrubbing.

Like many fag hags, Lou was an anything-for-a-laugh show-off and a daredevil who loved a good practical joke. One night, after getting locked out of her flat in Kings Cross, she woke up a neighbor whom she knew had a set of ladders. Batting her eyelashes, she demanded that he climb up into her flat and then open her front door from the inside. Seeing an opportunity for a good chuckle, Lou added an extra zing to the escapade by directing her Good Samaritan to climb into the wrong flat, thereby scaring the hell out of a sleeping senior citizen. This was deemed to be very funny. Lou lay on the sidewalk and laughed and laughed till she vomited.

Lou once shagged my roommate—a cross-dressing cabaret artist—and left big passionate scratches down his back. This whole incident shocks me even to this very day. When he arrived home the next morning and showed me these marks of passion, I nearly dropped my cigarette holder. Some fag hags had a knack for getting gay boys, even nellie cross-dressers, to shag them. Alcohol seemed to play a big part in these dodgy couplings. Even allowing for the booze, I did not really understand this. I never shagged a fag hag or a female of any description. No amount of alcohol would have been enough. This probably puts me at the far end of the straight-fag continuum.

Nevertheless, I had some odd experiences with women. There was a boring girl in a duffle coat called Leslie who used to pounce on me and tell me she was madly in love with me and that she was ready to leave her boyfriend. She was a specific genre: a gal who, out of the blue, randomly fell in love with a gay man and pined for him and stalked him. I never thought of these girls as fag hags. I thought of them as idiots.

I found the situation with Leslie incomprehensible and sinister. Whenever she came barging into the flat where I was living, I would jump out the kitchen window and run off down the alleyway in my Bata platforms and Mr. Freedom oxford bag trousers, leaving my roommates to console her. I used to hide in the nearby cycle sheds for hours waiting for her to bugger off home. Looking back, I realize now that the cycle sheds were made of asbestos. If I ever develop some horrible lung disease, I shall hold her personally responsible.

One day, fashion changed and those vintage dresses and poodle hairdos and MGM fox furs started to look démodé. Trendy girls were dyeing their hair pink and shoving safety pins through their cheeks and walking down the Kings Road wearing trash bags and ripped stockings. In one fell swoop, punk killed everything that preceded it, including the fag hag.

For me, it happened one night at the aforementioned Sombrero. It was 1977, the peak of punk, the year of the queen's Silver Jubilee. I was accompanied by several fags and a fag hag called Denise who was in full punk vinyl. Her hair looked like a tornado of bleached scrambled egg. It wasn't really a beehive. It was more like an explosion in a mattress factory. She had made a dress out of Union Jack tourist shopping bags and Scotch tape. She wore ripped white fishnets and black-patent porno shoes from a sex shop in Soho. She looked brilliant.

The pissy Spanish bloke on the door took one look at Denise and told her to take a hike.

"You hate me because I'm a woman!" said the combative Denise, trying out some poorly rehearsed, unfamiliar feminist rhetoric. (We fags and fag hags were very apolitical. We never owned TVs or read newspapers.)

"I bet if I was a man you would let me in," continued Denise.

"You're not a woman. You're not a man. You're a *mess*!"

Denise grinned from ear to ear.

"Finally, a compliment!" she said, and we all about-turned and left, never to return.

We jumped on a bus bound for the West End, and headed straight to a fab new place that Denise had heard about called Louise's where, thanks to the anarchy of punk, gay and straight and fat and thin and fem and butch had all started to mingle and merge. The punk movement was nothing if not inclusive: The only qualifications were the desire to get dressed up and to annoy people. We fags and fag hags were a shoo-in.

Overnight, the concept of the fag hag suddenly seemed as tired and dusty as a Judy Garland fan club membership card.

Will the fag hag ever come back?

It's hard to imagine a scenario where her services will be required. The world has changed. Men, straight men, have become much less obnoxious over the last few years. Some are even a bit nelly. The whole metrosexual thing has improved conditions for straight gals and eliminated the need to go screeching around with a claque of ghettoized gay men. And gay men in big cities are no longer marginalized. Hanging out with gay boys is normal and easy and does not require the kind of full-time commitment made by the great fag hags of yore.

So what happened to all my old fag hags? The Lous and Denises and Gingers? Lots of them got married or shacked up and had kids. Yes, kids. What could be more fun than having a fun-loving fag hag for a mother?

The biggest concentration of surviving fag hags—in the world, bar none—is probably to be found in Florida.

Look at that overdressed broad over there, strutting down Lincoln Road in Miami Beach, wearing leopard mules and capri pants. She's probably taking that scrawny poodle to the groomer. I bet you anything her best friend, Stephen, does her roots as a favor every other week, and her favorite Bowie album is still *Hunky Dory*.

THE COLLECTORS

● ● ● ● ● ● ● ● ● ● ● ● ● ● ● ● ● ●

K. M. Soehnlein

I had invited a handful of friends from Los Angeles—all gay men—to join me and my boyfriend, Kevin, for a weekend at my friend April's home, a small ranch house overlooking the Pacific. April hadn't previously met three of the four I'd invited, but she'd unhesitatingly agreed to host this reunion. We were a ragtag group. Jacob and Billy, in the early throes of romance, were positively moony over each other, almost to the exclusion of everyone else. Andre, struggling to sell a gay-themed screenplay, was feeling battered by the Hollywood hustle. Roger, a gregarious poet whom I'd had a distant crush on years earlier, hadn't previously met any of the others. Only April, happy to have a party delivered to her door, seemed to connect instantly with everyone.

I don't remember who suggested the game—it might have been me, trying to break the ice—but April was immediately handing out paper and pens. The game's premise: Describe your dream house. How many floors and rooms? What kind of front door? Is there landscaping? Everyone scribbled down answers before the key was revealed: Your house was your personality. The number of rooms showed how compartmentalized your identity was. The front door indicated how you greeted those who entered your life. The landscape illustrated the type of people you wanted to keep close. April's dream house was one story and sprawling, with large common areas and plenty of guest rooms—a more spacious version of the house we were in. The front door had a top that swung open, so that even strangers could be greeted face-to-face. And the landscaping? April laughed as she read what she'd written: "Fruit trees! My dream house would be surrounded by every kind of fruit tree."

We "fruit trees," circled around her, roared our approval.

Recalling that party recently, Kevin suggested that April was a "collector" of gay men. Wasn't it true that she had kept in touch with several of the guys she met that weekend? Hadn't she once claimed that her idea of heaven was a place populated by gay men (along with her husband and daughter, she had hastened to add)?

The idea of being collected, I replied, left me with a certain queasiness, as if I were an insect pinned behind glass by Dr. Kinsey, put on display for further study. "Really?" Kevin asked, knowing what an exhibitionist I am. "You don't *like* being on display?"

He reminded me of the artwork that April and her husband, Dean, have collected for years. They've made their home an eclectic grab bag containing everything from abstract landscapes to refashioned "found objects," such as a fetching party dress built from Junior Mints boxes.

To be collected in this way is to be *selected*, appreciated, chosen. To be selected means you might truly be known.

We know so little about ourselves when we are young.

I met Paul, my first boyfriend, in college, and I followed him to Manhattan, where we fixed up a rental on the Lower East Side: sanding the floors smooth, installing bars on the windows. Together, we became politically active in the queer movement; we socialized and screwed around as a couple. As my early twenties passed by, I began feeling a discontentment so strong I couldn't deny it, and so unfamiliar I couldn't define it. I let myself fall in love with someone who lived far away, courting this new boy with lengthy love letters. Six years after Paul and I first slept together, I told him I wanted to break up.

Soon after, on the subway, I ran into an acquaintance who blanched when I told him of the impending split. "I'm sorry to hear that," he said. "You guys have been my model couple."

My stomach clenched guiltily. I needed to get away from the relationship precisely because people like this fellow couldn't differentiate me from Paul—not physically, but conceptually. Even close friends sometimes slipped and called one of us by the other's name.

When I complained of this to my friend Maria, she shook her head firmly, her wavy, blonde-streaked mane shimmering in the light of an East Village café. Reaching out her hand, she assured me, "I've never had any problem knowing where Paul ends and you begin."

"You haven't?"

She smiled so endearingly I could only understand it as permission to shake off my guilt. Defining moments are rare, but this was one: I was being seen for who I was, apart from association with anyone else. I was being shown how to look at myself with the clarity of an outside eye.

I had known Maria since the summer of 1987, four years earlier, when I moved to New York. I first spotted her on a sweltering evening in an auditorium where she sat several rows ahead of me. We were there for a meeting of a recently formed activist group, the AIDS Coalition to Unleash Power. ACT UP had been gaining attention for street actions protesting the lack of government attention to the epidemic. On this night, the group was planning for the upcoming Gay Pride parade. Outraged by the Reagan administration's call for mandatory HIV testing—a thinly veiled attempt to identify, isolate, even quarantine "AIDS victims"—ACT UP would roll out a flatbed truck bearing a barbed–wire–wrapped concentration camp overseen by an actor in a Reagan mask laughing diabolically. Guards in masks and yellow rubber gloves would march alongside, keeping watch over those who'd been rounded up.

The meeting's facilitator called for volunteers. "We want as diverse a group as possible inside the camp," he said, "to send the message that the virus does not discriminate."

A few rows up, the petite woman with the humidity-rippled hair waved her hand. "You're volunteering for the camp?" the facilitator asked.

"No," she replied, "I want to be a guard."

Maria was unlike anyone I'd ever met: an intellectual whose fashion sense included leather jackets and boutique dresses, cowboy boots and marabou mules. In 1987, her nose ring seemed exotic and vaguely sinister, but her sense of humor was all embracing; she regarded everything New York had to offer as material for a (usually comic) story. She was only a couple of years older than I but seemed to have lived twice as many adventures: a girlhood in Africa, a brief stint at a Swiss boarding school, a year spent in Italy after dropping out of N.Y.U. She'd completed her undergrad education at a Seven Sisters school, where she'd had a series of tumultuous affairs with women, fueled by equal parts feminist theory and sexual energy.

Walking down lower Broadway on one of the first days we hung out socially, Maria complained about the afternoon's glaring sunshine. "It reminds me of L.A.," she said. "I hate L.A.! Too much sunshine makes people complacent. Plus you have to wear sunglasses, and you can't look people in the eye when you have something to say." Her tough talk was infectious. *I also hate L.A.,* I wanted to say, though I'd only been there briefly. *And I hate sunshine, and sunglasses, and people who don't look you in the eye!* I wanted to dispel received information as mercilessly as she did—be it about the weather, or about politics.

Maria was the first person I told about the affair I'd started; now I was telling her about leaving Paul. "I can't do this to him," I moaned. "I'm ruining his life, and mine."

She narrowed her gaze on me. "Karl," she insisted, "you're going to have many lovers in your life."

Her words offered the balm of perspective: You're not ruining your life, you're renewing it. You're reinventing yourself. I held those words close, a raft to keep me afloat through this sea change.

"Sweetheart, you'll be okay," she said.

"I don't even know where I'll live."

"You can live with me. Patrick is leaving in a month." Patrick was the latest in a line of gay roommates who'd rotated through Maria's tenement apartment ever since she'd moved in, knocked down the interior walls and filled the place with books.

"Are you serious?" I asked.

She was.

I couldn't believe my good fortune.

The idea of living with a woman was a great comfort to me. I'd grown up with sisters, and in college I had roomed with three different women, the most important of whom was Theresa.

I met her on the first day of freshman year, at a small private school in upstate New York. My roommate was an enthusiastic guy from Philadelphia named Chris, whose unfamiliar accent emphasized the *o*'s in *home* and *phone* until they seemed as round as doughnuts. With him was a girl from the same high school, another incoming frosh. She was dark-haired and cherub cheeked, just a breath under five feet tall, with dark, serious eyes that seemed unsure about this entire endeavor. I was used to befriending well-behaved, well-liked girls who carried sadness just below the surface. The girls I'd dated were like that, projecting happiness in order to maintain their high school social status, then letting down their guard with me, often while I gave them back rubs at parties. But this girl— she'd introduced herself as Terry—was offering no false cheer, as if she, and by extension we, understood that this was all just overwhelming.

Chris led us on an energetic campus tour that concluded at a highrise dormitory called the Tower. He brought us to the top floor, where a restaurant was open to the public. Since the campus sat at the crest of a hill, this marked the highest spot in the county. We could see miles of lush green farmland and the spectacular, long, blue lake that stretched north from the valley below. Chris pointed out the sights, then turned to go. But Terry, with a small sigh, announced that she would stay.

I took a chance and added, "Me, too."

Then it was just the two of us, side by side, looking at the haze-blurred horizon. "I'm not ready for college," she said. "High school sucked, but you only get to do it once. There's a lot I'd do differently. And now it's over, and we're on to college, and then that's going to be over . . ."

"We haven't even started," I protested, arms flung wide.

"I hate saying good-bye," she continued. "I hate it so much it can be hard to say hello."

"Do you have a hard time meeting people?" She looked at me, unsure. "Because I do. If I feel comfortable with someone, I'll just start talking, but there are a lot of people who make me nervous, you know?"

She nodded. She knew.

"At least the view is incredible," she said.

"On a clear day you could see forever," I joked.

She brightened immediately. "Do you know that movie?" I nodded. "I love Barbra Streisand," she added.

"Well, hello, Terry," I sang.

Our interaction was the only substantial one I had that weekend; still, when the fall semester arrived, our friendship was postponed. I would spot her in the company of the guy she was dating—a skinny preppie with thick hair and a stuck-up attitude—and I'd think, *We were supposed to be friends.* But I—not yet out, even to myself—was also absorbed with a new love, Petra, a moody film student who took my virginity and made me over in her image. Petra introduced me to Fellini, Plath, and the Violent Femmes; she wouldn't abide Streisand. Then she dumped me without explanation before spring break.

During a melancholy campus walk, I ran into Terry. She was in the midst of her own blue mood; her romance with the preppie was on the skids. Already nostalgic for the summer before, we decided to take the elevator to the top of the Tower to see if the view had changed.

I fell for Terry over a single conversation; I fell for April before I even met her.

Long before she started hosting Southern California dinner parties, April was a theater producer in Marin County, and I was a receptionist at an arts nonprofit in San Francisco. The organization was searching for a development director; it was my duty to process the applications. One after another, I scanned the staid cover letters, each outlining, in workmanlike prose, a commendable level of experience. Then one day I opened a letter beginning, "There are several reasons why you shouldn't hire me, but by the time you're through reading this, I hope I will have dispelled them all." The paragraphs that followed were saturated with so much personality that I walked the letter directly to my boss, announcing, "Here's the one."

April's first week on the job coincided with our annual two-day staff retreat. She showed up in overalls, with her shoulder-length auburn hair in pigtails, as if ready for summer camp. In the midst of one of those getting-to-know-you activities, she revealed that at age twenty-seven, she'd already been divorced, remarried, and excommunicated from the evangelical Lutheran church. April, it turned out, was fond of costumes, games, and self-disclosure for the sake of a story.

She quickly became my confidante at work, where she would escape from her desk to join me in the reception area with a bottle of blue nail polish. We'd fan our wet fingertips, gossiping in a cloud of cosmetic fumes. Soon we were hanging out after work as well, usually at my apartment. The first time she sat down on the toilet to pee, and left the door open so we could continue our conversation—something Maria used to do at our apartment in New York—I knew this was a friend I'd hold on to.

April and Dean's marriage was that rarest of things, a heterosexual union with a degree of permitted sexual openness. This meant April was free to pursue an occasional fling; she usually chose a butch, brooding dyke. Soon she developed a crush on Lucy, one of our part-time technicians. They would disappear together after work, and the next day I'd hear about the charmed, urban adventure April had cooked up: an evening walk through Golden Gate Park, a cliffside visit to watch the sunset. One morning, April arrived at the office in the clothes she'd been wearing the previous day—overalls again—her hair looking storm-ravaged. The night before, she'd been knocked over by a wave on a beach walk with Lucy. Drip-drying back at Lucy's apartment, April fell asleep. She awoke in the morning to an empty bed and a note from Lucy reporting that she'd run off to be with the woman she was really in love with. Then April somehow managed to lock herself out of Lucy's apartment without her shoes. I looked down, and sure enough, she'd come to work in her socks.

April didn't last long as our development director. Within a year, she had given notice and returned to what she did best—producing theater.

I've never wanted to be a woman, but I've often emulated the women in my life.

Maria was outspoken when I needed to discover my own strong voice; she was already the fearless activist I was determined to become. Theresa was able to articulate emotion in the midst of the superficial, party-centered life of a college campus. April brought me outrageousness when I was locked into routine. My women have unearthed in me the very qualities that I admire most in them.

But who am I to call these women "mine," even casually? Isn't possession exclusive to the lover, whereas friendship is ecumenical? Naked and kissing, hands roaming, skin wet: Put two bodies together like this and, yes, you make of each other a possession. But I have not made these women mine in this carnal way, except one, once—an isolated, delirious incident in an otherwise platonic friendship.

Yet these three women *are* to some degree mine, just as I am theirs. Doesn't Maria send me Valentine's Day cards? Doesn't Theresa leave plaintive voice mails saying, "I miss my Karly"? Doesn't April start conversations with "Hi, honey" and end them with "I miss you" in the most adoring tone? Meeting each of them had the dizziness of falling in love.

My earliest friends were the girls in my neighborhood. There was always more than one sharing "best friend" status. Even when I dated girls—they tended to be Catholic virgins whose overprotective fathers waited up with the light on—we spent more time on the phone, talking out life's troubles, than we did in person, getting busy. I related to these teenage girlfriends as I would a best friend. Now I treat my best friends with a romantic devotion usually reserved for lovers.

In college, only one friend's opinion really mattered to me: Terry's. Feelings were complicated, and Terry was my *feeling* friend. Never before had I known someone who could guide a conversation so quickly into the hilly terrain of the heart. One night during junior year, sharing a contraband bottle of wine in my on-campus apartment, I stuttered through the news I hadn't yet told her: "Paul's not just my friend, he's my boyfriend. I think I'm bisexual, but I'm with him now, so that probably makes me gay."

She responded by telling me of a night in high school when she dove naked into a swimming pool, followed by a girl named Carol and Carol's boyfriend. The three of them wound up fooling around. "It was Carol I was most excited by," Terry said. "She was definitely hot."

"Would you do it again with a girl?" She admitted she would. "Have you?" I prodded. In the delay before she said no, I guessed that there was perhaps more to this story, more to Terry's sexuality. Just how much more I wouldn't learn for another six months.

We were in London, spending a semester abroad, living in a tiny flat with four other students. Privacy was nonexistent. Terry and I discovered a dimly lit creperie in Soho that we'd steal away to, drinking glasses of port and pecking at a single dessert crepe for hours. Here, Terry confided that the excessive homesickness that had overtaken her in England had a secret cause: She'd left behind a lover back home, an older woman, a kind of mentor whom she'd been involved with since high school. This woman, Marguerite, held a prominent position in Terry's hometown, and had set the terms of their togetherness: No one was to know.

I was dumbstruck. The affair seemed to me politically retrograde and logistically untenable. Yet it also revealed a side of Terry so complex that my own sexual confusion paled in comparison—an ordinary weed alongside a night-blooming, bloodred flower. I wanted to know how this Gothic love had continued for so long, rooting itself in the shadows. I predicted it wouldn't last—surely Terry, a founding member of a college club called Feminists for Awareness and Action, would chafe against Marguerite's control—but I was wrong. It was a relationship with no future that showed no sign of ending.

I'd imagined Terry a substitute college sweetheart, our late-night shared desserts akin to old-fashioned malteds sipped through two straws at once, when in fact she was living the intricate, compromised life of an adult. In singling me out as the keeper of her secret, she'd bestowed adulthood on me, too. In return I offered a kind of antidote—an increasingly free-spirited playfulness made more wild through drinking binges and multiple bong hits, under the influence of which Terry was at her most carefree and nonsensical. During a weekend in Amsterdam, stupid on hash brownies, we explored the nightlife arm in arm, bug-eyed and laughing uncontrollably. "I'm not myself tonight," Terry proclaimed, adding thoughtfully, "although I am," which made us laugh even harder.

After college, living in different cities, we entered a period in which we clashed repeatedly. As much as I wanted Terry to explore her sexuality, I simply couldn't approve of Marguerite. When Terry asked me to lie to her mother about her whereabouts so that she and Marguerite could vanish for a weekend—their first vacation together, to homo-heaven San Francisco, of all places—I refused. My life at this point was an ongoing, vocal crusade, not just among ACT UP's activists, but as a journalist at *Outweek*, the magazine made famous for "outing" billionaire Malcolm Forbes upon his death. The women I was meeting, Maria most prominent among them, were didactic and commanding, aflame with righteousness. They were knocking down walls, not keeping secrets. Their influence was a gift I needed to pass on to Terry.

The bond between gay men and the significant women in their lives has often been painted as neutered, and thus safe: You both desire the person who's not in the equation, the straight guy over there. I first heard the term for this type of woman—"fag hag"—in college, tossed off by bitchy theater students, whose conversations rippled with barbed phrases like "drama queen," "beard," "breeder," and "bull dagger." The fag hag's cultural currency was so devalued that her only refuge was the company of girly men, who exploited her devotion for their own gain. This was disorienting news. Was it supposedly true that gay men kept women around in order to feel superior to them? Every woman whose friendship I'd sought seemed in some way superior to me.

I have shared with the women in my life a kind of perversity, a willingness to push at sexual limitations. These are women who have cast the net wide, sexually. They can be crude and challenging and sophisticated and compassionate. These are no withered hags. These are women to be desired.

By the time Maria and I became roommates, the headiest years of our activism were already behind us. For Maria, grassroots politics were replaced by the stimulation of N.Y.U.'s graduate filmmaking program, and in this new environment, she found her next lover. She had quietly begun seeing a man named Hal. In our queer circle, heterosexuality was deemed by some as "sleeping with the enemy," but I found Maria's situation romantic, a love seeking expression against the odds. And I was pleased that she'd chosen someone gentle, even dorky; a man, yes, but one who wasn't interested in screaming at her on the street, as her last two female lovers had done.

I, too, had a new boyfriend—Benedict, the letter writer I'd left Paul for. I recall the night the four of us—Ben and I, Maria and Hal—sat on her bed watching news coverage of the racially explosive L.A. riots; whole neighborhoods were burning, sending up wartime clouds of smoke. We talked about politics and fear of the other, trying to understand. Afterward, we slipped to our separate beds, Maria's just around a doorless corner of the apartment from where my futon sprawled on the floor. Beneath the Duke Ellington music that we occasionally blared to create a curtain of privacy, I listened to Maria getting fucked at the same moment I was.

It wasn't long after this that I moved west, inspired by Maria to make my own leap to grad school. A few nights after I departed, she called me in tears. She was standing over a kitchen sink filled with dirty silverware; washing silverware was a task that she abhorred, and so I had always taken it on. Only now, wiping off forks and spoons, did my absence fully hit her. But there was never any doubt that our friendship would continue, in intensity if not immediacy. My future with Ben, on the other hand, wasn't so clear. I came to realize I was more invested in a life-of-many-lovers than I was in a life with him.

I continued to visit New York in summers, when Maria rented a vacation house on Long Island, where she worked on her new career as a screenwriter. On one fateful visit, she and I found ourselves at an open-air bar for happy hour, taking in the sunset over the bay. We chatted up a couple, married New Yorkers visiting for the weekend. Greg had sleepy brown eyes and thick curly hair that bobbed as he nodded, listening earnestly. His wife, Gina, was a brunette with a lithe body and large, laughing mouth, who worked for a design magazine with a guy Maria and I knew. The discovery of a mutual friend and the two-for-one vodka martinis warmed us into camaraderie. After sundown, we invited them back to Maria's.

We opened bottles of red wine, as marinated chicken sizzled on the grill. The corn on the cob, fireflies, and cut-grass smell of summer lent a timeless, wholesome air to the proceedings, but there was nothing innocent about our intentions. Maria and I had decided to seduce them—separately or together, we weren't sure. We'd giggled conspiratorially as we'd driven back from the bar, Gina and Greg tailing us in their car.

After dinner, I announced that I had a joint in my bedroom. Greg drunkenly followed me. We sat on the edge of the bed inhaling smoke, while I lobbed out flirtation, but I soon understood that earnest Greg wasn't any more seducible high than he was sober. The pot on top of the wine on top of the vodka, plus the chicken in its tangy sauce, was a lethal recipe; the only physical intimacy I shared with Greg that night was our side-by-side puking into the toilet. Gina quickly took her messy husband away.

The next morning, Maria and I groaned about our foiled attempt to play Paul and Jane Bowles on the prowl in Tangier. That night we found ourselves curled together in my bed, the same one that had failed to lure Greg into a horizontal position, this time with no one to seduce but each other. One of us leaned in for a kiss, and who knows why, but ten years into the friendship, we decided to keep going, like lovers would.

All along, there have been women whose friendship might have lasted, but didn't. I think of my rowdy college pal Melanie, who ended up at a desk job she despised, insisting it was the right choice for her career. Each time we'd speak, she had only complaints about her life and jealousy about mine, which she deemed more exciting and "real." When I would suggest changes she might make, she inevitably answered, "I can't."

To say, instead, "I can," is something that my women share. For Terry, this came, at last, when she summoned the courage to cut Marguerite off. She marked the moment with an even more elemental shift. She stopped calling herself Terry and reclaimed Theresa—"Big Theresa" was our nickname for the still diminutive but more self-assured woman who stepped forth. Her next significant relationship was with a man, a gentle giant named Guy who treated her with great care. They were married in a Quaker-style ceremony, at which guests were asked to stand and testify when the spirit moved them. When I stood, I told the story of meeting her that first day of college. I wondered aloud what that vista would have looked like through the confident eyes of Big Theresa.

For my thirty-first birthday, April took me out for a fancy meal. We ate quail and drank wine suggested by the sommelier. The dessert arrived on a plate with "Happy Birthday" penned in liquid chocolate. From there we ventured tipsily into the Fairmont Hotel, sneaking onto the ancient glass elevator for a look at the San Francisco skyline. We hit last call at the campy tiki bar in the hotel's basement, where a band sang "Celebration" on a floating island as sprinklers spat rain onto indoor palm trees. On the walk home, I spotted a copy of the Book of Mormon in the street, and I eventually stopped kicking it obnoxiously along the curb and picked it up to bring home.

Back at my apartment, the romantic flicker of our four-star dinner morphed effortlessly into a raucous slumber party. April slipped into pajamas, and I took the opportunity to don what she'd been wearing, a mod minidress with a harlequin print. I pulled on a wig and heels from a recent outing as my drag alter ego, Brianna Cracker, and I posed like a drunken stripper against the orange walls of my apartment while giving a dramatic reading from the Book of Mormon.

The next morning, April walked to the corner for coffee while I cleaned up the night's detritus. She returned in under ten minutes, armed with a story about the stranger who had chatted her up at the café—a gay, homeless blues musician who had escaped from Czechoslovakia during the 1968 uprising. When she finished, I marveled, "Your story lasted longer than the actual time you were gone."

To adore this quality in April is to encourage her to nurture it. And it's also a way to grant permission. Because when April left my apartment that day, and went back home to Dean, I knew that she would tell him stories about *me*.

At each crucial stage of my life, almost without being aware of it, I have looked to women to help define the contours of my identity. Extraordinary, complex women have always appeared. Does some elemental characteristic unite them? To answer "complexity" is to suggest that there is no answer at all.

For Theresa, I am and have always been the one gay man in her life, though she recently reminded me that she didn't pick me because I'm gay, but because I helped her "drop her armor." Of course, it was she who helped me drop mine; throughout twenty years of sentimental education, knowledge has flowed both to and from. April seems to give any gay man she meets the benefit of the doubt, assuming that with him she'll find some rollicking adventure, some shared, misfit laughter. She's also been the person who, at my low moments, has accompanied me to a church service, the better to stimulate discussion about belief, contemplation, spirit. Maria has lived more deeply inside the queer community, though as her identity has shifted from lesbian to "hasbian," from activist to filmmaker, she has concluded that the only label that really fits her is "Maria." My most recent visit with her was in L.A., where she now lives and works, and where despite the numbing California sunshine, she has found stimulation among a new group of friends..

I have pursued my women and kept them close, the better to bask in the spell of their influence. Perhaps what unites them, then, is simply that I've entrusted each one with my story. My women are the portrait of my history, and the portraitists, too. I am, it seems, the real collector here.

To collect is to understand, to cherish. To collect is to demonstrate what you value, what you love. To collect is to extend the self, arms open, unguarded.

MY FAIRY GODFATHERS

* * * * * * * * * * * * * * * * * * *

Cecil Castellucci

17–18. New York City. Stefan.

I am at N.Y.U. I am going to be a filmmaker.

Stefan. Tall, elegant, handsome. Prone to wearing turtlenecks. Never flashy, always debonair. Big, strong arms. Impeccable taste. Studying theater design. Loves opera. Interned at Julliard.

I live in dorm room 1119. He lives in room 1118.

He and I are always walking down the street with our arms around each other's waists. He catches me midswoon when I discover my dorm room in flames because my roommate got overly exuberant with candles. I lose almost all of my Super 8 films. He lets me cry in his arms.

Stefan.

Sits on the warm spot in the space between our doors drinking illegally bought beer. Me with a pen and a composition notebook. Him with a paintbrush, painstakingly filling in hundreds of squares, going from white to black, doing his gray scales.

Club kid. On occasion he comes over, dresses me up, and takes me along to the clubs he frequents with more flamboyant acquaintances. Notorious names cross his lips: Michael Alig, James St. James, Michael Tron. Out all night. Limelight. He passes the club gossip along to me.

Often he finds me sitting outside my dorm room dressed up, like a geisha, white face, tiny red lips, dark eyes, wrapped in a 1920s red smoking jacket, drinking a beer. He never blinks twice at my dressing up to go nowhere. He sits down and joins me.

"You look gorgeous, Cecil. You are a real classic beauty."

And then he kisses me on the lips. Holds for a second. I linger. Soft lips. No spark. Means nothing. Feels like a brother. We pull apart.

Walking down streets in N.Y.C. in 1987. "Silence = Death" posters everywhere. Stefan goes to clubs and parties, but he does not smooch carelessly.

We agree on one thing: Love. True love. True deep passionate love. Romance. Wooing. Something real. Something beautiful. Love is a treasure.

Stefan loves a boy that he met at Julliard. It's an unrequited love. And me, I love Mitch, a boy from the fifteenth floor.

My favorite thing to do is to gather a group around me and tell a story. Usually it's a fairy tale. I love to spin a yarn sitting on top of my bed while my friends gather around me quietly. I love the look on their faces. I notice Mitch. He hasn't moved to the front with the others. He's in the back. Still just an acquaintance, but he is listening to me.

"Tell me the story again of the Little Mermaid," Stefan says when we are alone and I cozy up in bed with him, spooning. I tell the story. I draw it out. Make it longer with more details for him. He embraces me like a lover and we hold hands. I am safe in his arms.

Stefan is never afraid to point out my flaws or tell me where I could improve as a person.

Learn to listen.

Don't walk away.

Stop being so sensitive.

Stop being a baby.

Don't take everything so personally.

Learn to laugh at yourself.

I get angry sometimes and I slam doors. I cry and shake. I beat his chest and I sob. I tell him he is wrong.

But I know he is right. And I learn in little tiny doll steps, how to grow up.

I stay when I want to leave.

Listen when I want to yell.

Smile when I want to cry.

Zig when I want to zag.

We would plot out our future. Our fabulous future over cappuccinos and hot apple ciders and wine or beer when they don't card us at cafés on Bleecker Street or St. Mark's Place. Café Borgia. Café della Lanterna. Café Orlin. Dojo's. Edith Piaf always playing in the background. Like me, he knows the words in French by heart. We sing together and to each other. Our voices kiss in the air. Oh, why can't Stefan be straight? I could spend my whole life talking and hanging out with Stefan. Our babies would be beautiful. With dark brown eyes and a love of Princess Turandot.

"I love you," he says.

"I love you, too," I say.

"I will design the greatest sets ever for the most wonderful operas at the Met," he says.

"I will travel the world, become an expatriate, recruit a lover, and write novels!" I say.

Mitch snakes his way down from the fifteenth floor. Sitting with us at the tables in the student dining hall. My friends and I watch him perform with his guitar singing sweetly at the talent nights. He is a glowing light and we are moths.

"He's cute," we say.

"He's smart," we say.

Everyone we know agrees and we make more and more room for him in our social activities. Except for Stefan. Stefan is not so easily charmed.

Mitch has a girlfriend at another college in another state. He flirts with all the ladies. He likes to impress older women.

But he picks me.

Mitch begins to come into my room after midnight asking me to play pool at the twenty-four-hour billiard hall. Or to talk physics and fairy tales over black coffee and French fries and gravy. Or to kiss me awake and to make love.

"This will end badly," Stefan says.

But I am like the Little Mermaid. I am in love with a dream. I am convinced I am the only one.

Mitch is singing Handel's *Messiah* at Carnegie Hall. I get box seats for Stefan and me. We dress up and Stefan brings lorgnettes for us to share. I only look at Mitch. Beautiful Mitch.

After the performance, Mitch does not hang out with me. Our friend Gail has been sleeping with Mitch behind my back. I am in Stefan's room, crying. Stefan lets me fall asleep in his arms. He strokes my hair.

He whispers to me, "Someone will love you. Someone will."

He says, "I love you, Cecil. I do."

"I hate Handel," I say. "There can be no hallelujahs when my heart is breaking."

The next night, as usual, Mitch joins our table at dinner. I do not talk to him, but I move over to make space for him.

It is hard to be friends with Mitch. But I can't let him go. I always leave the door open. Sometimes there are still midnight visits. How I hope for the midnight visits.

Once, when Mitch leaves all of his love letters from his ex-girlfriend who attends a different college on my desk for a week, I am strong. I resist reading them. But my roommates, like evil stepsisters, convince me that I deserve to know what is in the letters.

They are too strong, these girls. I succumb. I open the first letter and bounce on my bed. Bounce right into the wall, unread letter open in my hand. A wobble. I black out for one second.

Stefan takes me to the E.R.

"A concussion," the doctor says.

Stefan shakes his head. He tsks. "That's what comes of reading love letters that are not yours."

Stefan takes it upon himself to follow the doctor's instructions to wake me up four times a night for three days to make sure I am okay.

I never know the contents of the letters. I press them into Stefan's hands to give to Mitch. To tell him never to leave love letters for another woman with me again.

Tuition is too high. I cannot make ends meet. There is no financial aid for me. I have to drop out of N.Y.U. I am devastated because I will leave my friends behind.

But mostly, I know in my heart, it is because of having to leave Mitch.

The little voice inside of me tries to tell me that boy from the fifteenth floor does not love me.

Stefan writes me a letter good-bye.

"Forget that guy," Stefan writes. "Only 'La Vie en Rose' for you."

18–19. Montreal. Jerry.

I am working in a video store. A college dropout. A going nowhere. A slacker.

Jerry comes into the store and we share a love of two movies: *Another Country* and *My Beautiful Laundrette*.

"There is a hollow at the base of his neck that wants me to pour honey all over it and lick it up," we quote.

"Eyelash!" we quote.

Jerry is always smartly dressed. It is winter and he wears his scarf well. He loves an ascot and leather gloves. In another era, he would have been called a dandy.

He lives in the neighborhood, so he just stops by to talk. And oh—how we talk about boys and boys and boys!

I have heard from Stefan and my friend at N.Y.U. that Mitch calls me a bitch because I stole his soft gray sweatshirt. The one that says "Echo Hill" on it. He always wore that sweatshirt. I wanted it. So I took it. Now I always wear it.

I pass it off like I don't care. But I do.

I hear that whenever anyone gets too emotional or sensitive, Mitch calls it "pulling a Cecil."

I pass it off like I don't care. But I do.

It is almost Valentine's Day and I get a card in the mail from Mitch. It is not the declaration of love I longed for.

It is the picture of a dunce looking straight ahead while walking off a cliff with jagged rocks below. The outside of the card says, "Another Romantic Enters the World."

Inside, Mitch has written the word *careful*.

He probably thought it was funny. But I feel like the dunce splattered on the rocks below. I am broken and hurt.

I show the card to Jerry.

"Jerk," he says.

He comes back to the video store later that day.

"Cecil, look your best on Valentine's Day. I'll pick you up at seven."

Jerry picks me up. He is wearing a tuxedo. I am wearing a vintage 1950s cocktail dress with my grandmother's fur stole. It is real fur, but I don't care. We both cut a fine figure.

My parents think he is a gentleman caller. I have to inform them that he likes gentlemen, too.

We drink champagne at a bar at the top of a hotel that spins us a view of the city.

"What are your dreams?" Jerry asks. He is interested in me. He really listens. He makes a video store clerk feel like a queen.

"I will recruit a lover, travel the world, and write novels," I declare.

"Sounds yummy," Jerry says.

My dreams like pearls, spilling on the table. He will make me a pair of earrings with those dreams. I will wear them. They will sparkle for the rest of the evening.

But maybe my dreams are stupid. Perhaps they are too flashy. I panic.

"I probably won't go anywhere," I confess. "Everyone is going to Paris next year for their junior year abroad, and me, I'm working at a video store!"

"Everyone is going to Paris?"

"Mitch is going to Paris."

"Well, if you want to go to Paris so badly, you should go to Paris."

"Really?"

"Hell, yeah," he says. "Go write your novel."

We toast our champagne glasses. I will do it. I will really do it.

Jerry opens his coat and pulls out a card from the inside pocket of his suit.

"What's that?" I ask.

He pushes the envelope toward me. I open it up. It's a sympathy card. It says "My condolences on this sad day." Inside the card are all the spades from a deck of cards and also the two of hearts. On the hearts Jerry wrote, "You and Me."

"Hearts Day is so silly," Jerry says. "I think we should call it Spades Day. I wish you a happy Spades Day, Cecil."

There is nothing else to do but order another bottle of champagne.

19–20. Paris. Jeff.

I am studying theater at L'Ecole Florent. I am a *fille au pair* to a two year-old named Aymeric. I am obsessed with a French play called *Feroe, La Nuit*.

My eyes are always scanning the crowds for Mitch, in the Metro and the cafés and the museums. I am always standing on the banks of the Seine. On a bridge. Casting my wishes across over to the ile Saint-Louis.

I sit in front of Notre Dame, reading poems. I have a theory that if I sit in front of the cathedral, the whole world will pass me by. I think that maybe Mitch will show up.

Mitch. He doesn't know I am there in the City of Light with a heart in my mouth that longs to cover him in kisses. I imagine that if we are destined to be together, then he or I will just emerge from a Metro station one day and find the other sitting there at a café, having a Pernod, smoking a cigarette, writing a great novel.

I have been in the city nearly six months and I haven't run into him.

Sometimes, you have to give up a little before fate steps in.

He said his name was Jeff.

He was American, like me, at the dinner party we both attended. He was handsome, had floppy two-toned hair with too-long bangs and an asymmetrical jagged edge that was so 1980s fashionable. He looked like he belonged in a new-wave band. A British one.

When we met, I had two broken hands.

"What's wrong with your hands?" he asked, pointing at the two claw-like casts I had on my extremities.

"Tumor," I say.

"Cancer?" he asks.

"No. Benign. I have to get a transplant. The bone won't grow back."

"Drag," he says. "But you still look fabulous."

We smile. I ask him to cut my turkey into smaller pieces. Someone has to cut my meat. I have claws for hands.

He told me he was doing his N.Y.U. semester abroad.

"Do you know a boy named Mitch?" I ask.

"No. Why?"

"I followed him here."

"Here to Paris!?"

"Yeah, kind of not really." I feel stupid. Want to take it back. What kind of girl admits that the hope of running into a boy made her go across an ocean? When I say it out loud, I know what I sound like. I sound like a crazy girl.

"Oh, that's soooooooooooooo romantic!" Jeff says.

We exchange numbers. I write mine down in his notebook. He writes his name on a scrap of paper along with his phone number:

> *Jeff. I have a summer house and*
> *a small Pomeranian.*

A few days later, Jeff calls.

"Let's go to the Marais! Let's go clubbing! Let's have a sleepover! Let's make you beautiful! Let's go see jazz! Let's go to the Bastille! Let's go to the Louvre! Let's go meet boys!"

We go to clubs and there are boys, beautiful boys. Jeff has a French boyfriend named Etienne. And they dance with their eyes closed. And the *umsk, umsk, umsk* of the beat pounds in my chest and makes my feet ignore the floor. And I fly. And the walls start to come down. I am free.

In the news, the wall comes down in Germany. I have a piece of it a friend brought back from New Year's in Berlin. She tore it off that wall with her own hands. It sits on the shelf with my books and my hopes that it means the Cold War is coming to a close.

I am cast in a play at school. Greek Chorus Girl Number Three, one of the supplicants in Aeschylus's play. The play is full of dancing, falling, and throwing. The director does not want to kick me out of the play because of my broken hands. He places me on a dais above everyone else so that I am alone, like a goddess.

I watch Jeff and Etienne from my perch as they hold hands and enjoy the show. They take care to watch the action, but always their eyes come back to glance at me. I can see that they brought me a dozen red roses. Over lunch they say, "You were the best one. You were the queen of the chorus."

We are all broke. There are never enough francs. I am hungry in Paris. It is the oldest story in the book. It is now my story, too.

"Oh, what a bummer that living on love and red wine is not enough!" we say, though the wine we have left flows freely and the stars shine brighter for us.

Etienne gets us all invited to the *vernissages* of his Beaux Arts friends. We haunt the tiny galleries around the city. We feast on hors d'oeuvres and free wine. The food is sometimes better than the art. When no one is looking, I fold finger sandwiches into napkins and put them in my purse.

At Shakespeare & Company, I buy a book of the letters of Héloïse and Abelard. All the other Americans we hang out with make a pilgrimage to Pere-Lachaise to see Jim Morrison's grave. I ignore it and head straight for the greatest letter-writing lovers of all time, Héloïse and Abelard.

I want to write a letter to a true love that lasts for a millennium.

I am a stage-door rat at the Theatre de la Ville and see Michel Deutsch's play, *Feroe, La Nuit*, three times. I am invited by the dwarf in the play to the closing night party. He and I have a postparty drink across from the Moulin Rouge. The red windmill blinks on and off.

I feel like a true bohemian.

It is Moliere in the mornings. Café Pompidou with my notebook at lunch. And Aymeric's dirty diapers in the afternoon.

I try not to get upset when Aymeric's parents get angry that he calls for me when he wakes up in the middle of the night. He calls for me because they are never around. Aymeric is like an accessory to them. Like a new coat of paint on the wall. Like their condo on the Riviera. Like a four-course meal at the hippest restaurant.

I decide the boys and I should have picnics once a week in front of the Eiffel Tower. We pack baguettes and cheese and fruit and watch the skateboarders do tricks. Jeff, Etienne, and I walk down the Parisian streets together arm in arm. They are both beautiful.

"Will you marry us and have our babies?" they ask me.

"Yes, oh yes," I say. "Can we have a chateau where they can run around and grow?"

"Yes, oh yes," they say.

"I will write novels. I will take lovers. I will put on plays in the garden. I will make experimental films. There will be feasts with wine and Chinese lanterns and everyone will stand up and speak poetry."

"Oh yes," they say. Jeff and Etienne make out passionately, and then take me in their arms and cover my face in kisses and we roll on the lawn of the Trocadéro laughing.

Months melt away with all the fun. I am not thinking about running into Mitch. The phone rings. I know who it is. It's Jeff. It's always Jeff.

"I saw him!" Jeff says.

"Who?"

"Mitch! Someone introduced me on the Sorbonne campus. He looks like Elvis with long eyelashes. I said, 'Cecil says hi!'"

I can hardly breathe.

"What did he say?" I ask.

"He turned white and asked for your number! I gave it to him! He's going to call you!"

A few hours later, I am at a bar with Mitch. A few hours with him. I am sitting with Mitch in Paris.

"What are you doing here?" he asks.

I don't say, *I am here because I love you*. Instead, I show him the pages and pages of my notebook. I show him my novel. I say I am an artist.

We walk down the dark streets and I am on pins and needles and every once in a while, he kicks me playfully on the ass. It makes me want him.

Then I am kissing Mitch in Paris.

Mitch comes over sometimes late at night, throwing pebbles at my window, begging to let him come upstairs. He sits on my bed, playing the guitar, singing me deeper into love with him. I love his hands on the fret board. I love his fingers running through my hair. I love his deep blue eyes. I love his hands on me. We tell stories to each other while laying on my single bed, picking up the tale where the other leaves off. A verbal exquisite corpse. I like his parts better. He should be the one trying to write a novel. Not me.

I fold him in my arms. I kiss him all over. I think he loves me. I really think he does.

"You are in love," Jeff coos at our usual picnic spot.

"Yes, Mitch is the love of my life," I say. I am certain. This is the big love. This is the one.

"But you'll still marry us, right?" Jeff asks.

"Yes. Oh yes," I say.

One day Mitch comes over with a gift for me. A typewriter.

"You should type out your novel," he says and then takes me over to the bed.

My days are spent on the typewriter. Clack, clack, clack. The pages come to life. It is the story of a girl like me who loves a boy like Mitch.

"Do you want to hang out with my friends?" I ask.

"No," Mitch says. He is just interested in putting his hands in my nooks and crannies.

As soon as I am completely his, Mitch cools off. He slows down. He doesn't come around as much anymore. He is busy with school. I have to try harder. Reach out more. I show him pages from the book, try to woo him with my work.

He tells me that I am not a gifted artist.

"You are not an artist, Cecil. It is you and the way you move through the world that is your greatest piece of art."

I yell at him. I scream.

Jeff and Etienne are there, to take me out to jazz clubs where women sing Piaf and other torch songs and we drink Billie Holidays—sugar, tequila, and champagne. They hold my hair back when I throw up. They tell me how beautiful I am. Try to convince me that I am a catch. Swear that if they weren't gay, they would love a girl like me. Remind me that I shouldn't forget the chateau and the babies and the novels. Tell me that I deserve better than Mitch.

Mitch is gone. I have found out the truth: I was not the girl Mitch loved.

It is Gail. It is always Gail. Gail has come to Paris. And once again, Gail wins.

It hurts so much. How can a breaking heart hurt so much?

It's best not to stay in a city of love when your heart is ruined. I know it is time that I leave. I have a continent to see. I have a Eurail pass. I have adventure on the brain. I'm ready to begin. I will start on the Orient Express.

They are sitting outside at the café at Place d'Italie. Jeff and Etienne are holding hands. They are beautiful. Smoking cigarettes. Looking lazy, as though they just fell out of bed. Light falls on them like a painting.

One last hug. One last good-bye. One last espresso and Gauloise.

"I can't believe you're abandoning us," they say. "What about our wedding? Our alternative lifestyle? Our chateau? Your novels? Our babies?"

"That lives right here," I say, and I point at my heart.

And I can feel that this is good-bye. *Casablanca* good-bye. We'll only have Paris good-bye.

I walk away, humming "La Vie en Rose."

THAT UNSETTLING FEELING

· · · · · · · · · · · · · · · · ·

Mike Albo

On a recent Sunday, I went to get a coffee at my neighborhood muffiny-coffee place in Park Slope. Inside, there were three young couples with baby carriages. One of them was Lorrie, an old friend from grad school with her new baby, Hamish, and her quiet husband, Drew. I moved to New York around the same time as she did, in our early twenties. It seems like yesterday that Lorrie had a birthday party and got so drunk she was flashing her tits at strangers on Avenue B. Now she had a son staring at me with a disturbed look, taking me in as if I were a flapping bird. She held his little pruney face up to me, I sang hello, and we all smiled.

Many straight women in my life are a lot like Lorrie now.

Colette was skinny, smoked constantly, and had a short blond hairdo that she kept greasy and messy in a good way. I would meet her at straight bars, go gay around 1:00 A.M., and then call her the next day to trade trashy stories. She would often go home with this crafty, straight British photographer who had fleshy, muscular arms and wore soccer jerseys. I did coke off Colette's coffee table with him. Her apartment was right across from a halfway house for homeless drug addicts, and they would call at her while she got dressed. She is still single but has a one-year-old now, lives in Maryland, and is a social worker.

Sylvia is a talented stylist, one of those people who have a special relationship with color. Once I went to Brighton Beach with her. We ate at a Russian restaurant that had a tacky live show. For some reason, we took Ecstasy. Actually she took two. Russian food doesn't taste good on Ecstasy, so we drank a lot. Sylvia passed out on the subway home, turning a light shade of periwinkle. I carried her to her apartment and held her hair back while she puked.

She met a guy in 2003, and I knew within a week she was going to marry him. In an easeful way, without seeming forced, everything in her life corrected itself to fit him in. Her career flourished, her clubby social life became boring, her rickety studio apartment's building was turned into a co-op and she had to move in with the boyfriend. Now she is an assistant fashion director at a magazine and her baby is turning two this fall.

Vida is Sylvia's best friend, gorgeous and robust like a Thomas Hardy milkmaid. One time I took her along to visit my gay friend and his straight roommate on the Lower East Side. We all got very stoned, Vida and the roommate hit it off, and she stayed the night. The next day on the phone she told me she gave him head and he came in her mouth. "I didn't want to swallow, so I just transferred it to the mattress," she said pragmatically. A year after Sylvia was married, Vida's life somehow fell into place, too, blessed by some natural law I can't seem to perceive. She got married to a professor of American studies, had a baby, and is pregnant with her second while working as a political fundraiser. The straight-guy roommate married a yoga instructor and is a father now, too.

I have always been a hag fag, since the first grade when I hung upside down with my girl classmates on the jungle gym at recess rather than running around the playground trying to kill and destroy things. I have maintained intense relationships with straight girls up through high school, college, and our sloppy drunk twenties. Our emotional lives were not always exactly synchronous, but somehow we suffered our love, sex, and career anxieties in complementary ways. But over the last five or so years, something has happened between my gal pals and I that makes our lives separately drawn.

I feel like I was on the phone, put on call waiting, and then the next thing I knew, many of my female friends became married mothers with solid careers. Their lives are, of course, much more complicated than I make them out to be here, but still it feels like they all suddenly, swiftly transformed their lives, as if they were in a Sandra Bullock film, full of plot-propelling montages. Around the time we all hit thirty-two or thirty-three, they radically changed from being confused single women worried about finding a suitable mate (how twee and immature it all seems now) to being busy, married decision-makers who dash to their jobs from their apartments after they deal with ear infections, preschool politics, and nanny guilt. Is it because they stopped producing new episodes of *Sex and the City*?

Meanwhile, I feel like the only things that have changed for me are that my jeans are more expensive and my emotions don't feel twentysomething-fresh. I have been circulating within the same gay narrative (meet a guy, have sex with guy, fizzle out with guy, worry about rent, repeat) like a bobbling buoy anchored to my spot, the weather moving over me chaotically. These women in my life are swiftly settling down in a megatrend of babies and weddings, and I am still in a dizzying maze of dating. I feel hapless and tangled and there is no way the world could speedily provide me with a family in a two-year extreme life makeover renovation. Something keeps me out of the market.

It's not easy to feel Walt Whitmanesque, liberated by my rootlessness these days. I walk out my door and down Fifth Avenue in Brooklyn, and I am drenched in the Settling Down lifestyle. I pass by Area Yoga & Baby, a new store on my corner where little crocheted toddler jumpsuits dangle in the window. Across the street is Lulu's, a newly opened hair salon for children, painted in an optimistic nectarine (it used to be a bodega). Down the street is Umkarna, a clothing store with Moroccan, organic-themed clothes for women and their kids. The inside of the store looks like you are walking into the tent of a nomadic tribe.

Settling Down is very marketable these days; it involves a lot of gear you need to purchase. This engine of couplehood controls a level of the economy that confuses me as much as hedge funds or the futures market. I pass by these stores and try to calculate how many hundred dollar infant hoodies or forty dollar haircuts they need to sell simply to pay their rent, much less turn a profit, and I can never wrap my head around it. They must be lucrative, because there are more and more of these stores all the time, a bulky diaper tsunami that threatens to drown us all.

I still know a lot of single, defiantly unmarried women. But I notice that they, too, pass by these stores and have to defend their childless choices to themselves. The weird thing is that even my new mother friends are stumped. These are women who trade their tots' clothes among each other and physically deflate when you ask them how much they spend on their babysitters. None of us understand who the hell can afford a five hundred dollar Bugaboo.

I open the paper and see settled, grounded couples smiling at me from the Real Estate and House & Garden sections of the *Times*, replete with articles about sweet straight architect couples who convert Methodist churches or missile silos into gorgeous minimalist homes for themselves and their sons named Cody or Bray.

And every now and then, I will see a feature on a gay couple and their clean, sharp-edged furniture in their beautiful farmhouse upstate. They are shown smiling in white T-shirts in front of a warped barn façade and a wildflower field that would inspire hundreds of watercolors. They look comfortable with each other and are talented with handicrafts: "Tim and Jorge converted the old slave quarters into a ceramics studio." I look at their serene faces and my apartment suddenly feels too messy and I fear that I drink too much and I need to stop being so adolescent and flakey and make a decision about the men I keep meeting. I wonder if I should have stuck it through with Stephen or called Sam back before he moved on and started dating Matthew so I could be shown holding a basket of snap peas next to my landscape architect husband in front of our modest three-acre organic garden.

I was on the beach last summer when two people sat near me and began talking loudly about a mutual friend named Sally. It sounded like she was making a triumphant comeback from some squalid single person time in her life: "Sally is doing great. She met her fiancé at Lisa's engagement party. She's really turned around."

"Yes," the other replied. "You have got to *want* it. Just *want* it and things will happen for you."

I remember my confident, curvaceous friend Ayn saying something to this effect when she married Scott. Ayn and I lived together when I first moved to New York, as she was just starting to study environmental law. Once Ayn and I had a party and someone brought hash. Ayn kept the door shut to her room and did a fair amount of it with this talkative filmmaker. I took way too many mushrooms with two hardcore gay guys. They wanted to go out, but I was afraid to get off the couch. Everyone left, and Ayn stayed up with me and we watched the E! channel. That night all I remember is seeing Demi Moore's face morph into Elizabeth Taylor's on the TV screen. That was my one dumb hallucination.

Now Ayn is married and pregnant and works for a senator. A year into her marriage, she told me that right before she met Scott, she had a strong feeling she was going to meet her husband. "I guess I just decided it was time," she said. I had never heard her say something this self-help-flavored.

Is it that simple? Is that what it takes to become part of the Settled-Down Set? I get so anxious when I hear that I could change my life if I just "wanted" it enough. I have tried wanting it until I am red faced, like I am straining on the toilet, and it never happens so brightly as it does for others. I become pissed off at the vague force called the Universe that seems to have less energy and time to be clear with me than it does with other people. I barely do drugs now, I work hard, I try to go out sensibly and not date jerks, but still haven't figured out how to want it enough. Maybe I have intimacy issues. But while I am here, at thirty-seven, in my stunted adolescence, before I succumb to the baby trend, get married, adopt two kids, and start shopping at a store called Rock Star Baby Couture, indulge me over this: Why are we all so powerless to this pricey pathway? Is there really no other alternative?

I am supposed to find that partner and living space and scramble for an adequate income to afford health care in an economic system that favors CEOs and HMOs, and then say things like "God, I am so out of it," "I never go out anymore," and "Remember that crazy PJ Harvey concert? Those were the days."? There is something limiting about the Settled Down paradigm. Don't misunderstand me—I adore all these new little beings my friends have brought into the world. I love making them smile, I love watching their crafty brains try to figure out a way to get what they want, I love talking to them about trees, confetti, and outer space. I just don't want to stop having fun.

And I miss my girlfriends.

Last Monday, I went out to dinner with Sylvia and Vida. They described their anxieties about buying property, having to liquefy their assets to afford a down payment, their concerns about schools.

I remember how in her last month of pregnancy with her second child, Sylvia was put on bed rest, and I went to visit her. She asked me how I was and I told her about some guy whom I thought I liked but we fizzled out. I realized it was the same conversation using the same "fizzle" word that I have had with her since I was twenty-five.

"Will you be patient with me while I still go through such square-one love conflicts?" I asked her.

"Yes. Will you be patient with me when I become a boring mother of two and have zero social life?" she said to me. We both slouched there on her couch, tired and hungover in our very different ways.

I had gone out with this "fizzled" guy the night before. He lived above a bar. I was very, very attracted to him. We went to an Italian restaurant; he had ravioli and I had tagliatelle with mushrooms. We shared a bottle of wine, and then walked to another place for two more glasses. I went to the bathroom and closed my eyes to check and make sure I didn't have the spins. He asked me if I wanted to buy some pot with him; his dealer lived nearby. I said sure, thinking that this would bring us closer to making out. The dealer was red-haired and affable; we bought a bag and talked for a time and then walked back to the guy's place. He pulled out his pipe, packed it, and I puffed on it. We began to kiss, and at least for me, it felt as if there was something electric between us, my lips into his neck, our exhales lengthening, his waist fitting in front of mine, everything communicating effortlessly.

Unfortunately I forgot that when you are this attracted to someone, your head reels and you detach from gravity. The little internal gyroscope that had been keeping me from spinning too much tipped on its side like a top. I felt that unsettling feeling like a prophecy as I got up, kissed the guy on the neck, calmly walked to the bathroom, and threw up a nefarious borscht of taglietelle and red wine six times. The guy, thankfully, was passed out by this point and didn't hear a thing. As I brought it forth, hovering over his grimy toilet, I tried to understand why this was happening, again. I honestly hadn't had that much to drink; I sure as hell have held down more. Maybe it was because I was hot, or had mild food poisoning, or was an alcoholic, or thought I was in love.

Maybe it was that pure moment of focus I had been waiting for—a time to be used to want it and imagine a spouse and nice house with a low mortgage rate. But vomiting up everything inside of me, I had an easier time envisioning myself splintered off into a million bits, that my body was a part of the porcelain and didn't end at its edges. For a brief moment I was emancipated from the Settle Down agenda and its pointless opposite. There were no expensive stores there, no *Times* profiles, no perfect lives to linger over. There wasn't even a bar or a cute guy or drink tickets. It felt freeing.

II

• • • • • • • • • • • • • • • •

Close Confidants

*"That first night, we were leaning in toward each other,
laughing at each other's jokes, finishing the other's sentences."*

—from "My Best Girlfriend," by James Lecesne

A HARVARD (FAG)
HAG-IOGRAPHY

● ● ● ● ● ● ● ● ● ● ● ● ● ● ● ● ●

Alexandra Jacobs

"*Eohhhhhh.*"

E This is how C. and I always greet each other: in a low, sardonic, world-weary sneer that succinctly encapsulates the good and bad that has accumulated over more than a decade of friendship like a pile of unread newspapers. It can be weeks since we've spoken on the phone—these days, when we live on opposite coasts, it's usually months—but it's always obvious who's on the opposite end of the line.

"*Eohhhhhh.*"

My husband calls it the Café Pamplona voice, referring to the white-walled subterranean restaurant in Cambridge, Massachusetts, frequented by pretentious, espresso-quaffing Harvard students, which C. and I used to be ("Speak for yourself!" he would say), and chain smokers, which C. was, until one day, shortly before he began medical school, when he gave up the habit with no fanfare whatsoever. I got the feeling he thought that people who needed a nicotine patch or hypnotism, *addicted* people, were morally weak. Another day, after he had become a surgery resident, he abruptly stopped eating meat, though not for any namby-pamby health reasons. "I like animals" was his nonproselytizing explanation. (Long before Brad Pitt and Angelina Jolie made it chic, C. spent months in Namibia, researching the cheetah.)

We met in an entryway when I was a sophomore; he, a year older, had transferred from a small liberal-arts college in Vermont because he thought Harvard's premed program was superior or, at least, more prestigious. We were both nursing heartbreak—we were always nursing heartbreak in those days—as we lugged our cardboard boxes into the large wood-paneled rooms with picture windows and working fireplaces that we'd been assigned in Adams House, the best undergraduate residential hall on campus. As we recently agreed, we've never had such good real-estate fortune before or since.

Back then, before the days of completely randomized living assignments, Adams was known for something other than its convenience to the Yard, its sumptuous library and billiard room, and its extravagantly tiled swimming pool: It was famous for its "artsiness." Subtext: its friendliness to homosexuals. In years past, the swimming pool was rumored to have vibrated with bacchanalian orgies; now empty of water, it was an echoing performance space. That semester, the putative social committee printed black-and-pink T-shirts bearing a mischievous cartoon face and the phrase: "Adams House: We're all gay and we're coming to get you."

There was a crushed-velvet decadence to the place; its dark corridors always smelled faintly like gin and clove cigarettes. But as C. pointed out to me on the phone, "Compared with other people's college experiences, it was actually kind of innocent." During countless parties in those wood-paneled rooms, classmates munched not tabs of LSD but strawberries dipped in chocolate; drank not Long Island iced teas but champagne. They stripped down to their underwear and danced to Madonna and Prince. One crisp autumn night, mysterious and benevolent forces planned and executed an elaborate Disco Masquerave Ball in the dining hall. There was also an annual official spring waltz with ice sculptures, a string orchestra, and red rose petals scattered on the floor. It was archaic. It was ridiculous. It was wonderful.

Most of those living in Adams House, as opposed to the rest of the country at that point in time—the Bush *pere* early-early 1990s—considered it cool to be gay or bisexual; it only enhanced a straight person's reputation to hook up with someone of the same sex. "All those kookaloos," C. said, sighing gustily as we minced down memory lane together. "I finally felt like I belonged, for the first time in my life." He had grown up in suburban New Hampshire. I was born and raised on the Upper East Side of Manhattan, a place that, as everyone knows, can be more provincial than Toledo, all flaxen-haired mothers in headbands and plaid skirts gathering at the church craft fair, their private-schooled daughters—Emily or Elizabeth—in tow, trailing muffin crumbs.

One of my own mom's friends, a renowned composer, was gay, but to my sheltered young self that was an exceedingly vague designation, perhaps indicating a fancy penthouse apartment with a white shag rug and a pair of pampered cats for companionship. Later, attending a progressive public high school, my knowledge of homosexuality was inextricably intertwined with education about AIDS and how to avoid it. Tragic figures like the actor Rock Hudson, whom I'd watched on *Dynasty*; the artist Keith Haring, with his boppy graffiti and sculptures; and nightlife impresario Steve Rubell of Studio 54 and the Palladium shared a free condom-strewn continuum in my subconscious. But these were just glossy abstractions till I reached Harvard's hallowed halls, where C. told me everything I had never known I wanted to know about gay male culture from the (apparently quite sticky) ground up: About what went on in the bathrooms of the Science Center. About poppers and hummers and glory holes and twinks. Barebacking, beards, and bears, oh my! About the fellatio that tall, lumberjack-looking guy with a girlfriend had administered one night to that slight, dark, perpetually hungry-looking visual and environmental studies major.

"Really?" God, I was so naive.

"I enjoyed your curiosity," my ambassador of alternate behavior said reassuringly, years later. "I felt sort of predatory or parasitic in college, going and soaking up everyone else's experiences and abilities, taste in clothes and books and socializing styles, and this made me feel like I had something to give in exchange. Something to bring to the table."

But what did *I* bring to the table? "You told me all about kosher food," C. said, laughing.

I am only half Jewish. My father didn't even have a bar mitzvah. To the best of my recollection, I didn't eat a single matzoh ball until I met my husband. But apparently, that was plenty Jewish enough. "I had known people from New York City, but they had gone away to prep school—I didn't know anybody who had gone to high school there," C. said. "It seemed very exotic and sophisticated to me."

Judging from appearances, though, C. was the more sophisticated one by far. Tall, dark, and handsome, with the high-cheekboned, melancholic-eyed, between-the-World-Wars look of a young Jeremy Irons, he was the perfect escort and the perfect ear when we were both between boyfriends, easily passing as straight when I needed him to make a prospective conquest jealous from across the room. Oh, the ridiculous tableaux we staged! When I *was* involved with someone, C. and his vicious gay circle provided merciful comic relief from a relationship's daily emotional roller-coaster rides. One day over lunch (Chickwiches and Constant Comment tea, no doubt), he looked at me, the only woman at the table, and triumphantly pronounced, "Fag hag!"

That was it. I had arrived.

Yet ours was never one of those double-snappin', Cosmo-swillin', shoe-shoppin' gay man–straight woman relationships depicted *ad nauseam* in popular culture. Nor was C. constantly administering Carson Kressley–style makeovers on my then lamentable wardrobe of flannel L.L. Bean shirts, Levi's, and hiking boots. He was far too masculine for that. He was obsessed with sports cars and airplanes and traveled often, with barely more than a toothbrush. He never cared much about what he was wearing, and in recent years has tended toward the tracksuits favored by Cinnabon-chomping Midwesterners suffering through long layovers in municipal airports. I was horrified when he shaved his head in tribute to his pop-music idol, Sinead O'Connor. I think he's even watched football from time to time.

If we had anything in common, it was our tremendous inner reserves of dorkiness. As a teenager I'd played the viola, taking the humiliating instrument on the crosstown bus twice a week to two successive different Upper West Side music schools; C., meanwhile, was lugging an enormous double bass through his own New Hampshire high-school cafeteria, where he was shunned by the people at the popular table.

All right, in college I was *still* playing the viola, as little as possible while still maintaining membership in the Harvard-Radcliffe Orchestra, an affiliation that pleased my musician parents. (They were, after all, paying the tuition.) The spring after C. and I met, this organization announced a tour of Eastern Europe.

"Go!" my parents said delightedly. I quivered in dread, wishing for a normal summer job, filing papers in a law office, lifeguarding, *anything* . . .

In a generous show of solidarity, C. announced that he would join H.R.O. in time for the trip. Together we would skip over the Charles Bridge in Prague, visit the Judenplatz in Vienna, take a relaxing soak in the famous baths of Budapest. For a few weeks he gamely showed up at rehearsals, ninety long minutes made suddenly bearable by our making faces at each other between pizzicati. At the last minute, the plan collapsed like the Berlin Wall, thanks to the merciless premed curriculum. After a miserable summer without him, touring the aforementioned sights en masse in air-conditioned motor coaches, subsisting on giant bowlfuls of post-Communist potatoes and phone calls home, I, too, finally found the courage to quit.

On another vacation, C. drove me to his parents' house for a taste of the suburban life. Now *that* was exotic. Burgers from the drive-through, an evening at the local multiplex (I fainted during a showing of *Aliens II*, occasioning a dramatic rendezvous with the local fire department in the theater lobby as C. obliviously masticated a bucket of popcorn inside), and—in one concession to the stereotype he never embodied—listening to his mother's Barbra Streisand records.

Like most dorks, we could be exceptionally cruel to those even lower on the totem pole. Perhaps the hardest I'd ever laughed in my life was the sun-dappled afternoon we spent pawing through my roommate's wardrobe, donning her teal vests and mimicking her Elaine Benes–style dance steps. Talk about hiding in the closet! We dripped with disdain for frat boys in baseball caps, for people who took too long at the ATM machines, for students sitting anxiously scribbling in class on the first day. "I hope the syllabus isn't too onerous," we mocked in our Café Pamplona voice.

It wasn't all acerbic bliss, of course. C. was always scornful of my majoring in literature, which he believed was mere entertainment. Senior year, he told me I would look "better in jeans" if I lost a few pounds. ("He's a *gay man*," a mutual friend reminded me. "They're not usually that into hips.") Once, a relative of mine—I am ashamed to say which—voiced concern that fraternizing with C. might result in my somehow getting HIV. (*"How?"* I hollered at the heavens.) Then there was the time C. "had relations," as they say, with an ex-boyfriend. Somehow, it didn't bother me nearly as much as a similar transgression by a female friend. Was that homophobic in some way, I asked him, using the politically correct patois of our age? Not really to "count" what had happened? "No," C. said. Our relationship, he said, had always been free of the competitiveness I felt toward women, or any sexual tension I might have had with straight men. This is why it worked.

When I began planning my wedding, half a dozen years after we graduated, C. complained that *he* couldn't get married, implying that I should've eschewed the institution's dubious privileges on principle (again, he was way ahead of Brad and Angelina). But there were no earnest boycotts; he sent over a shiny red KitchenAid mixer and a congratulatory note, put on his old tuxedo, and showed up to the party. He was the best-looking man—besides the groom, of course—and certainly the best dancer. (I got the feeling we both relished revisiting the Adamsian revelry of yore.) In one of the delicious life twists that it seems only New York City can hand you, his date was someone I'd known in high school.

When I announced plans to have a baby, C. expressed dismay that I was about to become a breeder, trying to get me to explain logically—

he is unfailingly logical—why I wanted to reproduce when the planet was overpopulated and my life was perfectly full already. But I couldn't. There's little that's logical about deciding to have children. And for that matter, there's little that's arch or sarcastic about little people, either.

It was a difficult pregnancy, and C.'s interest in the gory details was crisp, impersonal—like the new M.D. he was. I was grateful for his cool-headed counsel, and yet—

Then he came West to visit me in Los Angeles and met my baby daughter for the first time.

"Eohhhhhh," he cooed.

I laughed. And so did she.

MY BEST GIRLFRIEND

James Lecesne

Dearest Friend,

As I mentioned to you on the phone, I've been asked to contribute to a book of essays about gay men and their best girlfriends. Since I am most definitely gay and you are without a doubt my best girlfriend, I'm planning to write about us. But before I do, I thought it might be a good idea to run a few things by you to make sure that we are both on the same page where our story is concerned.

First of all, I'm a little unclear about the exact year we met. '92? '93? I do remember that it was Mark's birthday, so that would place it in February. He had invited us both to a celebration at a trendy little restaurant on the corner of Washington Square. (Or was it Madison Square Park?) It wasn't the first time he'd tried to get us together. We'd been refusing his invitations for years; we would just nod politely and smile whenever he insisted that we would absolutely adore each other and then move the subject along to something else. Neither of us really wanted or needed another friend; at the time we were both full up in that department. But that first night, even before the appetizers were served, we were leaning in toward each other, laughing at each other's jokes, finishing the other's sentences. Mark had been right.

A week later you threw a sit-down dinner party at your apartment on 16th Street to inaugurate our new friendship. You had just returned from your first trip to Bosnia (or maybe you were thinking about going to Bosnia for the first time?) and you were very much taken with gypsy music. You played it throughout the evening, the same CD, over and over, until finally, unable to contain our enthusiasm, we got up from the table, cranked the stereo, and began to dance. Next thing I knew, you and I were rummaging through your closet and you had me shimmying into an old Christian Lacroix pouf dress, which was (correct me if I'm wrong) the color of sea foam. You wore a bandanna and sported a moustache. Together, we created three separate gypsy-inspired looks that night, complete with makeup and jewelry. Each time we made an entrance, the guests were appropriately astonished. Didn't someone take pictures? Would you be able to put your finger on them? Maybe I could publish a photo or two along with the piece. Let me know if you find them.

Anyway, I feel it would be better for the purpose of my story to set our first meeting at the dinner party instead of the restaurant. The gypsy thing, the music, costumes—it all makes for a better introductory scene. But can you recall who else was at dinner? I mean, other than you and me?

Looking back, it seems as though everyone was jealous of our friendship from the beginning, because although we tried to include other people in our good time, our bond was as tight and exclusive as it was deep and obvious. People were astonished, impressed, and slightly horrified at how close two people could get in so short a time. We were a club that I finally wanted to be member of. Do you remember riding in a taxi from an uptown theater in Manhattan where we were working together to a downtown theater where we were also working together? (We were so busy.) You turned to me and said, "You know, you and I are so close that sometimes even *I'm* jealous of our relationship." Maybe I'll have you say that in the beginning of the piece, just as we're becoming friends.

We began working together right away. We had to. What else were we supposed to do with all that energy and all those sparks? It was either work or sex. Sex was out of the question, due to the obvious. I'm not sure that my readers will want to know too many details pertaining to our early theater careers. Somehow theater stories never read as well as they did during Dickens' time. In any case, I do think a contemporary audience will be interested to know that Barbra Streisand came back-stage to see me after a performance of that one-man play you wrote for me. I should mention that—for the gays. But do you remember anything Barbra said to me that night? About the play? About my performance? I was so *verklempt* at the time, I can only recall the large, floppy hat she wore in a desperate attempt to go unrecognized in a theater that had only fifty seats. And I've been meaning to ask you for years: Did Barbra come to the show the same night I leapt from the stage and into the audience to help that man who was having a heart attack, or have I conflated the two events? "Memory is such a strange and selective creature. It collects those details that put a gentle pressure on the heart and yet it discards the ones that pierce too deeply." That's a line from an earlier play I wrote, but I'm thinking of working it into the essay and ascribing it to you because I believe it will help to illustrate my point.

I also want to discuss the possibility of including some of your words in this piece. Of course, I certainly wouldn't want you to feel exploited in any way. For example, there is an e-mail that you wrote and sent to me in 1999. I printed it out, folded it up, and placed it in my wallet, where it has remained for years. Whenever I feel a little low or unloved or too desperately alone, I take out this piece of paper and re-read it. Though it is now terribly dog-eared and hardly readable in its original form, I still find it incredibly reassuring. Here's what you wrote:

> *It's Saturday morning and I just read your e-mail. As usual the depth of your self-understanding awes me, as does the struggle of your soul to evolve and become. I understood everything you said. How do we get loved when we don't appear to need love? How do we get held when we seem to be self-sufficient? How do we get attention when everything's okay? So much of my life was about acting out, drinking, drugs, fucking, being naked, depression, sui-*

cidal feelings, anything to get the big attention. Of course it was negative attention and that helped to keep me infantilized and little in the early state where my needs existed. Now I'm getting big attention in the world and I am strangely lonely and alone. I am me, myself, separate matter. I alternate between desires to go on mad drinking binges or a fucking binge or to just die. So I get a cold, a terrible cold and maybe that will bring my mother inside me or get my friends to see that I am still needy and broken, but it doesn't work. Coming to our loneliness, our death. Not being afraid or uneasy with it. And you're right—love is the only salve. It makes this journey into the center of our self/aloneness bearable. I love you. And as Rilke says, I stand as "a guardian of your solitude." That's what friends do—they see and honor each other's separate solitude. I want to reach in there sometimes and rescue you from the terrible pain of this aching separateness, but that would be undermining you, stripping you of your strength and value. So we bear witness to each other's standing tall. And I respect you as deeply as I have ever respected anyone. And I know you will eventually feel comfortable standing by yourself surrounded by those of us who see your insane beauty and brilliance and kindness and deep shiny black hair.

So beautiful.

But it just occurred to me that perhaps you'd rather not include the business about drinking, drugs, fucking, being naked, depression, and suicidal feelings. It's your call. But in the event that you *do* agree to publish this as part of the essay, I will need your written consent. I will forward the necessary papers to your lawyer. Are you and I still represented by the same law firm? Have you seen their new offices?

The other passage of yours that I'd like to include is a note that you slipped to me the day after I confessed to you that I was having suicidal feelings. I had just returned to New York from L.A., where I had run out of money and options. After years of trying to make my way in the world, I saw little visible success, and on top of that, I felt as though I would never find a decent boyfriend. Without real work and true love, I didn't see much point in going on. You stayed on the phone with me for a long while, trying to convince me, once again, that I was loved, that I did matter, that it would all turn out all right. Finally you got in a taxi and came to my apartment. It was eleven o'clock on a Sunday night, hardly an hour to go visiting, and yet you sat with me while I cried and cried and eventually cried myself to sleep. The next day you handed me this note:

14 Reasons Not to Kill Yourself

1. Coffee
2. The Trevor Project (The twenty-four-hour suicide prevention helpline for GLBTQ teens that *you* started!)
3. Pumpkins
4. Thanksgiving at my house
5. Me
6. Rilke, e.e. cummings
7. Great moments of discovery in the theater
8. Sex
9. Provincetown
10. You're going to die anyway
11. City buses
12. Great cotton, silk, shoes, hats, bags, accessories in general
13. Because things always turn around and you'll miss it
14. Because it would break my heart

I don't want to give the impression that you and I just sat around being depressed, discussing the intensity of our feelings and considering suicide, because that is not the case. As I recall, we were very busy creating things, trying to move the world, and helping our fellow humans. And I can honestly say that I never laughed as much or as heartily with anyone before or since as I have with you. I also plan to include a few amusing anecdotes about shopping sprees, makeovers, fabulous summer shares, pedicures, parties, and perhaps a list of celebrities with whom we have worked. If I can't think of anything in those departments, I may have to make stuff up, but I will run it by you beforehand for your approval so that you can pretend it really happened.

Perhaps it's not specific to gay men and their best girlfriends, maybe it's just a function of being a friend, but it seems to me that what you and I have always done for each other is (a) encourage each other's work; (b) remind each other that our lives may be determined by a shattered past, but we will not be limited by those events; and (c) love the very essence of the persons we are becoming. What *is* specific to gay men and their best girlfriends, however, is that we have always managed to look fabulous while we were busy with a, b, and c. I will be sure to make that point, and if possible I will publish a favorite photo of you and me together looking fabulous so that everyone can see what I'm talking about.

Finally, I plan to end the piece with a conversation we had not that long ago about the nature of friendship. I think it will make a good wrap-up. I can't seem to recall if it happened at Orso's or at Joe Allen's. Not that it matters, but maybe you can remember. We had either just seen a Broadway show or I was meeting you for dinner after one of your shows. I do recall that it was a lovely spring evening and it had just rained. Or was it autumn? In any case, we were talking about the nature of friendship and you said, "This is how it works. I love the people in my life, and I do for my friends whatever they need me to do for them, again and again, as many times as is necessary. For example, in your case you always forget who you are and how much you're loved. So what I do for you as your friend is remind you who you are and tell you how much I love you. And this isn't any kind of burden for me, because I love who you are very much. Every time I remind you, I get to remember with you, which is my pleasure."

And mine, as well.

Always,
James

P.S. There is also the issue of your name. Should I include it, or would you feel more comfortable if I gave you a made-up name? In the case of the latter, I have compiled a list of names for you to choose from.

   a. Kiki
   b. Meg
   c. Sid
   d. Anastasia
   e. Claire
   f. Brie
   g. Bette

MY DINNERS WITH TOM

• • • • • • • • • • • • • • • • •

Gigi Levangie Grazer

A lot of stars come into The Ivy; success and charisma breed at this fashionable West Hollywood bôite. But by far, my best sighting at The Ivy was always Tom Bailey.

You've never heard of him. Tom Bailey was my favorite waiter.

But Tom was much more than a waiter: Tom Bailey was The Way.

Tom Bailey in his life, and in his death, taught me a thing or two about how to live.

Just over a year ago, I wandered into The Ivy on Robertson at about eight o'clock on a Thursday evening, wrapped in the pleasant buzz of anticipation. I was seeing a close girlfriend—a comrade, the type of friend who knows you, knows your secrets, and still, loves you. You may have heard of The Ivy, if you're familiar with such publications as *US Weekly* or *Star*, or even *Elle Decor*. You may have spied its shiny denizens, human Christmas ornaments tucked safely behind a white picket fence that shielded them from the masses on Robertson Boulevard, its wood slats pitched out at odd angles, like rows of long, crooked fangs.

There was a time when climbing the uneven brick steps to the inner

sanctum of The Ivy—deceptively quaint, grandmother's house steps—
would require courage that I did not yet possess, a worldliness I couldn't
muster, and a sense of entitlement I was not born with. Those brick steps
were my Everest, and Tom Bailey was my gay Tenzing Norgay—on the
way up and on the way down.

The first time I met Tom was at The Ivy at the Shore, the Santa Monica version of The Ivy. I was seated across from my future husband. I
was young and awkward and unfashionably dressed and not quite pretty
enough to get away with my determined lack of style. Around me were
tables of blondes, thin and beautiful and assured and obviously (hope-
fully) idiotic, and God, I wanted to be just like them. As I sank into internal despair, longing to be with my brown-haired, near-sighted, Toyota
Corolla–driving sisters on the east side of La Cienega, a voice reached out
and wrapped its long arms around my hunched shoulders.

"Someone shut that woman up already—there's not enough Percocet
in the world to get me back to that table—can I take your order, doll?"

I looked up and placed the face with the voice. It was love at first sarcastic sound bite.

But by that night last year, I had been cradled in the heady, cosseted world
of the Hollywood inside track for close to fourteen years. I was married
to a highly successful Hollywood producer and I had a writing career of
my own. I knew the name, even the birthplace of the maître d'; he knew
mine. But there were times when I was reminded of my modest roots,
times when my club card was declined. I'd once made reservations under
my maiden name, and another for the same lunch, by mistake, under my
married name. Gigi Levangie rated a small, lopsided table in the back
room, squeezed in with the Orange County tourists and the low-level,
faceless development execs; Gigi Grazer was seated on an expansive, padded bench in the sun-streaked front room overlooking the patio, where
she could watch an unobscured Justin Timberlake chew diligently, two
tables away. Tom laughed and told me not to take it personally; I didn't,
and I learned my lesson about the value of a name.

So on that Thursday night, I was eager for the first margarita, as welcoming as a sunrise, the rich, dark bread, the specials that never change (they are not special at all, but reassuringly familiar), the ease of the experience. It was a warm, breezy April evening; I had not seen my girlfriend in a month and there was much to tell, much to hear. I'd arrived a few minutes early, and the maître d' greeted me with a kiss, a smile, words floating into each other in a Missouri drawl, the verbal equivalent of a languid backstroke. I looked over his shoulder for one of my favorite people, a man who had played the part of the Greek chorus to a man-eating party girl in my second novel. No one had better lines, in the book or in life, than Tom Bailey.

"Where's Tom?" I said. "Has he died?"

William looked at me. It was night; the light was gray. But I could see his face pale.

Jesus Christ, what have I done? I thought to myself.

"William," I said. "Come on, William. I was joking." What did I say? What did I say? My big mouth—

My table mate had just arrived. Her face was pink, lit up. A thick tassel of blond hair swept past her large eyes; she appeared carefree, breathless. "Darling," she said. (She's British, this is what they do; it's not an affectation.)

"We'll talk later, after your dinner," William said to me. Gently now, he spoke, every word standing alone, forlorn and unadorned, the drawl put aside for the moment. But my hand was fastened to his arm, his navy jacket, the gold buttons. My eyes were on his, carving inroads into those silvery blue mirrors. *Tell me, tell me, tell me,* I implored.

People were waiting. My companion's smile had faded and concern had replaced joy. Our anticipation of commiseration fueled by minor amounts of alcohol and heaving plates of picture-ready food had become something else entirely.

"You have to tell me, William. Tell me. I was joking. He's not dead. Tom is not dead."

You know those moments, when your brain is so far ahead of your words, the words are coming out—one, two, four, eight—but your brain is saying, *I just saw him, when did I see him, was he sick, he's always so . . . alive, vibrant, so funny, never ever ill, never a cough, so much energy, in great shape, skinny even, maybe he drank a little, but still, where is he, is he in the hospital? Not in a hospital. He couldn't possibly be in a hospital—the food, no alcohol—Jesus, God, what if he doesn't have a cute doctor—*

"Can I visit him?"

William just shook his head.

Tom had died the week before. In a hospital.

"Conform" is the telegraphed message of the glossy watering holes in and around the Westside of Los Angeles. Wear the right shoes, lug the right bag, buy the right bland nose if God didn't give you Jessica Simpson's. It is a true and frightening thing that any woman walking down Rodeo Drive around noontime is likely to have the same bridge, the same swollen lips, the same color and length hair as the three preceding her, all teetering with misplaced confidence on their uniform stilettos. "Conform" is something I've fought against and yet felt eerily attracted to—but I'm even more attracted to those who don't conform. Like Tom Bailey.

Maybe I'm kidding myself. Maybe he really cared about what people thought of him, about his skills, his looks, his "funny"— but I don't think he did. For one thing, he directed the majority of his pithy comments not toward my husband, a producer, but to me, someone who could not change his life with the wave of a script deal, the promise of a screen test. Tom wasn't interested in the next job, in other possibilities. Unlike other waiters, there would be no script awaiting us at the end of dinner, no headshot proffered after our coats. In a town where lines are drawn and crossed at the same time, he did neither. He enjoyed his riches; he never seemed to want more.

So picture this man, his head carpeted by tightly woven, neat brown curls angled back from a long, café au lait face, punctuated by startling, light green eyes—his was a face that wouldn't be out of place on a *National Geographic* cover, a Benetton ad. Even more striking than Tom's face had been his body. This body, in constant movement, tall, made taller by his sleekness, the lack of curve—a human exclamation mark—more of a liquid than a solid. His arms and legs, exceedingly long, seemed without bone, a yogi carapace with the comic soul of a Buster Keaton.

He was obviously American, but did Tom have Egyptian blood? Pakistani? Were his people from some remote mountain region of Afghanistan? I never asked—I don't know why—but when I learned Tom's last name at the memorial service, I had my answer. Exotic he was, and yet not at all. Tom Bailey: My God, he had the last name of the Jimmy Stewart character from *It's a Wonderful Life*. How could I not know this of him? Why hadn't I asked?

Was I afraid or unwilling to cross a line into a deeper relationship? And is this why I never realized he'd been ill? Did I not want to acknowledge the possibility? Had I become one of those people I write about, who are unable to deal with the darker realities of life, of death? What else did I not know?

When Tom died, my life was in flux, as they say, "they" being more polite than I am. My life was taking a hairpin turn on a bumpy road. I had turned forty-two; I was looking at the rest of my life and not liking what I saw. I had written a third novel about life in L.A., my hometown, and I was done with it. Done with this city. I no longer found excessive plastic surgery or materialism amusing; the erratic behavior of the Westside wealthies ceased to be rich fodder and became, instead, an annoyance, something to be avoided altogether. I even regarded the lifestyle as a danger to my children. I had, up to that moment, justified my existence in this fun house Oz by writing about it—but what would happen when I stopped?

Who was I now?

I was looking for an escape and I was looking for distraction and I was looking for a few laughs. Or so I thought. I was really looking for a new way to live, a new way to be. I hadn't yet had this conversation with Tom: Hey, what do you think I should do with the rest of my life? Got any ideas?

I was looking forward to having that conversation with him.

Instead, I went to Tom's memorial; it was held at a conservative Catholic church in a Republican enclave of Los Angeles, Pacific Palisades; irony was all around—and with it, humor—Tom, my Tom, had been an altar boy. I met his delightful mother and thus started putting together the pieces of Tom—the things I did not know and wished I had. I looked at her face, open and forgiving, while she, the bereft mother, smiled and comforted everyone who came forward. This was where those startling green eyes had originated.

I stared. I saw his smile in hers, and oh, the slight tilt of the head. I watched her and heard his loving words regarding his mother, saw his description of the trips with her to San Francisco, experienced the immovable bond of a mother who loves unconditionally and a son who accepts her love. Could we all bear a piece of this, her ultimate loss?

I put the memorial picture of Tom on my dresser. (He is so young in the photograph!) Instead of talking to him over a menu, I talked to his picture. As things in my life bucked and keened, as my marriage faltered and threatened never to recover, instead of asking "What would Jesus Do?" I'd ask "What the fuck would Tom Bailey do?"

Tom would keep his sense of humor. And so I did. Tom would be true to his nature. And so I was. Tom would ride the current until it brought him to shore or pushed him out further to sea. I pinched my nose and dove.

The rough tides of my emotional life have died down now. I am walking again. My marriage, our marriage, has found its footing. It would have been nice to have had Tom along for the ride—or at least for the wicked narrative. I can only imagine the things he would have said, though my imagination is no match for his words.

I don't know exactly what my relationship was with Tom. How would I classify it? Friend? Well, we were friendly—we certainly had a connection—but were there shared meals? Late-night phone calls? Serious commiseration over love's vicissitudes? No. But we weren't acquaintances, either. There was a service-clientele element, but often it was difficult to tell who was serving and who was being served. When seated in Tom's section, one was subject to the titillating vagaries of Tom. One felt lucky and so one wished to gain his favor. Look this way, Tom! Who's that at Table 9, Tom? Please, please gift us with one of your one-liners about "Ears," the restaurant manager who heard everything. You can finish my margarita, Tom—

I can still see his brows shoot up his forehead, his eyes widen and flash as he bestowed on us a zinger about the cheap, many-times-married studio boss ("He should tip more and marry less!") or the closeted action star. Nothing escaped Tom's senses, and everything was subject to his true acid wit—he would be so pleased by his own displeasure.

Anyone who was served by and served Tom loved him. Some relationships seem gossamer thin on the surface, but to look beneath, to see beyond, is to see a whole world. I'm sure I loved Tom more than he loved me, but in this case, I don't mind. I was happy to admire him like a besotted schoolgirl; I was satisfied with my lot as the rapt audience member, the girl in the first row, begging for attention from the lead singer. I would not have had it any other way.

The Ivy at the Shore, where I first met Tom Bailey, was shuttered and moved down the street days after Tom's death. The differences were slight: The menu was unchanged and the white uniforms remain, as do most of the staff.

To me, it has never been the same.

MAN'S BEST FRIEND

. . . .

David Ebershoff

Several years ago I got a puppy. When I brought her home she was ten weeks old, loose skinned and gangly, the color of cinnamon, with ears as big as her face. I named her Elektra. That's her real name. I'm telling you that because I've changed the other names in this story, including the names of the dogs.

I got Elektra for the usual reasons a single man gets a dog: companionship, affection, a living creature to care for. I wasn't really single; I was on a string of boyfriends whom over a period of three years I would end up treating shabbily—behavior I'm still ashamed of today. I chose a vizsla because—this is going to make me sound vain—they are lean and strong, a frame I had always aspired to at the gym but could never quite put into shape. One more thing about Elektra before I move on to Miriam—her name comes from the Strauss opera. Hence the Germanic spelling.

When I picked up Elektra at the breeder's I clasped a tiny pink collar around her throat and took her for her first walk. My best friend, Leo, and my boyfriend, Paul, were with me that day. By the end of this story I'll have gone through half a dozen boyfriends and my best friend will be off in rehab. That too leads me to Miriam.

Once I got Elektra back to my apartment, she hurried across the living room, turned around, looked into my eyes, and peed. That afternoon she went on to pee on every carpet in the apartment and in the elevator as I walked her to the curb. I put down paper, but she merely shredded it and then peed next to it. Within a few hours, she had slashed a hole in my sofa, pulled the toilet paper off the roll, and thrown up. I had read several books on how to train a puppy, but it was clear I needed live help. That evening, when I was out making a run to the deli for more paper towels, I saw a woman walking a stately golden with a plumed tail. The dog sat when commanded, walked calmly on his leash, and, most impressively, took an appropriate leak on a trash bin. A bit desperately, I explained my situation to the woman. Her face warmed up: "You have to call Miriam."

When I got back to the apartment I called the number the woman had given me. "Is Miriam there?"

"Who's this?"

I told her about Elektra.

"A vizsla, huh? Well, I'd have to meet her first."

I told her that was fine.

"And there'd be an interview with you."

"An interview?"

"I'm not going to walk just anybody's dog."

I asked her when she could come. She stalled and made a noise like flipping pages in an appointment book. "How's tomorrow?"

I told her that would be fine and gave her the address. I don't remember if Paul was there when I made the call. He must have been, because I remember he stayed over on Elektra's first night. I set up her crate in my office, but when she started whimpering late that night, I got out of bed. I went to stroke her and ended up falling asleep in her crate, my legs sticking out the door. Paul and I lasted about three more months.

At the time, Leo had a dog, a clever white twelve-pounder he insisted was a pure-breed poodle, but really was a mutt. Over the phone, Leo gave advice, his point of reference being his own dog, Adam. "It's cruel to put her in a cage."

"But all the books say—"

"Adam would never go in a cage."

"She doesn't think of it as a cage. To her, it's her house."

"Adam would rather die than go in a cage." Adam was a typical city dog: little and spoiled. On the line, I could hear Leo exhale a Marlboro. "By the way, how's Paul?" For the next several years, my friendship with Leo would be some variation of this conversation. It happened mostly on the telephone, revolved around our dogs, and then would meander into a discussion of my current boyfriend (after Paul, there was Phillip, then Jeremy, followed by Jonathan, Bill, and Jim) and Leo's obsession with one married man or another. What I didn't know, but now am aware of, was that Leo was almost always drunk when we were on the phone, spiking his Starbucks with minibottles of Smirnov, from six in the morning until he passed out. Sometimes I heard a slur in his voice and asked if he was drinking. He'd deny it with such irritation and a sniff of offense that I believed him. I mention this only because later—after Miriam and I had, for lack of a better phrase, broken up—did I figure out the subtext of this period in my life: that using had nearly destroyed one friendship, possibly two.

When I opened the door Miriam brushed by me. "Come on in," I squeaked as she moseyed around the living room. She shrugged at a picture on the wall, surveyed the sofa with a raised eyebrow, and went to the window to dismiss the view. "How long have you lived here?"

"Three years."

"Not bad." She looked down to the Oriental rug my mother had given me. "This rug's going to have to go."

"Why?"

"Where's the puppy?"

I went into the office, unlatched the crate door, and released Elektra. She ran through my legs into the living room, squatted at Miriam's feet, and peed on the rug. "Vizslas," Miriam said. "They're the worst."

I fluttered about with paper towels and a cleaning product called

Ur'Ine Trouble! While I was mopping up the puddle, Miriam took a seat. She was small and slender, in her late forties, with pretty, dark hair pulled back. Her voice had gone gravelly from cigarettes. "I'm very picky about my dogs," she began.

"That's good," I said.

She explained she had a longtime boyfriend who had made a lot of money repping jeans. "I don't need to be doing this."

"Of course not."

"This is about a relationship."

I nodded in agreement.

"We're in a relationship together with your dog."

I was so eager for assistance and blinded by my limitations that I let the interview continue. We went over the details of the walking schedule, Miriam's fees, her right to a glass of water or a soda from the fridge. A lot of what we talked about was what you might expect in such a situation—except that she was the one asking the questions and stating the demands. I know that makes me sound like a doormat, but one of the reasons I let her go on like that was that I knew nothing about dogs, while she was, as she put it, "a professional."

"How'd you come up with a name like Elektra?"

I told her about the opera and that in Greek mythology Elektra remained loyal to her father after everyone else abandoned his memory.

Miriam listened to this, frowned, and said, "I see."

Then for the first time she softened up. "Next to goldens, vizslas are my favorites. You know, I grew up with a vizsla. Ruby. What a nut job, that one. But I loved her. Did you know she was nine years old and running around like a mental case until the day she died? Someone rang the doorbell and Ruby jumped up and had an aneurysm. Dropped dead right there in the front hall. The poor girl."

This was my first glimpse into Miriam's sentimental side, which would go on to reveal itself in abundance over the next few years. Miriam was a dog nut. She preferred animals to humans, spoke to anything with four legs, and could simultaneously curse a fellow human being for "getting in my way" while calling terms of an endearment to a dog for taking a poop.

Miriam rubbed Elektra's ears and kissed her snout. The dog responded by rolling over and spreading her hind legs and showing us her, as Miriam would call them, "lady parts." "You got yourself quite a lady," Miriam cackled. "What a whore!" Elektra has surprisingly large genitalia, a trait Miriam immediately delighted in by declaring, "It looks like a Hershey's Kiss!"

She got on her hands and knees and started kissing Elektra's belly. For a moment I feared she might go down on my dog.

When Miriam was back in the chair, we talked some more about walking and training. "This city's full of lunatics," she concluded.

I took this to mean I had passed the interview. I don't remember if it was that first day, or not long after, when she said, "By the way, I have lots of gay clients. The gay dogs love me. There's Tiny the great dane. His daddies are gay. And Lilly the shar-pei, her daddies are gay, an Asian and his older lover. And Rita the bull terrier, her daddies are gay, too. And I mean really gay. You should see their apartment. I call it the Palace of the Penis. In their living room they have a giant plaster of Paris cock."

I laughed about this, and probably said something like, "Oh, how tacky." I don't know why it didn't occur to me to say: Is that true?

By the time Elektra was spayed, I was seeing Phillip. We were set up on a blind date by a coworker of mine. We met for drinks at a bar in Grand Central. About twenty minutes into the conversation, we realized we each had a dog. His was a sturdy black mutt, built like a bolster, propped up on four tiny legs. Her name was Elizabeth. A few days later, when they met for the first time, Elektra chased Elizabeth around the apartment and turned over her water bowl. "That's because she's a bitch," Miriam said on the phone. "You got yourself a real piece of work. So you like this guy?"

I said I did.

"I'm really happy for you. You deserve it. He sounds like a really nice man." She would go on to say this each time I started dating someone new. My relationship with Miriam had quickly evolved into almost nightly telephone conversations, when she would update me on Elektra's day: "Did I tell you what your daughter did today?" I heard her fumbling for cigarettes. "We were crossing the street, dashing to make a light, and she decided she had to pee right in the middle of the crosswalk. She kept going and going—it was like a river!—and the light changed and there she was, squatting. Such a slut. Even the cops were laughing. I love her, the big dope. Oh, there's my other line, hold on." She put me on hold, and I waited. Sometimes she kept me waiting for four or five minutes. Sometimes longer. Only after a few years did I start hanging up.

"I like Phillip," Leo assessed on the telephone, although it took months to get him out of the house to actually meet him. "He's the nicest guy you've ever dated." Leo and I spoke on the phone every night. Often he phoned from his bathtub, where he would soak for hours with the water trickling, his neck resting on an inflatable cushion.

"How's Elektra treating Elizabeth?" he would ask.

"The same."

"I'm sorry, your dog's insane."

"She's not insane. She's a vizsla."

"That's what it is."

"What?"

"Elektra thinks she's a dog."

"She is a dog."

Leo tsk-tsked liked I'd said something pathetic. "Not Adam. Adam thinks he's a person."

Phillip and I dated for about nine months. We broke up for my typical reasons—he wanted more and I wanted less. One night he summoned the courage to tell me how he truly felt: "It's like you're not really here with me, and I want you here." He was right of course but I didn't have the perspective to see what he meant. I didn't know I had passed out all my affection to Miriam, to Leo, and to my dog. We broke up amicably enough. I think the dogs missed each other for a few weeks.

"Oh well," said Miriam. "Another one bites the dust. At least you'll always have your girl."

"He wasn't right for you," Leo said on the phone. "Too domestic."

"What's that supposed to mean?"

I heard the deep but quiet exhale of a man who smokes four to five packs a day and lies about it. "How should I put this? You're not a nester."

"I'm not?"

"Not yet you aren't."

But hadn't I decided to get a dog to encourage my nesting ways?

"Yeah, right."

When I repeated this conversation to Miriam she said, "Well, you know, he's got a point."

Not long after I started dating Jeremy. It was an intense, summer-long relationship that ended badly, with the door literally hitting me in the ass as I left his apartment the final night. "I never liked him," Leo declared.

"That's because he was smart and he could see right through you," I said.

"He was smart, but not *that* smart."

But he was that smart. My relationship with Jeremy was so brief because he could see right through *me*: "You're so not available," he said bitterly, before throwing me out.

As for Miriam, I remember her saying something like, "Who needs him?" But to tell the truth, I can't be certain which guy she was referring to.

I met Jonathan a few days after September 11, when we were all reassessing our lives. We talked about how we were like a couple in London in 1940, falling in love while the smoke billowed over the city. It was a romantic notion for a very unromantic time, and it didn't last long. Fortunately we had something else in common: our dogs. Jonathan had a cockapoo named Muscat, an Arabic name that felt weirdly apt.

"If you ask me," said Leo, "you need someone with a dog."

"Why's that?"

"Because Elektra's always going to be the most important person in your life."

"That's not true."

"Darling. Yes, it is."

When I'd hang up from talking to Leo, often there was voice mail from Miriam. I'd call her back and she'd tell me about Elektra's day. "I took her to the bank and the park." While she was updating me, it was impossible not to think: Miriam clearly loves my dog. How lucky is that? "She was a very good girl," she'd say.

"Thank you."

"My mother was an evil person."

Over time Miriam's speech became filled with more and more of these non sequiturs. "Elektra had two pees and a poop," she'd report, immediately following with: "Steve's new beach house must've cost him a pretty penny. You should see the pool! Oh I'm telling you." Never mind that I had no idea who Steve was.

Or it would go something like this:

"I'm telling you, you've got yourself a real piece of work."

"Why, what'd she do?"

"I don't know why they think I would go all the way to the South Bronx for fifteen dollars."

Over time, I learned to ignore it. If I were to follow her lead, she'd have me on the phone for forty-five minutes telling me about the paint job of people I'd never heard of before and would never hear of again.

Why'd I put up with it? She adored my dog. She considered herself Elektra's nanny. She walked her, played with her, fed her, checked her water bowl, brushed her, gave her cookies, taught her tricks, took pictures of her, and cared for her exactly as you hope someone will care for your dog. She never let me, or Elektra, down. I suppose it's worth mentioning that during this period, when I had boyfriend after boyfriend, and a best friend a subway ride away, Miriam was the only person who had a key to my apartment.

Sometimes I imagined her in there after a walk: setting out a bowl of water for Elektra and glancing at my kitchen shelves. I know she looked around because occasionally she would mention a book on the table or a ticket stub in the key dish. She wasn't snooping: She was being a friend.

"So this Jonathan guy, is he the one?" she asked.

I don't remember what I said.

Sorry, but I have to backtrack: A week before I met Jonathan, Leo's dog died of cancer. I was in Australia and missed the whole event. I know Leo didn't forgive me for being out of touch during this time. He's right: I didn't make the best effort to phone. But what I'm even more sorry about is how I misjudged the tailspin it would send him into. After Adam's death, Leo slipped into a deep, lonely mourning. I called, but not enough, and I underestimated his acute loss. To make matters worse: September 11 consumed our sympathy and grief. After that terrible day there was little pity for the man whose dog had recently died. I can't say with any certainty that I ever saw Leo sober again after this, not until he checked into rehab a few years later.

Jonathan and I lasted until the following spring, when he broke up with me over sushi. "You can't give me what I want," he said. The pattern was becoming so apparent that I promised myself I would fix some things. I was embarrassed about my selfish behavior then and I'm even more embarrassed about it now.

"It's them, not you," said Miriam. By this point, I knew she was wrong. But that didn't mean I was capable of breaking old habits. I swore off dating. No dates, no phone numbers, nothing until I figured out what I was looking for. Maybe a hookup or two (or three) every now and then, but nothing that could end up hurting someone else. That's how I met Bill; we lasted seven months. We broke up over sushi as well. His blue eyes filled with tears. I'd done it again.

When I told Leo the news, he only said, "I'm not surprised."

"Oh well," said Miriam. "You've always got Elektra and me."

*   *   *

I decided to move. A new apartment in a new neighborhood seemed like a good way to force change into my life. I didn't tell Miriam until I had already bought a new place. My new neighborhood was downtown, too far for her to walk Elektra. I wasn't moving away from Miriam. It was more like I was moving away from myself. An astute observer might ask: moving away or running away? Probably both. And my draining friendships with both Leo and Miriam probably had something to do with it.

When I told her she began to cry. "You're moving downtown? But, but, but—" She couldn't finish. Eventually she managed, "You can't move. She's my baby."

We made promises of doggy visits and staying in touch, but about a year passed before I saw her again. I hired another dog walker, a guy named Rick who worked in a fish warehouse from three in the morning until ten, then walked dogs in the afternoon. A friend recommended him, I met him once, and that was it. He came, he took Elektra out, and on Fridays I left cash on the counter. Our relationship was so distant that one night when I was out walking Elektra she lunged across the street at a handsome man in a blue fleece vest. I apologized to the stranger but he said, "Oh hi, Elektra." Elektra clearly loved her dog walker, even if I didn't know his face. In the meantime, I started seeing Jim, an actor-waiter who had a cat named Oscar. Jim and I would last a year, and although it ended it wasn't a bad ending. With him, I began to open up. With him, I began to be less selfish. (It would take one more guy before I finally gave in and fell in love.)

During this time Leo crashed. He blew his savings on hustlers. He lost his job. An old trick beat him up. He got busted for making obscene phone calls. He passed out in bed with a cigarette and burned down his apartment. On and on and on, like a bad TV movie. And throughout I kept calling, visiting, cleaning up, begging him to stop drinking. Exactly the wrong approach, I now know, but at the time I was clueless.

One evening we made plans to meet at my office to go to dinner. When

I came down to the lobby I saw someone who I first thought was a home-less person. He hadn't shaved in several days. His hair was crusted and standing up. His clothes were rumpled and stained with hot sauce. He had a black eye. The man was wobbling and reeked so badly of alcohol that it seemed—although certainly this isn't possible—it was coming off him in waves.

I took Leo by the arm and got him in a cab. "How many drinks did you have?"

"I'm not drinking."

"How many?"

"You're always criticizing me."

When I got him home I helped him out of his raincoat. A dozen empty minibottles of Smirnov fell from his pockets. "I swear on Adam's grave I haven't been drinking."

"I can't believe anything you say anymore."

When I got up to leave he finally admitted he'd been drinking since the liquor store had opened at nine A.M.

A few days later I told him enough. "No more. Enough. I've had it. Don't call me until you go to rehab."

"But—"

I said good-bye.

And that's all it took: By the end of the month, he was in California drying out. If only I'd done it sooner.

Before I finish the story about Miriam, I want to say something about writing from memory. I'm presenting these events as somewhat simul-taneous or subsequent to one another. And they were, but not really. A whole lot of other things were going on at the same time too—other friends, my family, work, travel, Elektra. But in shaping this story, and teasing out its themes, inevitably I needed to whittle down the memories to a few incidents and lines of dialogue that fit into something that might, or might not, resemble a story. And so the impression I might leave you with is that my life during this time felt exactly like as I have presented it. And it did, but not always. Only now, with the help of perspective, can I see the major themes, and separate the important moments from the trivial. In doing so, I am forced to shape the past to meet my own requirements—the requirements of this story, to be precise. But life, as you live it, does not feel like a story, with characters, themes, and leitmotifs. Life feels like life—thrillingly shapeless and unknowable.

With that disclaimer I can now tell you what happened with Miriam. Somewhat, but not exactly, simultaneous to Leo's final days as a drunk, Miriam visited me in my new apartment. Prior to this we had started talking on the phone again with some regularity. During these conversations, she showed a keen interest in Leo. "How's your friend doing?" she asked over and over. It was probably indiscreet of me to tell her about him, but the way I looked at it was that Leo had already relinquished his right to discretion. I recognize that I'm rationalizing my disloyal behavior, but so be it. This whole story is disloyal, but isn't that always a messy by-product of writing things down? To all involved: Forgive me.

When I told Miriam Leo was finally on his way to rehab she said, "Oh, is that right?" I thought I heard a slur in her voice, but it was different from when Leo had slurred—more like the groggy sound of someone slipping into a coma. The non sequiturs had become more frequent as well. "How's my missy doing?" she'd ask of Elektra, breathlessly following it up with a (poor) opinion of psychotherapy or the mayor.

When she came to my apartment she looked around with a twist in her lips. I had moved from a doorman building in midtown to a loft in a neighborhood that was, as the real-estate ladies say, in transition. The apartment had been a former candy store, converted by the previous owner, a sculptor, into studio space. Now Elektra and I lived there more or less happily.

"You like it here?" Miriam asked.

I said I did.

"You think Elektra likes it here?"

I said I thought she did.

"I suppose it's very you," she said.

"Thank you."

"I guess you like it because you think it's artistic." She said something about not feeling safe in the neighborhood, which took her into a story about a friend's father in the hospital for some sort of blood transfusion. She talked on and on, slumped in the corner of my couch. Her eyes were glazed. Her skin was gray. She was very thin, probably ninety-five pounds. She held her purse tightly in her lap. She showed little interest in Elektra, who was sleeping at her feet. It finally occurred to me: She's on something. And she's been on something for a long time.

I'd had it. I had learned the hard way: You don't do anyone any favors by politely ignoring the obvious. So I called her on it.

"What?"

"You're acting very strange. Are you on something?"

"Oh, no," she said listlessly. "No. No, no, no. You know why?"

"Why?"

"I don't do that."

"Okay, but all I know is you don't look well, and you sound funny, and you come here and criticize my apartment and my neighborhood and you just sound strange and you're totally uninterested in Elektra, which isn't like you."

She closed her eyes, held the lids down for a long second, and opened them again. Her lips moved as if she was trying to say something but couldn't form the words. "I don't do that, you know how you can tell? I know what it does to people."

"All right, that's all I'm going to say about it. I've just learned with Leo that I wasn't helping him by not telling him what I think."

"How's he doing, by the way?"

I told her about his progress in rehab. I detected regret in her voice. "Is that right? That's just great. I'm really happy for him." She stared off at the wall behind me. Had I snapped my fingers in her face, I doubt she would've blinked.

I wanted her to leave but I didn't want to throw her out. I asked her about her other dogs.

"Gone. They're all gone."

"Gone?"

"Everyone's dead or moved away. Dogs aren't what they used to be."

The visit lasted about forty-five minutes. When she got up to leave, Elektra and I took her out to get a cab. She was disoriented and couldn't tell uptown from downtown. She had a blank, ashen look to her that suggested profound fear. "I'm really happy for you," she said. She said goodbye to Elektra, but it seemed to take a great deal of energy out of her, as if it was too painful to care.

I don't know if Miriam was on something that day, or ever. She said she wasn't and I suppose it's only fair to give her the last word. But the few times I spoke to her after, she sounded like something was off. She never came back to the apartment. Once, many months later, I asked if Elektra could stay with her overnight while I went out of town. I suppose this was my way of apologizing to her for not being a very good friend. Even though I had learned from Leo that to help an addict you pretty much have to turn your back on them, I felt guilty about it. And I suppose I wanted to be wrong: Maybe I had overreacted and she was fine—nuts, but fine. So I dropped Elektra off.

About an hour later Miriam left her alone in the apartment and Elektra ripped a slit in the sofa cushion. It was a funny thing to happen because Elektra had never done anything like that at Miriam's. I suspect that Miriam was acting oddly and it upset Elektra. I should make it clear that I don't know this for a fact, and I never will. This is only my opinion; I have no more evidence than what I've presented here. When she called to tell me what happened, she started crying. I told Miriam I would pay for the couch. I told her it wasn't worth worrying over. "But I don't want you to think Elektra can never come visit me again."

"She'll visit you again," I lied.

"No, she won't, you won't think she's good enough to stay with me."

She was weeping and sounded like a small girl. "You won't let her come visit me again."

"I will, I will," I continued, even though I knew it wasn't true.

After many months of rehab, Leo got sober. He stayed out West, moving in with friends from recovery. I call every few weeks and he takes a few weeks to return my calls. I know I remind him too much of the past. I understand that; even so, it's hard. I expect that in a few years we will renew our friendship. I hang on to this hope.

My exes: Three are friends, two are friendly, and one will never speak to me again. It's remarkable he's the only one.

I no longer live in the loft in the transitional neighborhood. Elektra and I moved in with my new boyfriend who, until recently, had a dog, a gentle champion golden named Joey. Not long ago, we were in a bind and needed a dogsitter. "I know someone," I said.

I called Miriam.

MARRIAGE MATERIAL

· · · · · · · · · · · · · · · · ·

Wendy Mass

When I first met Stu's mother, she pulled him aside and said, "You should marry this girl."

Thirteen years later, he did.

Just not the way his mother meant.

If you're lucky, really lucky, you have one friend in this life who feels like a gift. I've always felt the universe conspired to bring Stu and me together at a time in our lives when we needed each other most. In the summer of 1991, I had recently finished college and moved three thousand miles away from home to pursue my dream of writing for television. I had no experience save for a screenwriting class or two, and one entertainment industry contact whose power extended to getting me a lunch meeting with the producer of *Blossom*, which was in its last season. Needless to say, my career wasn't soaring.

Out of options, I got a job as a counselor at a summer camp. I became friends with another counselor named Paul who introduced me to his friend Stu, who was in town for a job interview. Stu could have been Ferris Bueller's twin. Not only because he looked just like Matthew

Broderick at seventeen, but an impish grin lit up his eyes in a way that immediately made me like him. I had just gotten out of a three-year relationship and wasn't looking for another. But after one night of hanging out with Stu, I knew I wanted him in my life.

He moved to town a few weeks later. His voice on my answering machine sounded both jolly and tired, a tone I would come to know like the inside of my head. He didn't have a car yet and asked if I would take him apartment hunting. I drove to meet him at the Hollywoodland Motel, where I almost tripped on the minifridge that had been pushed out of his room and left on the concrete walkway. I found him standing on the bed, throwing a shoe up at the ceiling and ducking.

"Thank God," he said. "I was so lonely I'd begun to name the cockroaches. The ones living inside the fridge have already met their maker."

That evening, as we wearily approached our tenth vacant apartment, we both stopped short. The sky above the small complex was purple.

We turned to each other and said, "This is the one."

Two days later, Stu moved into his new studio apartment in Reseda, leaving the cockroaches and isolation behind. To thank me for my help, he took me to dinner at a restaurant called Yamashiro. Located high up in the hills, the city lights sparkled beneath it in every direction. *Our first date,* I recall thinking, even though the word was never spoken.

Too many umbrella drinks later, I had to hide in a bathroom stall making unpleasant noises. When I walked out, Tina Yothers (yes, from *Family Ties*) asked if I was okay. She seemed genuinely concerned. I nodded weakly and thanked her. To this day, if one of us isn't giving the other the attention we feel we deserve, we'll say, "I bet Tina Yothers would care."

Stu and I quickly became inseparable. We went to Disneyland, where the look of wonder and excitement on his face was like a little boy seeing the happiest place on earth for the first time. In a whisper, he admitted it was his dream to work for Disney some day. It seemed the perfect job for someone who had a poster on his wall with the proclamation, *We don't stop playing when we get old, we get old when we stop playing*.

Stu and I played a lot.

I stayed over at his apartment as often as my own. We could never get to bed before three. We cooked together. We bought bikes and rode them all over Los Angeles. We went to amusement parks, on shopping trips, to concerts, parties, even temple on the high holidays only to swear we'd never go back (he hasn't).

We'd spend hours in bookstores, where it would be my turn to dream about writing books for kids. We'd go out for late dinners, which were usually accompanied by too many drinks and a random celebrity or two, and always ended with a lengthy discussion on the meaning of life, or at least the meaning of our lives.

We both desperately wanted to believe that true magic existed, and went in search of it at new age bookstores, psychic fairs, renaissance festivals, holistic centers, and magic shops. We took classes in Lucid Dreaming and Out of Body Experiences and stayed up late to write short stories based on *The Chronicles of Narnia*.

It didn't occur to me that we weren't dating until a friend of mine asked if Stu was a good kisser and I realized I had no idea. She said if he hadn't made a move in all this time, he was probably gay. I disagreed. How would I not know a thing like that after all this time?

Reasons I thought Stu was straight:

1. He had a Jethro Tull song as his outgoing message on his answering machine: *"I'm a tiger when I want love, but I'm a snake if we disagree."* (This was at the tail end of when it was cool to have a song on your answering machine.)
2. He told me about girls he dated in college.
3. I didn't know anyone who was gay, so I had no basis for comparison.
4. He never mentioned being interested in anyone, which I, of course, interpreted as meaning he was interested in me, just too shy to make a move.
5. We talked about everything. Surely he would trust me enough to tell me if he was gay.

Reasons I should have known Stu was gay:

1. He never mentioned being interested in anyone.
2. He always looked put together, like he walked out of a J. Crew catalogue.
3. He wore jewelry—a marble turtle or crystal on a piece of leather around his neck.
4. He was very neat.
5. He collected recipes and cooked.
6. He loved the Indigo Girls and got us backstage passes.
7. He was the only guy who would go to a Tori Amos concert with me.
8. He had a skin care regimen.
9. His morning grooming routine took five times longer than mine did.
10. Our back rubs never led to anything more. And a back rub is never just a back rub. Unless one of the people is gay.

When months of playful flirting on my part didn't lead anywhere, I finally asked Stu if he ever thought of us as more than friends. He said of course he'd thought of it, but that he had a habit of losing friends after he dated them, and our friendship was too important to him to risk losing.

I should have seen right through that, but I didn't. I actually thought it was pretty cool, and I realized I felt the same way.

Plus, I could never date someone who was skinnier than I was.

A few months later I began to date a guy named Aaron, and on our third date, I introduced him to Stu. That night, Aaron bet me a hundred dollars that Stu was gay. I told him I was sure I would know if he was because we told each other everything. Aaron stood firm in his offer. It was starting to bug me that people kept saying this, as if it made our friendship not as deep as I thought it was.

I assured Aaron that Stu was just one of those people for whom sex wasn't very important, and that's why he didn't talk about it much. Or at all. And it wasn't like he had much free time; either he was with me, or at one of his many jobs. By day he worked at a mental health clinic, by night at a bookstore. Aaron said if Stu wasn't gay, then it wasn't right for me to be hanging out with another guy so much.

The only good thing to come out of this conversation was that I finally had a chance to tell someone not to let the door hit them on the way out.

By the time our friendship hit the one-year mark, Stu and I had learned to recognize each other's quirks and habits. When I was crabby, he'd give me food; when he got tired, his left eye would start to droop and I'd make him turn out the light. I knew he blew his nose at least nine times a day, whether it needed it or not. He knew I had stashes of candy hidden in drawers all around my apartment. I knew he believed that the tree of life, which controls the universe and everyone in it, was actually behind a movie theater in Syosset, New York. He knew I believed that if I searched long enough, I would find buried pirate treasure. He gave me my most prized possessions: a tiny house made of twigs, perfect for a hobbit; a tiny castle made of clay that seemed to hold all the possibilities in the world; and a beautiful edition of the poem *Desiderata*. He was my standby date for parties and work-related events, and I was his. It was the perfect friendship, although a slight awkwardness arose when the topic of his love life came up. I never pushed it, because I knew that if he had a girlfriend, I wouldn't see him as much.

After yet another nonpaid internship ended without a job offer, I decided it was time to give up on the entertainment industry for a while. After a few days of my wallowing in self-pity on the couch, Stu presented me with a copy of *Writer's Digest* magazine, which listed graduate programs in creative writing. We pored through it, and found one at a university nearby. He helped me type up my application, and went as far as putting the stamps on the envelope that I was too nervous to mail myself.

Stu could be decisive about my life, but when it came to his own, he was paralyzed. I would buy something on a whim that I usually couldn't afford, while Stu would spend months researching the best toaster oven, and then more months worrying that he got the wrong one. Stu always knew where his keys were; I never did. He never bought anything on credit; I used my Visa to pay off my MasterCard.

When Stu's big, life-altering decision arose, he couldn't make it. He paced like a man possessed, agonizing between going to one of the top graduate schools in the country for a doctorate in psychopharmacology, which was the main reason he had moved to Los Angeles in the first place, or attending a community college to get an associate degree in animal training and wildlife education, an option he had only learned of the week before. He described the two places—one a lab filled with florescent lights, test rats, and competitive grad students, the other a sun-filled oasis of exotic animals from all around the world that he would actually get to work with, one on one. He put the decision in my hands. I knew I would be breaking his mother's heart, but I made the choice.

There would be no rat testing for Stu.

The week after both of our two-year programs ended, we went hiking together in Lake Tahoe to celebrate. We followed a path that led deep into the woods to a clearing where people were setting up picnics. We sat on the ground, our backs against a big tree, staring at the food others had been smart enough to bring. Stu picked up a stone and began scraping the bark, trying to draw sap out of it.

I asked, "Do you think that cloud looks like Homer Simpson?" and he replied, "I'm gay."

It took me a second to realize his response wasn't referring to the Homer cloud. When it sunk in, I put my head in my hands and said, "Crap. I owe Aaron a hundred dollars."

To my relief, he laughed. He said I was the first and only person he'd told in his life, and that it was the hardest thing he'd ever done. As we sat there, watching the sap drip down the crevices of the bark, something changed between us. The last layer of an invisible wall came down. Never again would I have to defend our relationship to the guys I dated—or to my friends who said I was wasting my time on someone who I wasn't going to wind up with. I gave him a long hug and could literally feel the tension drop from his shoulders.

On the way home, Stu was so electrified from our conversation that he bounced in his seat like a helium balloon. As we wound up and down the mountain roads, he poured out the story of the one guy he had dated, back in college. I listened, rapt, so excited finally to hear him talking this way. Lost in his memories, he didn't see the edge of the cliff that was rapidly approaching. He kept talking about how the guy was cute but immature; as he started reminiscing about their first kiss, I yelled, "Turn, turn, turn!" Surprised, he quickly yanked the wheel around to the right. The tires squealed and dirt flew. The side of the mountain loomed, the way it does in the movies when you know the car is going over. I learned that your life actually *does* pass before your eyes. We skidded to a stop about twenty feet away from the edge and he turned off the car.

At first, we were too stunned to talk. Then with uncharacteristic seriousness, Stu said, "If we had died just then, it would have been okay because I finally told someone. Well, I would have felt bad for killing *you*, of course."

The rest of the drive was quieter, each of us lost in our own thoughts. Any selfish resentment that I might have felt that he hadn't told me earlier disappeared. Hearing him say he could die now, finally having released this secret, was a big wake-up call. I couldn't imagine what it must have been like for him. I wished he had unburdened himself sooner, but he explained that it was a question of him accepting it himself first. Who could argue with that?

Not long after our trip, Stu started dating. At first he was tight on the details, but he gradually opened up more and more about the kinds of guys he was interested in and about gay culture in general. He now took pleasure in critiquing my boyfriends and telling me why they would never make it in the gay world, a world he complained was based too much on appearance. To fit in, Stu joined a gym, shed his chest hair, whitened his teeth, and started getting his hair cut in Beverly Hills instead of at Supercuts. I finally saw how much of himself he had kept hidden, and was so relieved he finally felt free to explore the missing part of his life.

For the next few years, I was his only friend who knew. I took this responsibility very seriously. I never told our mutual friends, nor did I pay my ex-boyfriend the one hundred dollars. At twenty-seven, I moved to New York for a job in publishing, the first of many moves between us over the next decade. Wherever we were, it was usually three thousand miles apart. In that time, we have traveled together on buses, trains, subways, cars, trolleys, trams, ferries, planes, Jet Skis, ski lifts, and cruise ships to see each other. Some visits are weeks long; others are only hours.

If Stu or I ever lose focus or get complacent, we kick each other back into gear. After we had both suffered particularly difficult breakups within a short period of time, he wrote me a letter that said, "Someday both of us will be exactly where we want to be, and it will only have been possible with all the unexpected twists and turns our lives have taken."

It was hard to see it then, but I held on to those words and one day, twelve long years after Stu and I met, it hit me: I was finally exactly where I wanted to be. I hadn't given up writing for kids, and my books were now on bookstore shelves. I had met the man I was going to marry. I finally had real furniture. Stu, who was becoming well-known and sought after for his work in wildlife education, had bought a house, and was living his dream of working at Disney's Animal Kingdom in Orlando. Ever since we wrote short stories together in the late hours of the night, we knew we made a good writing team. Working long distance, we sold a story idea to a popular television show, and coauthored a book about fantasy literature. In every novel I have written, Stu has provided key turning points when I got stuck. I connected him with an editor who was looking for an authority on animals, and he has since published twelve books on animals and the environment. Without each other, we wouldn't have taken the paths that led us to where we are today.

So when my mother slipped me the card of a rabbi to perform my wedding ceremony, I knew that wasn't what I wanted. I wanted Stu up there with me and my fiancé, Mike, and not just as an usher. In ten minutes, Stu got ordained on the Internet and was legal to perform weddings and funerals in forty-six states.

There we stood, Mike resplendent in his tux, me in the long white dress that made me feel like a Greek goddess, and Stu in the black robe that was actually a *Matrix* Halloween costume. After years of headlining shows at Disney, he was a seasoned public speaker who made us laugh and cry as he led us through the ceremony.

My husband and I sometimes joke about whether or not we're truly married, but it was perfect and apparently fooled a lot of the guests. To this day, some of my parents' friends tsk-tsk about the rabbi who messed up the Hebrew blessing over the wine.

The last time Stu and I saw each other was at The Cloisters in New York City. We took the guided tour through the medieval castle and gardens, but wound up whispering to each other the whole time. Whether the topic was the real possibility of time travel, the benefits of a high-fiber diet, a new book series we wanted to write together involving ancient books of magic, or the mystery of what keeps love alive, we could pause only long enough to briefly admire the ancient tapestries on the cool stone walls before one of us would think of something we couldn't wait to share. Then Stu flew home to Florida, where he was to appear the next day on a Discovery Channel special, and I drove over the George Washington Bridge and back to my husband, twin babies, and impending book deadline. I knew, from years of experience, that the lump in my throat that came with each of our good-byes would last about an hour. Soon I'd be comforted that the universe would bring us together again, the way it always did, in ways I'd never have predicted.

III

A Fine Romance

"He's gay, you know."

—from "Love in Other Lifetimes," by Anna David

EVERYTHING I ALWAYS WANTED TO KNOW ABOUT SEX (AND LIFE) I LEARNED FROM GAY MEN

● ● ● ● ● ● ● ● ● ● ● ● ● ● ● ● ● ●

Stacey Ballis

Ultimately, I have Judith Krantz to thank.

When I was nine, I discovered in our family bookshelves a novel called *Princess Daisy*. The flap copy promised a tantalizing story of a real-life princess, stripped of title and money, making her way in the world alone under mysterious and tragic circumstances. Within minutes, I was hooked. The book had deposed Eastern European royalty marrying Hollywood ingenues, great beauties and handsome powerful men, and women who rise above the worst the world has to offer with grace and dignity. And sex. Lots and lots of sex. It made me all tingly in my prepubescent girl parts.

By the time I hit seventh grade, my life had changed in three very important ways. First, I had become a compulsive overeater and was putting on weight more quickly than I was putting on height. Second, I had become completely boy-crazy, obsessed with the idea of having a boyfriend. I learned pretty quickly that the fat girl doesn't get the boyfriend, at least not in junior high. Fortunately, I wasn't a social pariah: I had plenty of friends, and the boys, even if they didn't want to go steady with me, at least didn't groan in disgust when the bottle spun my way.

The third thing, one that was entirely the result of my reading endeavors, was that, at age thirteen, I was determined to get myself a gay friend. In so many of the sexy books I had been reading, the women had at least one very close, very fashionable, very witty gay male friend who gave them the hard truths and made perfect martinis. I was a few years away from needing a martini, but a gay friend seemed like just the thing. He would be a boy I could pal around with, a boy who would simultaneously understand my obsession with young men and have the sort of male insight to help me land one. Someone who would ensure that I wouldn't face yet another Chicago winter without someone to snuggle with.

Within two months of starting my high school career, I had found a wide circle of friends, but had not yet landed a relationship. Apparently the fat girl doesn't get the high school guy, either. I had, however, met Jody. Jody was in several of my classes and played flute in the band with me. He was tall and porcelain-skinned, with green-blue eyes and strawberry-blond hair. He was much, much prettier than I was. He was experimenting with drag and had mastered applying foundation without getting that dreaded visible mask effect; he was doing this master makeup blending on a jawline with *stubble*! He wore a delicate rhinestone earring in his right ear, a subtle smear of sapphire blue eyeliner, and a perfectly tattered tweed trenchcoat. He was my age, and totally, completely out.

Jody sat directly behind me in algebra. On the third day of class, I felt something slip into my hand. It was a note.

> *I swear to God, this man is making my ass twitch, he's so boring. At what point do you think he will realize we are all smarter than he is? X = Y are we wasting our time with fucking algebra. What are you doing for lunch? P.S. I LOVE LOVE LOVE your boots, so sassy! I just want to lick them.*

I had agonized over those boots, black leather with floral embroidery. They were right on the edge, either deliciously cool or totally dorky, and while I was convinced of the former in the store, I was equally convinced I had made a huge mistake as soon as I got them home. With that one compliment, I was his forever. We picked up hot dog lunches that day and sat on the mall in front of the school, eating and talking a blue streak about our common lack of current male companionship.

"Babycakes, the way you work that hot dog . . . you're going to make some boy very lucky indeed!" he said.

This made me blush furiously, as I swelled up with pride. He laughed. "And you look good in red!"

"Fuck you," I laughed, punching him lightly on the shoulder.

Jody sighed dramatically. "Oh, darling, wouldn't that just be the simplest answer for both of us."

Thus began my official career as a fag hag. Jody took me shopping in Chicago's bustling Boystown and helped me find my own perfectly tattered tweed trench. Jody took me to Berlin on Belmont Avenue for my first gay nightclub experience, teaching me that if I made really great faces while I was dancing and kept my upper body swaying to the beat, no one would be able to tell that my feet didn't move too much. Jody introduced me to my first drag queen, and explained about the pull-and-tuck method of hiding her package so as to be able to pull off the skin-tight Lycra jumpsuit she was wearing.

Jody became my tutor in all things male, as well as many things female; he wasn't just prettier than me, he was in many ways a better girl than I was. He taught me how to put my makeup on properly; he taught me how to kiss. But I wasn't longing for Jody to be my real boyfriend. While I thought he was beautiful, I wasn't physically attracted to him. Mainly I loved how he made me feel. He told me I was wicked in a tone that implied that I was a film noir vixen of devastating sexual power. He said it in such a reverential voice that I knew he really believed it.

If I had been profoundly wrong about most of my decisions where boys were concerned, I was dead-on in one respect: Getting a gay boyfriend enriches life immeasurably.

I became better dressed. "Honey, those pants are ghastly. Come over here and look at these instead. See how this cut is going to make you look taller?"

My vocabulary increased. "The taint? You never heard of the taint? It's that little piece of deliciousness between the balls and the butthole. T'aint the package, t'aint the tushie . . ."

I began to pepper conversation with witticisms. "He is from the Chinese province of DarLing!"

I learned more about the penis than previously thought imaginable. "No, just lick *underneath* the rim of the head, that's where the really sensitive part is."

Under Jody's tutelage, in addition to the ever-growing list of naughty books I'd read—not to mention that I was sporting an awe-inspiring D-cup rack—I became the queen of party hookups. I never lacked for male attention, albeit drunken, at any of our weekend gatherings or after-school get-togethers. But no matter how charming my conversation, how deft my kissing, how readily I allowed access to second base, none of those encounters ever resulted in my party playmate pursuing anything further. Making out drunk or high at a party? No problem. Furtive gropings in the back of the bus on the way back from a band competition? I was always popular. Escorting me to the homecoming dance? Not so much.

High school moved along at its petty pace as I stopped getting taller, continued getting wider, outgrew my awkward stage of glasses and braces and an unfortunate short haircut, and entered into an awkward stage of overmoussed hair and royal blue mascara. I had the requisite fake ID to get into clubs or buy beer at local liquor stores, and the tits to ensure no one ever actually asked to see it. I had a car named Bippy, a part-time job as a receptionist for my parents' real estate business, and a large collection of rhinestone pins and Salvation Army jackets. I had lost my virginity by design to a good straight male friend, having lost patience waiting for a true love to show up and deflower me. Jody had come up with the idea; he said he would have done it himself, but he had looked pretty nauseated at the reality of it.

Jody was the perfect playmate, and while we weren't friends to the exclusion of others in a *My So-Called Life* kind of way, we spent a reasonable amount of time hanging out together. We went dancing at Medusa and the Mars Bar. We went shopping on Halsted and at the Water Tower. We ditched a whole day of school to watch a sneak preview of *The Unbearable Lightness of Being* at the Fine Arts Theater. We tried cruising for boys at the mall, but that never worked; straight boys always assumed we were a couple, and if Jody ever actually found another age-appropriate gay boy, I quickly became extraneous and bored.

By senior year, Jody had been joined by Mikey, a less effeminate, less flamboyant (but no less gay) boy whom I'd bonded with while working on the literary magazine.

Still, I had no boyfriend.

I never saw my size as an imperfection, and neither did Jody or Mikey. We brashly viewed my weight as protecting me from shallow guys who wouldn't be worth my time or energy. I pitied the skinny girls as much as I envied them. They might have an easier time with the cool clothes, and they never lacked for boyfriends, but could they ever know that those boys liked them for who they were inside? All three of us wanted what they had, those magical girls: the handholding, the never worrying about having someone to dance with, the ability to buy a pair of boots that went over the calf. The secret jokes and huge class rings from boyfriends that were made small enough to fit delicate fingers with layers of tape.

Still, I believed I was both lovable and physically desirable, and Jody and Mikey believed it, too. As much as I longed for a real boyfriend in my life, for someone to devote myself to, for the romance I had been reading about for so long, I never thought losing weight was the way to get there. I just needed to meet a better quality of guy. While much of this confidence was acquired from a lifetime of loving support from my family, and some was a part of my natural personality, a great deal had to do with Jody and Mikey and their constant reaffirmation of my good qualities and desirable attributes.

"You totally need a real *man*," Jody would say. "These little boys just don't *get* you. You're too *smart* for them. You need someone *mature*."

"I *know*!" I would reply every time. "These children we go to school with are nice as friends and all, but I mean, really! They have no idea what a *relationship* is about! I just need to find someone more on my own intellectual level, you know? Someone who doesn't care if there are only eight band uniforms after me, and six of them are being worn by football players."

Band uniforms, you see, were numbered according to size. Unisex, they got both taller and wider as the numbers went up. There were 115 uniforms owned by the band. I was number 107. This fact was gloriously listed for all to see on the large assignment sheets in the uniform room. And yes, most of the defensive linemen from our football team filled in 108–113, joining band being an easier way to complete the school's music requirement than music-theory or -history classes. The pants on 107 were so long on me that they were hemmed to my knees, but the jacket at least fit over my ass.

"You're built like a *woman*," Mikey would rail. "*Women* are supposed to have *curves*. You're not supposed to be some stick. You aren't Edie Sedgwick, for Christ's sake."

"I know that, and *you* know that," I replied. "But these idiot *boys* don't know that. And frankly I need to get *laid*."

"Can I get an amen to that!" Jody threw his hands in the air like he was receiving the Holy Ghost.

Anyone who thinks the boys' locker room is the center of the lewd and crude universe has never spent time with a sexually active girl and her favorite gays. At seventeen, I was a teenage girl who had given up the goods, and now I had the good fortune to be dishing with my gay boyfriends. The three of us would turn instantly from mooning, cooing romantics into lust-driven psychotics, with language that would make sailors blush. We bandied about words like *girth*, engaged in the age-old debate about spitting versus swallowing, and had competitions to see how many different positions we could name in one minute.

"He doesn't exactly fill out his track pants in a meaningful way," Mikey might say in reference to a new student teacher in gym.

"One never knows for sure," Jody would pipe in. "Bobby was the same way. Looked like a total absence of junk unless we were fooling around, and then when it came down to business, it was like he was smuggling three pounds of grapes in his briefs."

Mikey was the one who first suggested that I look outside of school for someone a little more mature. We both had agreed that someone older wouldn't expect a girl to be the size of a French fry, and I embraced that ideal with all the fervor of a Grail-tormented knight of yore.

Ah, the older men of my youth.

Some of these guys had graduated when I was a freshman and were now in college, but still showed up at the parties when they were in town. There was a particularly handsome twenty-something waiter at an ice cream parlor where our crew hung out. I dragged my friends there twice a week for four months so that I could flirt with this devastatingly cute guy. (This did wonders for the size of my ass.) I finally got up the nerve to leave him my number on the table one night. But he never called. I assumed he must be gay, and I worried that I'd never find a straight guy.

Mikey consoled me by telling me that the eighties were a tough time for gaydar, what with all the androgyny in fashion. "It's Robert Smith's fault, princess, all these boys in eyeliner—anyone would be confused."

Despite our best intentions and well-laid plans, when prom time came, it was Jody who escorted me, dapper in a tuxedo with a cream silk scarf jaunty around his neck. He and Mikey took turns dancing with me all night and telling me how beautiful I was. And while I would have loved to spend the night after prom in a hotel room in the arms of a lover, I consoled myself with the knowledge that at least my escort genuinely loved me, and I wouldn't have to worry about prom-night date rape.

I emigrated East for college, and set about immediately to fill the void in my life formerly occupied by Jody and Mikey. Jody decided to travel for a time instead of going to college, and Mikey headed to California. In a time before cell phones and e-mail, and with our new adventures taking precedence, we fell out of touch the way high school friends often do. But when one door closes, another opens: Eli lived exactly one floor below me in my freshman dorm, and we sniffed each other out within thirty-six hours of our arrival. He had been wandering on the girls' floor and stopped in my open doorway to make a window treatment recommendation.

"You might want to extend that left side a bit beyond the actual window," he purred in a slight Southern drawl from the doorway.

"Really? Over the wall? Why?" I asked.

"Your window isn't centered on that wall. It is over to the right six inches or so. If you add six inches to the curtain on the opposite side you'll give the illusion of the window being centered, that's all."

We looked each other up and down. His khakis were pressed, his loafers battered artfully, the blue oxford well-worn and fraying delicately at the sleeves and collar, with a wide brown belt worn a little low on slim hips. He took in my full size-18 amplitude, the baggy black pants, the freshly minted Brandeis sweatshirt, the wrestling shoes.

"Are you a budding interior designer?" I asked coyly.

"Maybe." He grinned. "Or I could be a florist."

"Or a caterer," I offered.

"Hair stylist is always an option," he laughed.

"Don't sell yourself short, you could be a lawyer." I paused for dramatic effect. "I hear Lambda always needs good people."

This cracked us up, and within two hours he had completely rearranged my furniture, referred to three other guys from our dorm as "she," "Nancy," or "Miss Thang," taken a scissors to my sweatshirt, and given me a thorough tutorial on the art of the blow job.

"Don't give up the goods too quick, honey. These college boys will move on to the next girl in a heartbeat unless you give them a reason to come back. And getting them off without getting them naked is a guaran-damn-tee of a follow-up phone call. Now, you wanna start by firmly shaking hands with the monster . . ."

Eli assured me that by parceling out my gifts, I could be reasonably sure of three to four dates, by which time, "They'll have fallen in love with you despite themselves!"

Eli wasn't wrong, and with his guidance I managed to spend the better part of my freshman and sophomore years having intense mini-relationships of anywhere from one to four months.

A few choice tips from Eli worked wonders. It wasn't all about sex, either. Eli helped bring out my inner seductress, even when I wasn't in the bedroom, and I quickly gained new confidence.

I learned new social skills. "You're a natural flirt, kiddo, but you lack mystery. Get 'em hooked with the humor, the light stuff. But when it comes to real information, be cagey. Watch me, a little I-know-a-secret kind of smile, no teeth, a lowering and slow raise of the eyes, and a shrug. Then some innocuous comment like, 'You know how it is,' or 'Let's speak of more pleasant things,' and he'll be chomping at the bit to really *know* you."

I appreciated it even when the truths Eli told me were hard to hear.

"Dollface, I adore you. And I think you are the most beautiful, sexy, spectacular broad on this whole campus. But as much as you want boys to love you for who you are and ignore that you color outside the lines of conventionally accepted physical beauty, you yourself are a total looks queen. All these boys you moon over are handsome and fit and shiny like a damned Calvin Klein ad. When have you ever gotten a crush on some little schlubby guy with sloped shoulders and a weak chin, hmm? Your ideal of attractiveness is just as fucked up as theirs, and if you don't open your horizons a bit, you are going to miss out on some men who are just as extraordinary as you, and just as alternatively beautiful."

Eli spent his junior year abroad in Israel, and then transferred out of Brandeis to pursue a career as a rabbi. I missed his warm wit and caustic observations on life. His time in the Holy Land had reinforced his personal commitment to Judaism, which was wonderful for him, but put something of a barrier between us, as I am not religious. And it is difficult to talk about sex with an about-to-be rabbi. But his sage advice to me about my tastes in men broadened my criteria. I threw myself headlong into a relationship with my future ex-husband and lost my drive to pursue a constant companion of the homo variety.

However, once a hag, always a hag: After returning to Chicago and enduring graduate school, a wedding, and teaching high school English, I found myself working for a professional theater company, running their education programs. In one fell swoop, my social arena broadened to include more gay boyfriends than even I could juggle. My circle of gays even had subsets:

There were my shopping gays, who introduced me to the thrift stores where shabby was indeed chic: "It's got great lines, kiddo, just strip that yellow paint off it. Cross my heart."

My bitchy gays, who would sit for hours in my living room drinking wine and dishing the dirt on everyone: "I'm serious, he actually showed up to rehearsal high as a kite, and fell asleep during table work!"

My dancing gays, who kept me out far too late, and took me back to Berlin for the first time since Jody and I had last gotten our groove on, the summer after graduation: "Baby, it's already two in the morning, you might as well keep dancing!"

My dinner-party gays, who took my natural love of cooking and entertaining and sent me into the stratosphere: "I found the best place for wild mushrooms ever, come get me and we'll practice risotto tonight!"

My hang-at-the-bar gays: "Well, we could either go sing show tunes at Sidetrack or shoot pool at the Four Moon. Your choice."

My sub-for-the-couchbound-husband gays: "Of *course* I want to go to the opera tomorrow!"

And of course, there were my sex-coach gays. The latter attempted to assist me in rekindling, albeit unsuccessfully, the spark in my marital boudoir: "Have you tried the spanky spanky? He's a corporate guy, they always like the submissive role." The failure therein was not their fault but my own. (Do not ever marry someone to whom you are only peripherally attracted and who is boring in bed. It won't get better with time. No matter how many wise homosexuals offer guidance.)

After my divorce in 2001, my gay boyfriends became more essential to me than ever before:

"You are taking out a personal ad. I'll help you. And I promise not to laugh if you meet a couple of losers."

"I'm coming over. No one should watch a *Thirtysomething* marathon alone."

"Get off the couch and come meet me. This place is crawling with straight boys and martinis."

"It isn't your job to make someone happy if they aren't making you happy. Of course you're not a failure!"

"I'm sure it was just the beer, sweetie, of course he's attracted to you."

"I think we need new shoes."

They pushed me with firm directive back into the dating world and schooled me on how things had changed since I was last single.

"It's all about the online research. Google him, baby, Google him!"

They talked me through how to get over my first-time-naked-with-a-new-boy anxiety: "Wine, not liquor, two glasses, not four, and candle-light, not electric."

And how to delicately handle a limp lover who has been overserved: "Take his face in your hands, kiss him gently on the lips, and tell him that you'll blow him for the same number of minutes he goes down on you."

They built up my self-confidence and my lingerie collection: "Of course you can wear a garter belt! On those luscious, creamy thighs?"

They encouraged me to discard all the devices from my nightstand that had gotten me through the last years of my marriage, and helped me acquire a totally new set of toys that were not only functional, but yes, pretty, too: "Oooh, look at this one, it's lavender!"

They helped me buy a new bed, introduced me to six-hundred-thread-count sheets, and then showed me how to find and attend to the male G-spot: "Okay, first, shower him—you know how lackluster straight-boy hygiene can be. Then use some lube and your middle finger . . . about two and a half inches in, make a motion like you're beckoning him . . . and for heaven's sake, don't make that face when you do it!"

For all the wonderful support of family and colleagues and friends, it was my gays who really got me through the dark days and back out into the spotlight, both in and out of the bedroom. A pink spotlight, no less.

So when a recent new lover gasped to me, "I think I lost conscious-ness for a second there—that may be the best sex I have ever had," I just snuggled up to him and said, "Yeah, I know. Thank God for gay men."

Judith Krantz would be proud.

LOVE IN OTHER LIFETIMES

• • • • • • • • • • • • • • • • • • •

Anna David

"He's gay, you know," Bonnie said.

We were sitting on stools at a then trendy, now long-gone bar on Melrose, surrounded by Amstel Light bottles and cigarette smoke, and I'd just confessed that the guy she'd introduced me to a few moments earlier had made me feel like I'd been struck by the love-at-first-sight lightning bolt.

Of course, I'd felt such bolts before. I was twenty-five years old at the time and I couldn't fathom relationships built on trust and mutual compromise; I saw only fables or romantic comedies, Cinderella's prince or the lead actor rushing toward his one true love at the ninety-minute mark. I had no interest in what would happen post-happily-ever-after: Love, I was convinced, happened in a lust-filled instant, and there was no mistaking it for anything else.

"Really?" I gasped.

"Really. And not just gay—*very* gay."

While I nodded at Bonnie, Brian and I caught eyes again and gazed at each other the way only two people who are dying to tear each other's clothes off can. "I'll be right back," I said to Bonnie, making my way across the room to Brian's side.

"Oh, my God, Bonnie just told me," I blurted, knowing I didn't need to finish the sentence. I felt absolutely confident that the lightning bolt hadn't only hit me—from the moment Bonnie had introduced us, Brian and I hadn't taken our eyes off each other. The news about his sexual orientation felt worse than disappointing; it actually seemed intrusive, like it was infringing on the course nature wanted us to take. "Is it true?"

Brian nodded but continued to look at me in a way that I can only describe as deeply heterosexual. "It is—I mean, I always have been. But maybe—I don't know . . ."

That opening, combined with the sight of his sparkling hazel eyes and perfect cheekbones, was enough for me. "I'm buying us shots," I announced, fully confident that my bar order was the only thing we needed to get us to the next step and erase any notions he'd had before this point about his sexuality.

I know all about falling for gay guys. Since college, it had been my way of swooning over unavailable people without having to get involved with married men, and it's safe to say that in the ensuing five years, I'd been attracted to more than my fair share of guys who preferred guys. My previous biggest crush in this arena had been on Martin, a tall, spectacular British boy I met during my junior year in Cambridge, when we were in a play together. Everyone in the play—the entire cast of straight women and gay men—was in love with Martin. Not only was he charming, hilarious, and beautiful, he also didn't seem distinctly oriented one way or the other. Finally, at the cast party, I'd had enough of unrequited love so I confessed my feelings to him. And then Martin—charming, hilarious, beautiful, and, as it turned out, gay—told me that I had actually helped him to come to terms with his sexual orientation because, subtle though I'd thought my crush had been, Martin had been well aware of it, and when he compared the attraction he felt for me with his attraction to a short Asian guy whom he didn't think was as attractive as me, I lost. (Whether or not this was true, it was a brilliant rejection on Martin's part, as I walked away with my ego more than intact.)

But this was different. With Martin, there had been signs. He had loved Bananarama. (I'd justified that as a British thing.) He wore pink. (It looked good on him, I told myself.) He was in a musical with only straight women and gay men. (You can't label someone just because of his circumstances, I'd thought.) Though Brian was, in fact, out, he also happened to be sartorially straight, dressed in a button-down shirt and gray slacks, basic black, nondesigner shoes, and no product in his hair. Plus, there was the matter of the eye contact we kept having—not to mention that he seemed far more interested in cornering me for one-on-one conversations than the gay men I'd met before, who would start off talking to me alone but then trot me over to their friends like I was something they'd found outside and wanted to display in show-and-tell, usually urging me to be "fierce" and funny.

At the end of the night, I had all the confirmation I needed. "I can't believe it, but Brian is into you, too," Bonnie said, shaking her head. "This is just too bizarre."

With that, I went up to Brian to say good-bye and he asked if we could go on a date the next night. I nodded, giddy, and we kissed good night—on the lips, in the bar, with seemingly no worries over who might see. What kind of a gay guy does that?

I figured the conversion process was more than halfway through.

When I was getting ready for Brian to pick me up the next night, I found myself more excited than I'd ever been for a date before. Perhaps it was my desire for thrilling, dramatic, romantic-comedy love, but there was something fabulously intense about an attraction so deep that it penetrated the standard definitions of sexual orientation. The notion of a date with a regular old straight guy, who wouldn't have to sacrifice or defy anything to go out with me, seemed downright dull in comparison.

At dinner, Brian and I wasted no time in psychoanalyzing his past. Over steak and red wine, Brian told me all about how his older brother had stolen his teenage girlfriend away from him. Brian had been devastated and had found himself obsessing over thoughts of his brother and the girl together, and especially the thoughts of the two of them in bed.

And then—this part's a little vague, as I think we were well into our second bottle—he started obsessing over his brother sexually. He knew it was incestuous and wrong and horrible, but it felt better than obsessing over wanting to kill his brother for stealing the girl away from him. Soon after, he hooked up with his first guy.

I listened sympathetically as I poured him more wine. "My God," I said, feeling as I imagined Freud must have when he first coined the word *hysteria*, "You're not gay—it's just that a traumatic event made you *think* you were gay."

Brian shrugged, and I leaned in so that our faces were inches away from each other. "Maybe I'm bisexual," he said.

I was willing to accept that for the moment. After all, this transition back to straightness might be slow for my new boyfriend.

I nodded and he kissed me—a real, passionate, entirely straight kiss.

After dinner, we went to a bar across the street and though it wasn't a gay bar, the minute we walked in, we ran into two gay guys we both knew. One of them, Matt, was decidedly hostile to me, even though he'd been quite friendly when I'd met him a few months earlier and he'd been hitting on one of my gay male friends. When Brian went to the bathroom, Matt turned to me. "What the hell do you think you're doing?" he asked.

"What are you talking about? You mean, with Brian?"

"Of course I mean with Brian. What kind of game do you think you're playing?" With that, Matt got up in my face (though he was a few inches shorter than me, so he was really more up in my neck).

"We're just hanging out, nothing to get worked up about," I said. Even though in my heart I imagined that Brian and I were setting new standards of what love could be, I knew Matt wouldn't make an appropriate confidant. Actually I felt angry over his attitude. Shouldn't I be the one concerned with whether or not Brian was playing games with *me*? I was doing what I'd always done: going out with a man. Brian was the one betraying his group, and while I was personally thrilled with Brian's decision, I didn't appreciate Matt treating me like I was some wanton woman out to trap gay guys in my tangled web of heterosexuality.

When Brian came back from the bathroom and Matt went off to smoke, I told him what had happened. He shook his head. "We used to date," he said of Matt. I should have figured; Matt probably wouldn't be the last of Brian's exes to have a problem with us.

Brian and I went back to my apartment, where I opened a bottle of wine and we both lit cigarettes. After we were done smoking, we started kissing. As we kissed, I started to move Brian toward my bedroom, but when we got to the door, he suddenly stiffened. "I don't feel comfortable doing anything more," he said.

While this was the first time I'd heard a guy say anything remotely like this, I was even less prepared for my reaction. "Why?" I asked, feeling like he was suddenly backing out on the courageous and important journey we were taking together.

"Look," he snapped, showing me for the first time shades of a less-than-perfect personality, "that's all I want to do. If you have a problem with it, I suggest you go to the bathroom and masturbate."

"Stop," I said, kissing his neck. "No pressure." Brian calmed down, and after kissing for a while, we cuddled and I was able to erase from my mind the notion of my being someone who puts pressure on men in bed. After a while, we just lay there trading cigarettes and sad stories about our respective dysfunctional families and the times we'd been in love or thought we'd been in love, doing the postcoital thing without any coitus. When he described his utter confusion in the face of romantic relationships, it seemed like he was stealing dialogue from my own inner script, and the conversation felt more intimate than anything that had transpired thus far.

I fell asleep with Brian spooning me and dreamt about being in Washington, D.C. I couldn't remember any of the specifics in the morning—just that it somehow felt, as dreams sometimes can, deeply meaningful. When Brian woke up, I told him I'd dreamt about our nation's capital, and he mentioned that he'd been born there. That's when I came to the conclusion that I'd been working toward since the moment Brian had first caught my eye in the bar two nights earlier: We were soul mates and had been together in previous lifetimes. Given my fondness for story-book love and my well-established history of spontaneous passion—my third date with an ex was, essentially, a move from San Francisco to Los Angeles to live with him—this seemed the only possible explanation for our unlikely and illogical connection. When I shared these thoughts with Brian, though, he only smiled warily.

Over breakfast at the café across the street, Brian took a deep breath and gave me the apologetic look I realized I'd been dreading from the beginning. "I think you're fantastic," he said, his eyes intensely fixated on his over-easy eggs. "But I have to tell you: I really think I'm gay."

"But . . . but . . . ," I sputtered, unwilling to give up on this fantasy so quickly. "What about what you were saying about being bisexual?"

"I know I said that," he said, smiling his perfect pearly whites, his beautiful mouth making this rejection that much harder to take. "But after last night, I think I realized that it's not true. I'm just gay."

"But you're attracted to me—you said it! A few times!" Horrifyingly, I found myself on the verge of tears.

"I know," he said, sipping his latte. "And I think you're very attractive. But I just can't do this."

That's when I realized that there wasn't a whole hell of a lot I could do. While I felt positive that what he was saying couldn't possibly be true, a part of me also knew this was not a battle worth fighting. How could I accuse someone of being wrong about how he felt when our individual feelings, by their very definition, have to be correct?

Later that day, I stopped at a spiritual bookstore in West Hollywood that I'd passed many times and barely noticed. They sold the usual collection of crystals, affirmations for inner children, and books about creating your own destiny. I was looking for some comfort, some explanation, some confirmation that what I'd experienced with Brian was as real and important as I thought it was. I saw the book I'd subconsciously been seeking: *Only Love Is Real: A Story of Soulmates Reunited* by Brian Weiss, M.D.

That the author's first name was the same as my potential soul mate's was all the impetus I needed to buy the book.

It had been a crazy few days and I'd slept probably a total of about seven hours over the past couple of nights. But I stayed wide awake that day, riveted by every word of my new book, even though I'd never been one for self-help or spiritual books of any kind before. It explained that not everyone was comfortable with the notion of previous lifetimes, let alone the concept of meeting and falling in love with the same person over and over again. Brian will come around, I thought, as I underlined and dog-eared passages and pages that I found significant. I brought the book along to dinner that night with Bonnie, certain she would support my exciting new discoveries.

But she, as logical and wise about love as I was dramatic and superficial, just shook her head. "Anna, you're going on no sleep, ranting about how you've fallen in love with a gay guy, clutching this crazy book. I'm worried about you."

I wanted to shake my head right back at her, but hearing her summarize my behavior brought just the tiniest bit of perspective back. I put the book back in my purse and willed myself to talk about something besides Brian over dinner.

I wish I could tell you that Brian came around and we were able to go on our journey hand in hand, while teaching the world not to be so hung up on labels like gay and straight. It would be wonderful to report that the other Brian was right and my Brian and I had ended up as together in this lifetime as we had been in the previous few. But the truth is that Brian and I didn't speak again until we ran into each other a few months later, when he glanced at me with embarrassment—the kind of look I'd imagine a straight guy might give a gay guy he accidentally ended up in bed with one night when he was feeling experimental. "I'm so sorry for getting you all mixed up in my confusion," he said. "I was going through a rough time then."

boyfriend's expensive sheets, even though he was lying six inches away from me.

I would also be turning thirty in two months, which terrified me—in retrospect, a triviality, but no less dire a situation at the time. When the darkness is closing in on the mind of a depressed person, when everything seems bleak, when there is a gray, mushy tint clouding his vision, he will do anything to fix the problem.

I did something most would consider crazy, though I did it to get out of the crazy. I booked myself on a flight to Boca Raton to see a psychic healer who was renowned for shifting people's energy around and getting them out of all sorts of maladies. I was, and am, aware that this puts me in a small fraction of the population that has believed in such mystical dogma. But I figured no harm could be done; all I had to lose was money and time.

Or so I thought.

Sondra had come highly recommended by some family friends on the West Coast; she had reportedly cured their infant daughter of a life-threatening illness. Surely a garden-variety depression would be easy. After speaking to her on the phone for about fifteen minutes, I scheduled myself, with incredible blind faith, for three days of sessions, which was the amount of time she recommended.

I imagined my little trip to Florida as an esoteric rest cure, a departure from my life in the West Village.

Traveling alone isn't easy when you're despondent. But once on the plane, I started feeling hopeful; I pictured myself journeying to an exotic healing mecca, like Lourdes or Bath or Rajasthan.

The only people who knew where I was going were my boyfriend and my mother. For anyone else who asked, I was in Florida on business. Because it was terribly likely that a novelist working on a book set in New England would be doing research in Boca Raton.

I arrived on a Sunday evening at a grand, palatial hotel that wasn't too far from being a Floridian version of the Taj Mahal. It had a pink exterior, with magnificent 1920s architecture and a lobby decorated with palm trees and monkeys. Except for the staff, everyone else was at least thirty years older than I was.

The next morning, I met Sondra at her home office a few miles away, where she lived and worked in a condominium complex. While clean, it was extremely modest, a far cry from the waterfront luxury of the resort. The room where she practiced was decorated with stuffed animals, images of angels, and the other types of new age paraphernalia that tend to offend me more on an aesthetic than a spiritual level.

I sensed, though, that she was a good person. She was a slight, wiry woman in her early sixties, with curly brown hair. She gave me a hug upon meeting me, and I felt her bony spine. She might have weighed ninety-five pounds. Her accent was Florida by way of south Jersey; while her message could have come out of a holistic wellness center in Santa Monica, her delivery was that of a sassy Brooklyn diner waitress.

Some would be put off, but I found it charming.

We sat down, and she explained her philosophy. Most of it—apart from the hands-on healing part—didn't seem terribly different from concepts I had encountered in various self-help books over the years. She had healed people all over the world; articles had been written about her and her work.

"Do I believe in this?" she said to me. "I know it works. We need to keep your energy field as clear as we possibly can, because that's what we're in charge of."

When I asked her about her use of the royal "we," she said she was referring to herself and her spirit guides. I dismissed it as a quirk of the profession, in the same way that I would ignore an auto mechanic's or manicurist's improper grammar.

We did two healing sessions a day, lasting about thirty minutes each; I lay on a massage table, clothes on, eyes shut. The basic concept was that we all have an energy field that extends eighteen inches in every direction; some people, like her, have the power to move this energy around, unblocking it, refocusing it. As she moved her hands over me, I could actually hear a crackling in the air. I would feel alternating sensations of heat and cold over my body; I could hear her murmuring as she did her work, as if she were communicating with some higher power.

I was exhausted after the first day, though I also felt as if a tremendous weight had been lifted. Still, I had my doubts. During the drive back to the hotel, I stopped at an intersection of strip malls and fast food restaurants; I was behind a truck with a bumper sticker that read, "Welcome To Florida. Now Go Home."

Maybe I should have.

"I don't think you should write this essay," my mother tells me on the phone, calling from San Francisco. I have asked her to verify some of the chronology of it, which has unfortunately necessitated telling her what it's about.

"Why not?"

"Because people might think you're crazy. And do you really want everyone to know you were that depressed?"

"What does it matter? Most writers are a little bit crazy. It's about having interesting experiences; that's part of why I did it. And I'm not depressed anymore. Besides, if you're going to talk about depressed writers, I think I'm in pretty good company. Most of the writers I respect have been at one point or another."

"It just seems ungrateful, after everything she did for you. She helped you." Though I would hardly describe my mother as new age, to her, if something works, who cares how it works?

"I'm not being ungrateful. I paid her. I don't owe her anything. I'm telling my side of things. I'm not writing anything that isn't my truth."

"Okay," she says, in a voice that tells me she's not convinced. And then, more quietly: "I just don't want you to get hurt."

"I'm not going to get hurt," I say. "Trust me."

The healing sessions were one thing, but what I wasn't prepared for were Sondra's psychic abilities. If I encountered a psychic on the street, on television, or on a hotline I was supposed to call, I would be suspect. But there in Florida, away from my everyday life, and after paying a considerable amount of money, I wanted to believe.

We had long, intense discussions when we weren't doing the healing sessions, in the morning and afternoon, breaking only for lunch, when I would go back to the hotel. They were very much like therapy, except that they incorporated Sondra's psychic talents. Whenever I asked her a question that had to do with the future—and she made it clear that I shouldn't ask her anything I wasn't prepared to hear the answer to—her eyes went to my left side, her pupils skittering off to some other, unworldly place. She started by talking about a lot of stuff that had happened to me in the past, all events she had no way of knowing about. As I feasted on these little crumbs of truth, she began telling me about my future. When I would break up with my boyfriend, whom she said was not right for me (I already knew that, thanks). How many books I would publish. And when I would meet the next guy, who was going to be the love of my life, a man with whom I would truly connect.

She told me many things during those three days, some of them nutty, some of them sane, many of them prophetic, and quite a few that turned out to be dead-on accurate.

Of course, I focused on the guy.

She was quite specific: I would meet him in September of the following year. We would be at a dinner party, and he would be wearing a white shirt. Or giving off some kind of white glow. She couldn't be sure. Given my growing faith in Sondra and the absolute despair from which I was emerging, I believed her.

I finished up the three days in Florida feeling tired, but hopeful and relieved. She instructed me was that I wasn't to go to the gym for seventy-two hours after the last session, and I wasn't allowed to have sex, either. The former was no problem; as for the latter, I think I lasted two and a half days.

The real proof was in the coming weeks and months. I got through the rest of the fall, the holiday season, and my thirtieth birthday with relative happiness. My dark mood, seemingly without fanfare, had lifted.

I finished a first draft of the new novel. By the end of winter, I was strong enough, sad as it was, to break up with the boyfriend. I thought, somehow, that Sondra had made it all happen, that she had banished the negative energy that was keeping me down. I went into spring feeling free.

My regular therapist, a woman named Molly who is the exact opposite of Sondra—blond, robust, fair-skinned, and from the heartland—was not happy about any of this. She didn't say it outright, but I knew. It wasn't so much that she was threatened by my seeing another therapist; I think she didn't trust Sondra's methods. But I had become a believer. And when you are a believer, every bit of evidence serves as proof of your faith while you ignore anything that might sway you to the contrary side.

That is, until something royally fucks up.

I would continue to seek Sondra's advice over the next year, twice when she made visits to New York, and during several phone sessions. She assured me that the psychic line was even better over the phone. There were fewer distractions than in a face-to-face meeting. The phone line was pure electrical energy. Logical, right?

I thought so at the time.

She became my fast-talking Florida guru, the woman I turned to—more than my friends, parents, or therapist—when I needed advice at a critical juncture. I grew addicted to finding out what she thought about people or situations or business dealings. I started feeling guilty, in fact, that I had an inside line, though she assured me she would never reveal information that would hurt anyone. Sondra, after all, could tell me things about people I knew! I learned about their sex lives, their family troubles, their shady transactions. What could be better than that? It was like overhearing gossip without any of the drawbacks. And at only $150 an hour!

I didn't always take her advice; when making decisions, I relied on intuition, friends, and the powers of Google as well. But more than anything, I wanted to believe what Sondra said was true, because it would validate that one event I was holding on to: the guy I would meet in the fall.

Those summer months were happy and productive, if only a bit lonely. I dated some, but eventually decided there was no point. After all, it was in September when I would meet him, not earlier. And my God, if I got serious with anyone much sooner than that, I might jinx the whole thing!

So when I did meet a young man whom I liked very much, and though it was not in September, but at the very end of August, and he was wearing not a white shirt but a yellow one, and we were not at a dinner party, but on a first date at an Italian restaurant on Hudson Street that admittedly did have a long line of tables close to each other along a window banquette that was *almost* like a dinner party, I fell for him.

Over the next two months, I stopped seeing my friends as often, spent nearly every moment with him, sent and received gifts, went out to long dinners, even took a trip to Los Angeles where we vacationed at the Chateau Marmont.

He told me he loved me, gave me silly nicknames, said he could imagine never dating anyone else again.

He suggested things that meant real commitment in my mind, like getting a couples membership at an independent film society or taking a weekend road trip to the Berkshires. When I came back from eight days in San Francisco celebrating my parents' wedding anniversary, he said he never wanted to be apart from me for that long again.

My confidence about my new boyfriend was so high that I let myself plunge headfirst into those murky, deceptive waters of early-stage love. I paid no attention to contradictory signs: the fact that he'd never had a relationship lasting more than four months; that though he was enormously talented, he had no steady employment and was bouncing from one friend's couch to another; that he had an annoying fag hag who constantly hung around and openly admitted her jealousy of us. I ignored it all, because I was convinced we could overcome these problems.

What I also ignored was the lingering thought that I should call Sondra to ask if he was the right person.

I was afraid what she might say.

All I knew was that he made me happy, happier than I'd been in a long time, and I didn't want anything, or anyone, to ruin that.

So when this young man turned out not to be the love of my life, but rather a bit of a creep, when he left my apartment one night after slamming the keys I had given him down on the kitchen table, when he told me he wasn't cut out for relationships, that there had never really been anything between us, that I was too difficult, too much of a perfectionist, too high maintenance, I was not so much sad as I was angry. A very expensive psychic, after all, one whom I had flown down to Florida to see, had told me he would be the one! The one is not supposed to slam keys down on the kitchen table. The one is not supposed to walk out of your life two months after you start dating him.

The next evening was Halloween. I felt pathetic as I walked home through the cacophonous, revelry-laden streets of the Village. I had left my friends behind for this guy, and though they would all eventually be there for me, I wasn't ready to go crawling back. I was still in too much shock.

A month later, after a bleak November, it occurred to me to call Sondra.

"He looks like the one, feels like the one," she told me. "But you went too fast. You changed the script. You expect everything at once. You want it all. The romance is the icing on the cake. You have to build a strong foundation first."

Good advice, I thought. Maybe he had been the one. Maybe I had gone too fast. (Yes, I had definitely gone too fast. That much, even without a psychic, was obvious to me.)

"I see the number seven," she said. "It's not seven days, but it might be seven weeks, or seven months."

He would be coming back, she said.

Seven weeks seemed preferable, but I would have settled for seven months.

I held on to that damned seven, keeping it in the back of my mind as seven weeks and then seventy days passed, with no word from him. My mood became even more despondent than it had been a year ago. I stopped going out, stopped dating, was writing less than I would have liked.

I was also intensely angry at the young man and at Sondra. But mostly, I was angry at myself for screwing up so completely, for ignoring all the conventional wisdom about relationships I usually try to follow: *Go slow. Weigh out your options. Don't expect too much, too soon. Don't try to change him. And for God's sake, don't give him the keys to your apartment three weeks after the first date!*

Then, in March, the young man did come back.

Aha! I thought. Sondra was right. This is it. He's changed.

No, he had not.

He wanted to be friends. He was sorry for hurting me; he wrote me several long, sweet, romantic e-mails talking about what a good time we had had together. But long, sweet, romantic e-mails are not the same as getting back together.

I was convinced, though, that if we saw each other in person, all the feelings would return. We had an awkward dinner during which I had nothing to say until I finally let loose everything I had been feeling for the past five months. *What makes you so fucking special that you don't do relationships? And what makes you think you can treat someone this way and then just walk out of his life?*

He had no good answers for these questions. He was rude, defensive. Though I was still physically attracted to him, I was sad to realize he was a person I no longer wanted to know.

At the end of our nondate together, I ran into a friend who was out with a girlfriend of his. "Save me," I whispered to them. "Don't ask questions—we're going out for drinks now."

I turned back to the young man, gave him a big hug, lied that it was great to see him, and said good-bye. It was the last time I spoke to him.

*   *   *

When Sondra sent a postcard and left me two voice mails telling me she would be seeing clients in Manhattan in June, I didn't respond. She sent an e-mail a week later—"a loving reminder," she called it— asking me again if I would like to make an appointment. I wrote her back, saying I wished her the best on her trip, but I would not be booking a session.

I wondered, if she could see the whole story, why she didn't sense my unhappiness with her advice. I wondered why she had needed to contact me four times. And I wondered, after more than a year of knowing her, if she was so psychic, why didn't her number accept blocked caller IDs?

When I asked my mother these questions, I could almost hear her shrugging over the phone. "Well," she said, "maybe she's not psychic about everything."

Friends who've heard this story always ask me whether I thought Sondra was an elaborate faker. I don't think so. She did get me out of my depression. Perhaps it was by unblocking some of the negative energy in which I was mired—I'll never know for sure—but mostly I believe it was by giving me hope. By telling me that I would meet someone new, that my career prospects were bright, that my family loved me, she helped make lucid my perception of the future.

She went wrong, of course, in her specificity. Thanks to her, I focused on a man in the fall who may never have existed. That fantasy got me through the year, but I shouldn't have relied on it once September came.

I decided, after the actual young man left for good, that life was best lived moment by moment, that I was the only one who could give order to it.

Still, I am reminded of those three days in Boca Raton: the balmy weather, the pink hotel, the strip malls, the apartment complex, the departure from my everyday life. The fact that so few people knew where I was, I could have disappeared entirely. The idea that I was leaving a piece of myself behind and returning a new person.

And I admit, despite everything, that a part of me still holds on to that narrative, the one all single people have in some form or another, the one Sondra gave me, of meeting that knight in white-shirted armor.

I know he's out there.

It doesn't have to be in September.

Really, any month would be fine.

A MANHATTAN LOVE STORY

Melissa de la Cruz

"I love you."

I tell this to Morgan in a cab as we zoom up the West Side Highway after a night spent at the Sound Factory, the illegal after-hours gay dance club where vogueing was invented and where we have spent the last six hours high on Ecstasy, our arms and legs wrapped around each other while a drag queen circled us and pretended to take photographs with an imaginary camera: "Click! Oh, yes, gorrrrgeous!"

Now, it is eleven o'clock in the morning, and the bright, flat sunlight makes a mockery of our garish outfits—my fishnet stockings, his shiny Dolce & Gabbana shirt.

"I love you, too," Morgan replies, squeezing my hand. I feel tears in my eyes, because I do love Morgan—so fiercely and passionately that it sometimes borders on hysteria.

We are both twenty-two and Morgan is gay, but that is completely irrelevant.

Morgan and I met during our freshman year at Columbia, instantly bonding over our mutual appreciation for Madonna. At that point, having gone to an all-girls high school, I had little experience with boys; I was also awkward and shy. My strict Filipino Catholic background had drilled into my head the importance of remaining a virgin until marriage, which resulted in a twisted obsession and repulsion toward sex.

I wanted nothing more than to be with a boy, but I also wanted nothing more than to have him never touch me.

So when my roommate told me she thought Morgan might be gay, I didn't believe her. Nor did it seem an obstacle—if anything, it was a plus! Morgan was everything I wanted a boyfriend to be—sophisticated, erudite, charming, with good hair (a caramel swoop over a tanned forehead), and about as sexually dangerous as a potted plant. He was Australian, had lived all over the world (Singapore, Paris), spoke fluent French, and yet was still refreshingly down-to-earth. He liked *Star Wars* and fatty mustard-laden pastrami sandwiches, as well as Alabama slammers, having spent his last two years of high school in that great Southern state.

Also, Morgan taught me how to smoke. His long, thin fingers handed me one Camel Light after another. I was a sheltered girl from the northern California suburbs who wanted to reinvent myself as a jaded city girl. Peer pressure? Is there such a thing when one is so eager to be corrupted? Morgan was a mentor and ally, and we were terrible influences on each other. Together we ran up thousands of dollars on our parents' credit cards—charging exorbitant restaurant meals (opting for sushi and sake rather than the plebian offerings at the college cafeteria) and weekly shopping sprees at Charivari as we amassed avant-garde designer wardrobes. Issey Miyake. Claude Montana. Christian Lacroix. It was the late eighties, early nineties. Fashion was not yet the mass-market reality television phenomenon that it is now; it was the province of the design elite, the aesthete, and we wanted to be part of it.

Precisely because I was a financial aid student with hard-working immigrant parents, I wanted to shed every bit of my image as the underprivileged, earnest striver in twenty-dollar cotton sweaters from The Limited. Upon meeting my prep-school roommate, with her casual attitude toward Bergdorf cashmeres and offhand invitations to fly to London or the Caribbean on a whim, I had intimated very early on that there was absolutely nothing sexy about being poor.

My family was once financially and socially prominent in Manila but had suffered from the economic bust that affected the country in the mid-eighties. We had been forced to start anew in America. The downturn in our fortune was something I was deeply embarrassed about, and one night found myself telling a bald-faced lie to kids on my floor that none other than Corazon Aquino, the then-president of the Philippines, was my aunt (she was not blood-related but a close friend of my family's; to me, that was close enough). I was careful to project a confident, popular persona, even going so far as to invent a devoted boyfriend at home, con-cocted from a senior-prom-date picture with a cute guy I was set up with by the popular girls in my class.

Only to Morgan did I confess the unglamorous truths about my life—that my family ran an employee cafeteria at Sears in San Bruno, that we rented and did not own our house, that I had absolutely no friends from high school. The photo that adorned my college pin-board of a group of attractive kids with me in the middle? Taken during the one party I had ever attended, after graduation, when sentiment overcame snobbery, and for once, every girl in our forty-person class was welcome to a beach bash in San Rafael.

With Morgan I felt safe enough to be myself because he had secrets of his own. His aunt had committed suicide. His parents didn't get along. He wasn't happy, but he wasn't unhappy, either. He never thought my not having money was a barrier to living the high life. In his mind, we were young, smart, and attractive, and should have New York at our feet. Morgan always figured out a way to get on exclusive nightclub VIP lists, or invited to cocktail parties at swanky penthouse apartments on Park Avenue, or asked to art exhibits in vast Tribeca lofts. We ogled celebrities together (Isaac Mizrahi! Christy Turlington!) and availed ourselves of numerous open bars. When we weren't out, one of our favorite pastimes was to talk on the phone for hours and eviscerate everyone we knew in common—catty character assassination that only two people who weren't getting any action could excel at.

He was my very best friend and the most important person in my life. By junior year, I had accepted his avowed asexuality. Part of me knew Morgan was gay, but another part didn't accept it. I was still holding out for the day when he would realize we could be *everything* to each other. In the meantime, I began dating a sweet boy, a year younger than me and as inexperienced as I was. Next to Morgan, my feelings for Kevin seemed wan and puppyish, though it was nice to have someone to kiss. We would be fooling around in my stuffy dormitory room, the two of us half-naked and sweaty, and I would find myself wishing I was watching *Beverly Hills, 90210* with Morgan instead.

Did I wish I were kissing Morgan? I'm not sure. In the fantasies I spun in bed at night, we were entangled in the most romantic and erotic of love affairs; yet when I saw him in the morning, reality would blow those gauzy images from my mind. Morgan was a good-looking guy, but there was no sexual tension between us. If any did exist, it was a one-sided projection of mine. Still, I persisted in the illusion that I was Morgan's quasi girlfriend. I even got him to admit that if he ever felt like dating a girl, the only girl he would date would be me. He had a series of complicated excuses to explain his monklike behavior: wanting to focus on school, not feeling ready for the next step, cherishing his independence. It was such a shame, since we made a good-looking couple. Everyone said so, and even if our so-called romance was as fabricated as the airbrushed images in the glossy magazine pages I modeled my life after, it was enough to sustain me.

It never occurred to me to raise the issue of his sexuality, not even when we spent every weekend checking coats at the Lesbian-Bisexual-Gay Coalition dances together our senior year (yes, he was literally still in the closet). Nor did I find it odd that our circle of friends grew to include several flamboyantly gay men, all of whom told me in no uncertain terms that they believed Morgan was gay. They could see I was hopelessly in love with him, and nothing good could come of the situation. I was blithe, blind, and refused to listen. I convinced myself that Morgan was simply an open-minded straight man, a quality I cherished in him, albeit mistakenly.

When Morgan came out to me the night before commencement, I crumpled to my knees and cried. (Later he would tell me my reaction was worse than his mother's.) I was shattered and in my grief proposed a Bloomsbury-type union: We would marry each other but allow ourselves lovers (although we were still both virgins at the time). He happily agreed, and the thought of such a European-style arrangement made us feel very worldly indeed. That evening, it even briefly occurred to me that I might be a lesbian. What could explain my complete and total denial? Was I so repulsed by the idea of sex with men that I was hiding a nascent homosexuality that I subsumed in an attraction to a man who had no sexual feelings for me?

Yet the next day, during the graduation lunch attended by both of our families, when we exchanged presents—gold cufflinks for him, Tiffany earrings for me—I understood that it could no longer be the two of us against the world. The look on our mothers' faces said it all. They were already planning the wedding, and I couldn't be part of such a farce. I didn't want to play Dora Carrington to his Lytton Strachey. I was a bourgeois girl from San Francisco. I would have to make new friends, get myself a real boyfriend, and leave the cozy cocoon of glamour and gossip that we had built for each other.

But to my surprise, our friendship didn't change all that much after Morgan came out. If anything, we clung even more tightly to each other. We continued to share and dissect each other's every perverse secret, poisonous thought, or insecure assessment of our looks and personalities, and indulged in books and movies of questionable origin. The Danish art film *For A Lost Soldier*, a movie that celebrates the sacred love between a nineteen-year-old Canadian serviceman and the eleven-year-old Danish boy who becomes his lover and helpmeet? One of our favorites. We saw it in a darkened theater in the Village with what looked like grizzled escapees from a NAMBLA convention.

We made our way through the city and began to grow up—quitting our wild nightclubbing ways along with the coke and Ecstasy binges once we became junior professionals—coming home to a shared apartment where I would cook inedible meals that we would wash down with liters of vodka and 7UP.

We even fought like lovers, with me crying and saying I didn't think he loved me the way I loved him (as a best-best-best-friend), and I needed him to treat me better, while he, remote and aloof, arched his eyebrow and remained silent, causing me to cry even harder. Neither of us were dating at this point; our world was still so small that there was only room for the two of us, as if we were living in a hermetically sealed bubble.

Like an old married couple, we knew how to get under each other's skin.

"Those chairs you bought from IKEA which you think are so stylish are nothing but cheap cafeteria trash!" he would taunt, knowing I was ultra-sensitive about my interior-decorating aspirations, while I would counter with insults about his once-glorious crown of hair.

"Thinning, isn't it?" I would sneer.

I like to think these gruesome fights were a consequence of trying to make sense of what and who we were to each other, now that he had come out of the closet and we could never have a romantic relationship. Could we simply be friends? Somehow, we understood that our relationship had become suffocating in its intensity, and we pushed and pulled on each other, alternately encouraging the other to *Date! Date! Forgodssakes, date!* or to meet new friends to widen our social horizons. Yet each new friend or potential boyfriend only brought a gnashing of teeth and a feeling of abandonment and jealousy.

As the years went by, Morgan remained the most significant man in my life. Now that I had finally lost my virginity, I would sleep with the guy-of-the-moment at night but look forward to brunch with Morgan in the morning, brunch being a more important meal than dinner. I had a succession of loser boyfriends. There was the failed forty-year-old playwright from Queens whose latest work was a series of technical manuals; the racist investment banker who dumped me due to a misplaced sense of political correctness (his last girlfriend was Asian, and he didn't want to seem like he had an "Asian fetish," so he would have to dump me, because I was unfortunately, um, Asian); the handsome lawyer with an annoyingly high-pitched, whiny laugh. But it was still Morgan whom I spoke to every night before I went to bed, his clipped, cultivated accent as soothing as a bedtime story. He was my security blanket, my other half, my conscience.

Our relationship never progressed to the physical, except for one drunken semi-orgy with two of our close friends during a dinner party in the dead of winter. It was January, and we were huddled in an East Village tenement walk-up. After we had consumed several bottles of wine and moved on to vodka, Morgan cheekily suggested we take our clothes off, so we did. As we danced to Abba, naked and giggling at our daring in Lauren's living room, as free as wood nymphs, I thought the impromptu nudie show would be as far as it would go. Then I ended up on Leo's lap, Leo being the ex-boyfriend of my best girlfriend and a boy I'd had a passing crush on for years, and suddenly it wasn't so innocent anymore. When Leo moved on to Lauren, I found myself on Morgan's lap, and we grappled tongues and touched, my hand stroking his upright member. I still remember how hard and thick it was—and how odd that after all these years, I was finally getting to touch it. But I knew Morgan's excitement didn't come from kissing me, but from seeing Leo naked. We were comfortable with each other and laughed at how absurd it all was. I was surprised to find that fooling around with Morgan felt obligatory, while I was more turned on by being with Leo. It was probably safe to say that everyone in the room was.

Then one night, four years after Morgan first came out to me, and eight years after we had first met, he stopped returning my calls.

The night it happened was the week I had gotten my first article published ever, and my close friends, all twenty of them (by then, I had successfully expanded my social circle), were taking me out to celebrate. I called Morgan to let him know what time to meet us at the bar, but he never called me back. I kept calling and calling, and finally, he took his phone off the hook. I was aghast. What was going on?

The article we were celebrating was a personal essay published in *The New York Press*. It was an incendiary article, written in the in-your-face-antiestablishment voice of the paper. It was called "I Hate White Women: A Second Banana Speaks" and detailed my anger at how society depicted women of color as secondary sidekicks to the (tongue-firmly-in-cheek here) "Caucasian master race." I cited the movie *Clueless*, in which black Dionne sucks up to white Cher. It was meant to be satirical and ironic because of course, I didn't really hate white women. Several of them, in fact, were taking me out for drinks that evening. I had shown it to Morgan before I had submitted it, and he had pronounced it "genius."

I assumed that whatever it was that was keeping him from being at my side that night had something to do with my finding a small footing in the literary world. We had each harbored dreams of making it big in the city. For years, Morgan had been supportive as I tried, and failed, to get a succession of novels published while working a day job as a computer programmer. He was trying to crack the film and television industry but was stuck working in marketing and finance for a cable network.

A level of competition had always existed in our relationship—in college, we were anal grade-grubbers, keeping a scorecard of who had gotten a better mark in the classes we took together. For me, it was partly an economic convenience. If we took the same classes, I could borrow his books and spend my parents' money on shoes. Later, we would compete over salaries, even though we loathed our jobs.

I assumed in my vanity that his absence that night meant it had been too painful for him to realize I had finally received professional validation for my writing skills. It was an explanation I clung to because I would have no other way of knowing why he acted as he did.

You see, Morgan dumped me that night.

He never called me back, not that night, not a week later, not *ever*.

I called his apartment repeatedly for weeks and left tearful, angry messages. But nothing happened. Finally I gave up.

His betrayal felt like being blindsided by a cab—I was hurt, dazed, vulnerable, weightless. I didn't realize until then how much Morgan grounded me, how much having him in my corner meant that I could face the world confidently. Morgan's love was like armor—he told me repeatedly that he thought I was beautiful, and more fabulous than Madonna (*oh c'mon!* I would say, thrilled to my bones).

More than anything, I didn't want to be alone in the world.

But most of all, I was *furious*. In a rage one evening, I went through all my photo albums and tore up all the pictures of the two of us, taking out my anger on the Polaroids. How could he do this? How could he throw away eight years of friendship? Hadn't we always said "I love you" to each other in cabs after parties? Didn't that mean anything?

I was stunned. It was as if Morgan had died. I had just started dating my now-husband at the time, and all of a sudden, Mike had to be everything to me, just as we were getting to know each other. But my husband was a practical man; he admitted that he was intimidated by Morgan's hold on me and relieved that he was no longer a factor. Mike knew Morgan was the first man I had ever loved, and was worried that this meant I could never love him because he was so different from Morgan. (For the record, my husband is sophisticated, charming, erudite, and has good hair, but is from Ohio, not Australia, and so secure in his heterosexuality that he is not at all threatened by our large coterie of gay friends.) He was threatened by Morgan as a romantic rival for my affections, not because Morgan was gay.

From our mutual friends—a gang of gay men who took my side after the "divorce"—I learned that Morgan was explaining his actions by painting me as a psycho-bitch-controlling-harridan. That he had felt trapped in our friendship and felt like he couldn't get his life on track if I was always around, trying to one-up him. At the time, I was still so angry that I didn't process any of this information in any rational way. I just saw it as name-calling and did my fair share of splattering mud on his reputation. Morgan, calling *me* "controlling"? When he was so jealous of every new friend or boyfriend of mine that he came up with nasty nicknames for all of them?

In the end, I won custody of the friends. Okay, so maybe they didn't have much of a choice, since Morgan dumped them a few months after dumping me. I suppose he didn't quite feel comfortable sharing, since our friends were determined to remain neutral for as long as possible. But I like to think that he saw the writing on the wall, figured out which way popular opinion was beginning to sway, and ceded them to me. To the fag hag go the gays.

About six years after he dumped me, I bumped into Morgan at New York Fashion Week. I was a full-time journalist by then, and he had landed at job in production at MTV. I went up to him with no hesitation. "Morgan!" I said, my voice breaking. The emotions that washed over me were complicated and strong. Joy. Relief. Pain. It was so good to see him again.

"We need to get a drink," he said, in his cool, ironic tone. But his eyes were twinkling.

The two of us jumped into another cab and repaired to the nearest hotel bar, the Algonquin, which seemed appropriate since we had always idolized the Round Table wits. Dorothy Parker's and Robert Benchley's ghosts hung over us as we hashed out the remains of our friendship.

It was so easy to go back to the way we were—as if the six years of no contact had all but disappeared, we joked and laughed and drank vodka cocktails and caught up with each other's lives. He had actually met Madonna! (Through work. The bastard. And the one thought he'd had was, *I wish I could tell Mel.*) I told him about covering Fashion Week and of now being privy to all those red-carpet, velvet-rope events we had always dreamed of attending, while he regaled me with stories about music industry mayhem—all the rock stars he'd had to fish out of limousines and babysit backstage at *TRL*.

Finally I asked him the question that had been lingering in my mind for six years: "Why?"

"Couldn't you guess?" he asked.

The article?

The article was an excuse. Yes, it had been hard for him to see me finally published. But it was more than that. It was that I had finally landed a good boyfriend in Mike. "You said *he* was your best friend, after two months!" Morgan said. "So where did that leave me?"

I'd *said* that? And suddenly I remembered. Morgan and I were having our usual Saturday brunch (Mike was home in Ohio visiting family over Thanksgiving) when I nonchalantly told Morgan I thought of Mike as my best friend, and that I was sorry, but I couldn't go see *The People vs. Larry Flynt* with him because Mike had asked me to wait and see it with him when he got back. Morgan had given me an odd, angry look. We always saw movies together—at least, before I met Mike. And what I'd said was true. I did consider Mike my best friend. Even then, I knew he was the real partner I had been waiting for in life. But what I'd said to Morgan had been deliberately unkind, although I had tried to pass it off as a casual comment at the time.

Morgan took a sip of his cosmopolitan and handed me a Camel Light, just as before, and told me he had left *for my own good*, since if he had stayed, he would have tried to poison my new relationship.

"It wouldn't have lasted, if I had still been in the picture," he said.

I didn't think he should give himself that much credit, but I saw his point. It would have been too difficult to balance Mike and Morgan—already Mike had chafed at having to spend so much time in Morgan's company. Ultimately I would have had to choose between them, and I wasn't about to lose Mike. So Morgan's pre-emptive disappearance was an answer to the question he and I had been struggling with for years: who and what were we to each other, now that he had come out of the closet and I wasn't romantically interested in him anymore.

Could we be friends someday? I still hope so.

When we lived together in a low-income apartment (we didn't know it was low-income at the time), on Friday nights Morgan and I would come home from our dreadful jobs, turn up the air-conditioning in his room, sit on his unmade bed, and drink homemade, heavily spiked piña coladas. We called it *going on vacation* because the air-conditioning was such a luxury for two people who had weathered several New York City summers without one, it reminded us of being in a four-star hotel.

We would dance around the room to whatever new house music CD he'd bought off the street, and his large conch-shell ashtray would accumulate a mountain of cigarette butts. Most nights we would hardly even bother to leave the apartment, let alone his room. We were young and frustrated, stalled in love and our careers. But looking back, those nights when we did nothing at all were some of the happiest and most carefree times of my life. Who needed St. Barth's? We had each other.

In my mind, even today, Morgan will forever be the continental sophisticate who introduced me to a world beyond the college gates, to a city where yellow taxicabs spell promise and glamour and the VIP list always has our names on it.

SUPER COUPLE

. . . .

Sarah Kate Levy

O ne night in a crowded bar in West Hollywood, my dear friend Ed, the great unrequited love of my life, bought me an appletini and smiled like he was glad to see me. It had been more than a year since I'd been graced with that smile, so I imagined it meant Ed actually *was* glad to see me. This was big news in my personal universe, because I'd been moping after him since we were teens. Ed had come up to L.A. from his home in San Diego to attend his brother's birthday party, and since it was the first time in ten years that he'd invited me anywhere without my asking, I let myself pretend it was a date.

At the time, I was a champion pretender. My robust fantasy life had sustained our relationship through high school (*Someday he'll realize he's just fooling himself with those other girls—he really loves me*), college (*Just because Ed never calls me doesn't mean he's not thinking about me*), and my recent decision to move all the way from New York to Los Angeles in large part to be closer to him (*Okay, so he still never calls me—but it has to mean something that I've come all the way out here and it hasn't made him freak out and move!*).

That night I was sure there had to be a special reason Ed had asked me out. I was twenty-four years old, and lately it had seemed to me as if I'd aged past the realm of casual dating. When I met men now, I looked past the one-night stand to the long-term possibilities—after all, my mother had been married at twenty-five. So I couldn't help wondering if Ed's asking me there didn't presage something greater, if maybe the power of nostalgia might not nudge us toward a shared future. I enjoyed the free drinks and got a little high off his smile. When he leaned across the table to whisper in my ear, I went warm imagining what he was going to say to me. I even unbuttoned another button on my shirt.

"Do you think my brother's gay?" Ed said.

Those six little words changed my life.

Ed had pointed out his brother Moises when I arrived at the bar, but for most of the evening, Moises had registered as little more than a face in the center of a loud and happy crowd, a flicker in my peripheral vision while my gaze stayed locked on Ed. But I had reason to search him out now, and I easily picked him out among the mass of bodies on the dance floor. I say "easily" because Moises looked so much like Ed they might have been twins. They shared the same compact build, the same golden skin, the same short, short curly hair, the same mischievous smile and sparkling eyes. I watched Moi dance, and I watched the way he looked at the tall brunet man he was dancing with, and I knew that look cold. That look was the same look I'd seen Ed give every girl I'd ever brought him. It was the look I'd waited more than a decade for Ed to shine on me.

But I didn't tell Ed that. What I said was, "Do I *think* he's gay? Ed honey, this place is packed wall-to-wall with dancing men."

I'm still not sure why Ed couldn't see what I saw. In fact, I should have known right then that if Ed could be so clueless about someone so close to him, so completely oblivious to the obvious, then the chances were pretty slim he'd ever really come to understand me. But if Ed was suffering his own case of massive self-denial, then, man, did I have him beat: There I stood at the end of the evening, waiting for the valet, popping Altoids like they were candy, because Ed had suggested he come back to my place to crash.

Ed was inside, talking with his brother, but I wasn't the only one in the valet line. Bryan, the man Ed knew as Moises' roommate, was out there, too. I thanked him for the party, he thanked me for coming, and then he asked me how I knew Moi.

"I don't," I said. "I'm a friend of Ed's. I've been in love with him since I was fourteen."

Bryan did not give any indication that this was an odd thing to tell a stranger. "You know the secret is getting in with his mother," he said. "All she wants on earth is for Ed to end up with a nice Jewish girl."

"I've tried that, but she never seems to remember me."

"Try her again. Call her over Thanksgiving. She won't be there—you'll get her machine—but then she'll have to call you back, and the two of you can chat."

"You're not a Jewish girl. Does she like you?" I asked.

"She has to," Bryan said, "because I'm not going anywhere."

"How long have you been with Moi?" I asked him.

"We're going on eight years," Bryan said.

Ed might not have known they were lovers, but eight years together sounded pretty married to me.

Just then, a fight broke out in the street, white boys lunging at each other as if they'd been choreographed.

"Look," I said, *"West Side Story."*

Bryan sang a rousing verse of "Maria."

"Ed's going to flip out that I'm getting on so well with the family," I said.

"Let him," Bryan said. "We have to inject some edge into this."

Bryan's enthusiasm was infectious. No one else in my life had expressed the slightest interest in my feelings for Ed in a very, very long time.

I've always struggled to explain how it was possible to feel so strongly for a man who was completely out of my reach, how I could consider Ed my love, or even my friend, though he rarely visited or wrote or called.

Ed was one of the first people I'd met my first day at boarding school, just minutes after my parents had finished unpacking my suitcases, climbed back into their car, and driven away. That afternoon, Ed and I had walked down to the town side of the lake with a girl from my dorm and a boy from his. The four of us rented a rowboat, which the boys rocked back and forth on the water, trying to make us girls scream. Out there on that lake, I felt like these three strangers would be my friends for life. Then Ed announced his plans to run away.

"How are you going to pull that off?" I asked him.

"I've got a credit card," he said.

I was impressed. I'd run away once, for about six minutes, but I'd only gotten halfway down the driveway before I changed my mind. Ed's plan involved actual funding and a real destination—he was heading back to Florida as soon as possible, because he couldn't live without water, and by water he meant the ocean, not some stupid lake. There was a mystery and darkness to his personality that enthralled me. I was the sort of girl who wanted to plumb that pain.

I was also flat chested, frizzy haired, and prisoner to a pair of exceptionally thick-lensed glasses, while Ed at fourteen was tanned and muscled, the only boy in our class already proportioned like a full-grown man. It's no wonder, then, that despite periodically mortifying us both by declaring my undying adoration for him, I was never Ed's girlfriend; he was drawn to manicured blondes, Southern belles in padded bras. But I was his confidante. Mostly he talked to me about other girls. He'd tell me which ones he liked, and he'd ask me to introduce him to them, and once he had those girls, he'd come to me for advice on how to keep them, or if I thought he should let them go. I thought I knew Ed well, which made me feel special, because those other girls did not.

As I got older, I discovered underwire, hair products, and contact lenses. But I never stopped loving Ed. I thought knowing him like I did had to mean something. I thought he'd figure that out, eventually, if I waited long enough, if I just put in the time.

*　　*　　*

Ten years later, I was still waiting. After that night in West Hollywood, months would pass without a word from Ed, but Bryan started to call. He behaved as if my friendship with Ed was as important as I imagined it, as if my place in Ed's life was special and secure. Bryan was optimistic and encouraging, completely convinced that he could help me win Ed. His plan was simple: He integrated me into his and Moi's life, which was, by extension, Ed's life, and waited for Ed to wise up. He invited me to parties, and I went, even when Ed wouldn't be there, because being with Bryan and Moi did spectacular things for my self-esteem. They showered me with attention; at their parties, I was never alone for a moment, never allowed to retreat to a corner chair. With Bryan and Moi, I was a woman I barely recognized, fun and flirty, even hot. A lot of that had to do with how Bryan spoke to me—he called me *Sexy*, as if that were my name. (Thanks to ten years of unrequited longing, I was a sucker for anyone who called me that, straight or gay.) When I was with Bryan and Moi, I *was* sexy, and the thought that I might one day end up in Ed's arms seemed less and less improbable.

Maybe this was because Bryan and Moises had done the improbable themselves: They had found each other and fallen in love, a Southern man and a Latin Jewish man in a domestic arrangement that both cultures might view askance. It didn't escape me that they'd been hiding their love from Ed almost as many years as I'd been shouting mine from the treetops at him. But despite those difficulties, they'd built a relationship so vibrant and loving that it spread to everything they touched. They'd created a beautiful home that they filled with friends, and they were building a business empire together, buying and selling and developing properties on both coasts.

We all know them, the Super Couples, those couples that all other couples measure themselves against, those couples whose health (or dysfunction) act as markers for the rest. Bryan and Moi were my Super Couple. The way they behaved around each other—their intimacy, their generosity toward each other, their good humor—made me want all those things for myself. I fell for Bryan and Moi almost as quickly as I'd fallen for

Ed all those years earlier. Now, when I let myself fantasize about Ed, it wasn't just the two of us in the picture. It was the four of us: me and Ed and Bryan and Moises, double-dating. I wanted us to be family: me and Ed and my perfect brothers-in-law.

Ironically the closer I got to Bryan and Moises, the more distant Ed and I became. We exchanged calls at our birthdays, but the only reason I knew how to reach him was because Bryan sent me Ed's new contact information every time he changed his number, or moved. If I knew when Ed was coming to town, it was not because he told me; it was Bryan who did that, suggesting dinners for the four of us that would never come to pass. Bryan's commitment to the dream rivaled my own, but he wasn't just my cheerleader—ultimately, he was a true enough friend to be my reality check. One afternoon, he broke the news that everyone else had been keeping from me: Ed was back together with the most significant of his high school girlfriends, the Southern belle to beat all my nightmares of Southern belles. This time it looked like it was for keeps.

Lately I'd been thinking my entire strategy toward Ed was flawed, that no amount of time could make Ed love me the way I wanted. He wasn't naturally constant, he wasn't easily intimate, he could never give me what Bryan and Moises had. I'd assumed he simply wasn't as driven to build a coupled life. But it seemed while I was waiting for him, he'd been waiting for this other woman. For the first time in a decade, I could see through my fantasies. It wasn't love Ed had no interest in. It was me.

I'm not sure which of us was more disappointed, me or Bryan. "Just thought you ought to know, Sugar," Bryan said. *Sugar* was what Bryan called me when the news was less sexy than sad.

Three years later, I'm not *Sugar* anymore. Now I'm *Hon'* or *Darlin'*, which I suppose are more fitting terms of endearment from one married person to another. I'll admit to missing *Sexy*, but gone is the single girl at parties. I'm all grown up, paired off, a shockingly contented wife.

It was while my fiancé, Dave, and I were planning our wedding that

Bryan called to tell me Ed was sick. "Sugar," Bryan said, "if you're in your car, pull over to the side of the road." He told me Ed had just been diagnosed with an advanced, aggressive cancer, and that afternoon he'd be leaving San Diego for treatment in New York.

I couldn't follow him across the country this time, so I sent e-mails and letters, placed upbeat-sounding calls. But I didn't feel upbeat. Sometimes I was so scared for Ed I couldn't even manage to ask Bryan about him. Dave did it for me, often without my knowledge, only passing on the news if it seemed good.

We were married while Ed was still in chemo, so he missed our wedding. Bryan and Moises were busy traveling from L.A. to New York to see him, so they missed it, too. But Dave ensured they were all there that day. He toasted absent friends at our reception, and surprised me by singling out Ed by name.

Loving Dave is easy, and mostly painless. I don't adore his habit of spinning long, punny riffs from the names of our cats, nor do I appreciate being pressed to do the same. The way he moves through our house, shedding socks and soda cans and newspaper pages all over the floor in his wake drives me nuts. But there is no man on earth who can make me feel so much myself when I'm with him, no person I've ever met who is so fully invested in my happiness, who is so convinced that I am a woman who can achieve every imagined success. Dave may be completely incapable of doing a load of laundry without written instructions reminding him that *drying* our clothes is an essential part of the laundering process, but loath as I am to admit it, that's a small price to pay to secure what I really wanted: a love like Bryan and Moi's.

It took two full rounds of chemo, but eventually Ed got better. Dave and I are ecstatically married; we're looking forward to having children and recently got a dog. And after years of waiting, I finally have a partner for my Bryan and Moises double-dates.

A few weeks ago, the four of us had dinner at our favorite Los Feliz Italian place. We talked about real estate, work, traveling. We didn't talk about Ed, because we didn't have to. For the first time in ages, I have Ed's number because *he* gave it to me. If I want to know what's he's up to, all I have to do is call.

Over dessert, Dave asked Bryan and Moi if they ever thought about having children—now that we're pregnant, Dave wants everyone we know to reproduce.

"I don't know that we're there yet," Moises said. He looked at Bryan.

"Maybe when we're forty," Bryan said.

I don't want them to wait that long. Every time I see them, I am reminded how much I owe them for my own happiness, how they ushered me away from my fantasy and back toward a much more full, real life. In some small way, I like to think that I've returned the favor. I hope I'm a little bit responsible for Moi's finally confiding in his brother the whole truth about Bryan, as he did only a few weeks after that first night in West Hollywood five years ago, the night we met.

Now I want to pull them forward into a life with kids. I want to raise our families together, I want our kids to grow up together, I want them all to be best friends. I want them to grow up, fall in love, get married.

And maybe then, with the next generation, I'll get my perfect in-laws, after all.

GET THIS

. . . .

Cindy Chupack

I was finally getting married. That's what I kept telling people. I didn't say I was finally getting married "again," because bringing up a first marriage during the planning of a second marriage seemed to be a major buzz kill for everyone involved, especially me. I suppose this is because it reminds the bride and groom, at a time when their biggest worry should be buttercream versus spun sugar, that these partnerships don't always work out. That love does not always conquer all. And I didn't want to hang that cloud over my fiancé, Ian, because this was his first wedding (a term I didn't like for him either, because it implied he might have a second wedding). So in the same way that World War I was known as the Great War until World War II, we were simply planning our Great Wedding, and we tried not to talk about first anythings until our first meeting with the rabbi.

Ian called our rabbi "the hot rabbi," because she was young and hip and, okay, let's just say it: hot. I didn't mind him calling her hot. In fact, I found it reassuring, because it was a clear sign, exactly when I needed one, on the brink of our Great Wedding, that Ian was not gay. The one wedding detail I was certain about was that I did not want to publicly declare my love for someone in front of my closest friends and family only to have that someone, two years later, realize he might be gay. Again.

Yes, okay, yes: That's what happened to me the first time around, and that's what I told the hot rabbi at our first meeting when she asked if either of us had been married before.

The hot rabbi blinked, then nodded. Like I said, she was hip. She lived in New York. What woman today doesn't have a guy-who-turned-out-to-be-gay story? Admittedly, it's a smaller, and somewhat stupider, subset that has a husband-who-turned-out-to-be-gay story, but my point is, the hot rabbi was appropriately not shocked. She said she didn't need to know all of the details, although she was happy to listen if I needed to talk. But I didn't need to talk about that. I have talked about it so much, the story is on Audible.com. (Seriously.) It was more than a decade ago. It was amicable. We labeled index cards with our meager belongings and divided them up. We shared a cat for a while. It stung me a bit when I realized he was going to have a husband and kids before I did. I think it stung him a bit when he realized I was getting paid more to write sitcoms than he was getting paid to save lives. So we gave each other space to have—or have not—without judgment.

The hot rabbi then asked if my ex-husband was Jewish. This seemed like a moot point to me, but I told her, yes, he was Jewish. She nodded again and made a note.

I remember how happy my parents were that I was marrying a Jewish doctor. It was like winning the Jewish lottery, until he turned out to be gay. After that, my parents cared less about my boyfriend's religion than his ability to name at least three pro ball players. Therefore, it was nice, but not essential, that Ian turned out to be Jewish as well. Ian was a bad-boy motorcycle-riding tattooed lawyer-poet-chef who proposed to me on a beach at sunset, riding a white horse, dressed as a knight. The fact that he was Jewish was the least remarkable thing about him.

In the spirit of full disclosure, Ian told the hot rabbi that his mother had converted to Judaism before he was born, but she might now consider herself more of a Buddhist, and while we were on the subject of the gays, she was also a late-in-life lesbian who had recently married a woman. The hot rabbi made another note, then mused that it was perhaps fitting that our wedding was taking place during New York's Gay Pride weekend.

This fact, I have to admit, had somehow eluded me. As I started contemplating the irony of this, and wondering which of our carefully laid plans might be derailed by the parade route, Ian went on to explain that his dad was Jewish, and although his dad died when Ian was young, Ian still considered himself a Jew, and wanted a Jewish wedding, so here we were. Ian and the hot rabbi smiled at me. I smiled back, pretending to have been paying attention. Then the hot rabbi had this question for me: "Did you ever get a get?"

I had heard of a get. I knew it was some kind of Jewish divorce certificate, but it felt like Number 1,764 on my list of priorities when my marriage ended—slightly less pressing than figuring out what to do with all of our wedding photos, and about as exciting as informing my credit card companies that I needed to change my name back. Our Jewish divorce was definitely less urgent than our non-Jewish divorce, which was complicated enough, especially since I was attempting to fill out the forms myself with the help of a do-your-own-divorce book and a gay production assistant from the show where I was working.

I mention the gay production assistant not only because he was very helpful, but also because at that time in my life—when my marriage was ending for the most irreconcilable of differences—it seemed like everyone in the world was gay. It wasn't just my husband: Two of his groomsmen came out after our wedding, and, in a very unexpected twist, one of my bridesmaids. Looking back, I'm not sure if it was a wedding party or a White Party.

I was tinkering with stand-up comedy then, and onstage I only talked about things like why a clerk at the ninety-nine-cent store would shout, "Price check!" Offstage, however, I would talk to my friend Rob, a fellow aspiring stand-up, about everything else. Rob was a big guy with big glasses and a big personality. He was also the first person who tried to make me laugh about the fact that my husband had realized he was gay. Rob was endlessly fascinated and amused by my story, and asked me a lot of questions like: *What were the signs? Has he told his family yet? How did he tell you?* A year later, Rob came out. He also lost about half of his body weight, since he wasn't hiding anymore, and it became clear to me that in Rob's eyes (now in contacts), my husband was the hero of my story.

My story: Every time I told it, someone came out to me. I was telling it at a Hollywood party to a cute guy who I thought was flirting with me only to realize he was married. To a man. He explained that he had never even dated men until he met his husband while traveling abroad. Then I told *that* story to my friend who hosted the party, and he confessed to me that he considered himself bi, which he said was difficult for any potential partner to comprehend. For example, he said, how would I feel about dating him? When I realized his question was not rhetorical, I blushed and respectfully declined. Then I told *that* story to a male friend whom I knew was straight, and he also confessed he was thinking of dating men, but after coming out to his stunned Beverly Hills parents and getting a couple of gay relationships under his belt, so to speak, he decided he was actually more interested in women, and he's now married to a woman who had previously considered herself a lesbian. My feeling, at this point, when everyone's sexuality seemed to be in flux, was simply: *Pick a side! I'm fine with it all! Just declare a major!*

I was thinking about what a relief it was that I could finally tell my story without outing anybody when the hot rabbi announced that I should "get a get."

She explained that Ian and I did not technically need the get in order to get married, but without it, under Jewish law, our children would basically be considered bastards. This might be a problem when and if they wanted to marry a nonbastard Jew or go to a Jewish school for nonbastards. (She didn't use those words exactly; she may have used the term "illegitimate," but that was the idea.) She also thought the process might be good closure for me.

It sounded like the opposite of closure. It sounded like it would require reopening the lines of communication that my ex-husband and I had finally and, I would say, mercifully, shut down, after trying for years to prove that we were actually the friends we kept saying we were. We *were* friends. We wished each other well. It was just easier, I think, to wish each other well from afar.

Also, we'd had a version of closure. At one point, when his parents were having a hard time accepting the idea that their son was gay, that it was something he was born with, they cut him off financially. He was in med school at the time and rather strapped for cash, and the one thing he really wanted was to buy a house. So I decided to help him with the down payment by giving him back the extravagant emerald-cut engagement ring that he, out of guilt, had told me to keep. I had stored it in a safe deposit box, not wanting to wear it, not ready to sell or reset it. I would occasionally visit my ring, visit my old married self, but even with nobody present to witness it, I was aware how pathetic I looked sitting in a bank cubicle modeling my wedding ring. So when I had the opportunity to return it to its rightful owner in the spirit of forgiveness and friendship, I jumped at the chance. I said, "With this ring, will you not marry me?" And we had a little moment, and he bought a little house, and that was that. Until now.

In order to get a get, I would need to get back in touch with my ex-husband and persuade him to go before a panel of three rabbis and officially "release me." The process is actually more offensive than I am making it sound. The tradition is based on a completely sexist biblical verse (Deuteronomy 24:1), which states: "A man takes a wife and possesses her. If she fails to please him because he finds something obnoxious about her, he writes her a bill of divorcement, hands it to her, and sends her away from his house."

First of all, I do not think my ex-husband found me obnoxious. He might have wished I had a penis, but if anything, I was the one who had grounds for "sending him away from my house." However, with my Great Wedding less than three months away and the hope of legitimate children on the horizon, I decided this was not the time to go Gloria Steinem on the Old Testament.

When I called my ex-husband in Los Angeles (I was living in New York at the time), he was surprised to hear from me, happy to hear I was getting married, and a little dubious about what I was asking him to do. I assured him I would pay the fee and do all the homework; his only responsibility would be to show up. We decided that although it was possible to get a get without being in the same place, we would try to get ours the next time I was in Los Angeles. He even suggested we have a "get-together" afterward so I could meet his kids. I started to like the idea of a get. It sounded like it might actually be good closure after all.

Our awkward reunion took place outside a barely marked industrial building that served as an office for the Orthodox rabbi whose name I got through an online organization that facilitates gets. (Yes, there is such an organization, it's based in Brooklyn, and operators are standing by.) We made small talk while I pressed the buzzer. (*You look good. You, too. How are your parents? How's New York?*) It slowly became clear, as we ran out of small talk, that nobody was responding to the buzzing. We called the rabbi's number, which was his home number, and unfortunately he answered, and that's when we learned that there was confusion about the time, and we'd have to reschedule. We explained that we couldn't reschedule. It had taken us over ten years to make *this* appointment. The rabbi said he would try to locate two witnesses, and we should give him an hour.

That's how it came to pass that we had an hour to kill, and my ex-husband said his partner and kids were nearby shopping, so maybe we should have our get-together now. It was too late for lunch and too early for dinner, which seemed appropriately symbolic of our relationship, but we found a faux-French café nearby that would take us.

It's not often a girl gets to sit down with the man she thought she would have kids with and the man he had kids with, but the truth is, they were a pretty perfect family without me. I had met my ex-husband's partner at a Christmas party years earlier, and I liked him immediately. He was handsome and smart and kind and funny, and whether it was accurate or not, I found it flattering and comforting to imagine that he was the male version of me. Now they'd adopted two beautiful boys who looked like they crawled out of a Baby Gap ad. As I watched my ex-husband juggle juice boxes and crayons and children's menus, he smiled at me and warned: "Get ready."

Finally the rabbi called and said he could see us. When we arrived, all of us, he explained the process might take another hour, so my ex-husband told his family he would call them when we were done.

The rabbi was old, and his two witnesses were even older. They sat on one side of a table and we sat on the other. We had to say our names in Hebrew, which already was a problem because mine was supposedly Ariel, but I was told in Sunday School that the female version of Ariel is Ariella. Feeling strongly that *somebody* should be the female version of me in this process, I went with Ariella. We also had to state that we had come freely without coercion, and then we watched in respectful silence as the rabbi, who was also officially a scribe, wrote our divorce document by hand, with pen and ink, in Hebrew.

After what seemed like an eternity, the document was half-finished. When my ex-husband left to feed the meter, the rabbi fixed me with a stare and asked the question that had clearly been bothering him since we arrived: "Who was that other man who came with you?" Since I wasn't sure what the official Orthodox stance was on homosexuality, I said it was my ex-husband's friend. "And whose children were those?" he asked. I didn't like where this was going. I asked if this would affect the get process, because we had been there a long time as it was. He assured me it would not, so I admitted that my ex-husband was gay, and that the other man was his partner, and those were their kids. The two ancient witnesses looked at each other, which was the first and only indication that they spoke English. "I think that's sick," the rabbi said flatly.

"It's not sick," I said. "They're very happy."

Then, in a terribly unoriginal attempt at a joke, the rabbi said, "Which one is the man?"

"They're both men," I said. "They're both very good men."

When my ex-husband came back into the room, I felt ill. I had flown cross-country and paid five hundred dollars in cash so three old holy men could sit in judgment of him for an hour. And the irony was, he was much more Jewish than me! I barely remembered when Passover was every year, while his partner had converted so they could raise their children as Jews. I was fuming, wondering if we should forget the get, get out, get while the gettin' was good. I was composing an angry letter in my head, venting to the hot rabbi, praying this wasn't representative of my faith, when we were informed that our document was complete. Then we were asked to stand. And face each other. And then my ex-husband was asked to look into my eyes and repeat some phrases that meant basically: "With this document, I release you."

And as we stood there, just as we had on our wedding day, he looked even more handsome. And grown-up. And happy. And I thought about why he had married me in the first place. Yes, he loved me, but also, he was probably afraid he would never be able to have a family if he didn't marry a woman. And now he had that family without having to compromise any part of who he was. And I thought about what he gave me all those years ago when he had unofficially released me. He gave me my single life back. And as much as I hated the heartbreak and longing, it became the basis of my writing career, which led me to a job on *Sex and the City*, which led me to New York, which led me to my bad-boy motorcycle-riding tattooed lawyer-poet-chef.

And then I thought about how this tribunal, this ridiculous judgmental tribunal, is what my ex-husband faces every day, sometimes when he least expects it, sometimes from family, sometimes from within, and how hard it must have been to overcome that judgment in order to be honest with me and with himself. So as he dropped the get into my open palms, which made it legally binding, I felt proud of him, and proud of us, for releasing each other to our proper destinies.

"I'm happy you're getting married," he said. "Now I can finally stop feeling guilty." I told him he had no reason to feel guilty. But he said he couldn't help it. Some things, I guess, we're just born with.

IV

Growing Up, Coming Out

"Every straight girl in high school needs a boyfriend—
to ogle the baseball team with."

—from "Life Before Gays," by Elizabeth Spiers

THE GOOD GIRLS

David Levithan

I n high school, I was one of the good girls.

My parents didn't know what to think. Every night, there would be the parade of phone calls, me slipping out of the room and going behind closed doors, to talk about friends and homework and *relationships* and, every now and then, the meaning of life. My parents didn't know all these girls' voices like I did, so they were never really certain who was calling, or why. Either I had dozens of girlfriends or I didn't have any at all.

The truth was that most of my friends were girls. Groups upon groups of girls. Mayling, Elana, Joanna, Carolyn, Lauren, and Marcie were the good girls. Lynda, Dvora, Rebecca, Susannah, Dina, Meg, and Jinny were the good girls who drifted into the boy thing when we got to high school. Eliza, Jodi, Jordana, Jeannie, and Mariam were the good girls one grade below us. Jennifer and Sami and Tracey were the good girls who didn't do the group thing as much. There were boys, too—but there weren't that many of them. The girls were the nucleus of my social life.

We didn't talk about sex; we talked about love. We never, ever used *party* as a verb. Awkwardly mixed drinks and the occasional beer or wine cooler were as alcoholic as we got. Pot was a big step. Cocaine was unimaginable. We were the kids for whom VCRs had been invented. We watched *When Harry Met Sally* ... over and over again and pondered its lessons like it had been filmed in Aramaic. The central question, of course, was: Can guys and girls really be friends? I liked to think I was the proof positive, because even though I fell for one of my female friends every now and then, friendship always managed to win out in the end.

It hadn't yet occurred to me to like boys.

We good girls coveted our clever turns of phrase like they were SAT flash cards. We honed our wits like Dorothy Parker at the Algonquin lunch table. We were smart and we knew it. We were dorks and we knew it. Instead of hiding both things, we embraced them. We created our own form of popularity. In our town of Millburn, New Jersey, where the football team never won, this was surprisingly easy to do.

Many of the girls were in the Millburnettes, the girls' singing group. If they dated, odds were that they'd be dating one of the Millburnaires. I myself had auditioned for the Millburnaires in falsetto, because I'd been obsessed with the song "Bring Him Home" from *Les Miserables* and thought I could pretend my way through "Impossible Dream." Mr. Deal, our fussy, testy diva of a chorus director, was half appalled and half amused. He gave me another chance, but I decided not to take it. I hadn't wanted to wear the ultrablue polyester Millburnaire outfit, anyway.

Instead I became a Millburnette groupie. And a school musical groupie (memorably playing the one-lined doorman in *Kiss Me, Kate*). And I joined the fencing team—because all my friends were there, because I needed a sport for my college applications, and because at practices the girls and I talked much more than we thrusted foils at one another.

I have learned over the years that it's decidedly uncool to say I enjoyed high school—many people were lucky to have survived it, while others who didn't have as bad a time like to say they did. Since I was one of the good girls, I found life in high school to be, well, good. It wasn't always easy, and it wasn't always nice. But through it all, I felt a passive happiness that would break out sometimes into an intensely active happiness. This could happen in the most random of ways: Mayling pulling her long sleeve to her nose and proclaiming "I am an elephant!" with the rest of us following suit; Lynda and I holding up signs to each other in the middle of the Metropolitan Opera House, since I was in the balcony and she was in the orchestra, and we couldn't go the length of an opera without passing some word to each other; Jennifer and I leaving lunch early and sitting on the fenced-off stairway that led to the auditorium, remarking on the people who passed us and, when the hallway traffic was slow, talking about books. If we never felt the full swoon of romance, we often felt the giddy buoyancy of friendship. It was a counterbalance against all the tests we faced—tests in the classrooms, tests in the hallways, tests in what we wore and what we said and who we were.

The good girls were a sisterhood, and I was the brother. There were some conversations I wasn't a part of; you would think that hanging out with so many girls would open my eyes to their side of the sex thing, but with a few exceptions, this rarely came up when I was around. Instead I was exposed to the girls' emotional landscapes and, even more important, I was allowed to have one of my own. We wore our feelings so openly, whether it was annoyance or distress or delight or anger or affection we felt. I would never have learned such openness from the boys. There were certainly times when everything seemed like a big traumedy, but I learned to deal with that. By talking it through. By talking it out. And, if none of those things worked, my friend Lynda always advised a haircut. When you wanted to change your life, she said, a haircut was often the easiest way to start.

The good girls—the ones who hadn't split off in tenth grade—didn't date much, for the same reason that I didn't clue in to the boy thing as fast as I might have: In our not particularly large high school, there weren't that many bookish, articulate, cute, sensitive, clever, crush-worthy boys. In retrospect, I can see a couple of crushes I had without labeling them as such—tangential boys, nobody that close to me. They were usually a year or two older than I was and talked about philosophers and writers like other boys talked about sports or computers. It's not like I dreamed of kissing them or dating them—I was just *fascinated* by them, mostly from afar, with occasional glimpses up close. I was looking for River Phoenix in a Tom Cruise world.

I also had friendship crushes—on boys and girls—but those were different; those friends I liked because of what I knew about them, not because of their mystery. I didn't want to be their boyfriend. I wanted to be their best friend. I learned early, and learned well, that the person you talk to about the crush is much more important than the crush itself.

Instead of dating, the good girls and I were one big date-substitute. We played a lot of Pictionary. Sober Pictionary. We ruled the school newspaper and the lit mag. B. Dalton's was our favorite store in the mall, although we were never above dancing around the aisles of KBtoys. We went into the city on weekends and waited in the half-price ticket line for Broadway shows, or went into the Village to shop for secondhand clothes. We went to museums. Once we got our licenses and could drive around town, we rotated our evenings among Bennigan's, TGI Friday's, Chili's, and La Strada, the local pizzeria. When we weren't at the Morristown multiplex, we were at the Lost Picture Show in Union, which showed art films and looked like someone's garage on the inside and had a roof that leaked. We read Margaret Atwood and J. D. Salinger and Kurt Vonnegut. (Some of the girls even read Ayn Rand, but I could never get into it.) We talked about art without realizing we could treat it as Art. The more theatrical of us signed our yearbooks with Sondheim lyrics.

So many gay boys—whether they know they're gay yet or not—go through high school feeling like they're the only ones. They think they're the only ones who will never find love, the only ones who don't really fit in, the only ones who aren't coupled off. With the good girls, I was never the only one. Not in that way. I was sometimes the only boy. And I'm sure there were times when I thought it was ridiculous that the "dates" I had were fleeting at best. But because so many of my female friends were in the same boat, I didn't really feel alone. There were no long, dark nights of the soul, because my soul was keeping pretty good company.

The girls and I flirted and bantered. Nonstop. We passed notes. Lord, we passed notes. String these notes together and you'd get the full symphony of my high school years, an almost minute-by-minute re-creation. Constant observation, reflection, honing life into prose.

Everything remained peaceful until the senior prom came along. It wasn't a particularly big deal to me—I had already gone my junior year, the date of a girl I barely knew, who clearly had gotten to the bottom of her draft list before asking me. I'd had fun, but I'd also figured that it wasn't a night that would change my life forever. Going into prom season, I was, as always, unattached, and while the question of who I would ask was hotly debated when I wasn't in the room (or so I was later told), when I returned to the room, I was left to my own obliviousness.

I decided to ask Jordana, a member of the junior posse of good girls. Bizarrely I decided to ask her while watching her play Mother Superior in our high school's production of *The Sound of Music*. Seriously. While she was busy exhorting Maria to climb ev'ry mountain, I was thinking, *It would be fun to go to the prom with Jordana.* Not as a date-date. But in lieu of a date-date.

I knew another boy, Josh, probably wanted to ask her, too. But I figured, hey, I'd give Jordana the option and see what she wanted to do. We went on a nondate to Bennigan's, and I stalled. I pondered. I worked myself up into an existential crisis while I ate mozzarella sticks and debated whether or not to ask her.

Which is when Roxette came into the picture.

I almost didn't ask Jordana to be my prom date. But then a Roxette song came wafting down from the Bennigan's speakers, and it told me to listen to my heart. I figured this was a sign. My heart at that moment said to ask her, so I did. I even told her I wouldn't mind if she wanted to go with Josh. And she said she wanted to go with me.

I was relieved to have it over with.

I was unprepared, however, for the fact that I had just created more problems than I'd ever intended. By choosing a prom date, I was the one who had stopped the music and sent all of my female friends flying toward the musical chairs. Many, it seemed, had thought it at least a possibility that I would ask them. I had, to put it indelicately, fucked everything up.

Now the good girls had to grab hold of the nearest boy and hope it would work out. By and large, it didn't work out well, even for me, since Jordana ended up wanting to go with Josh after all, causing awkwardness all around. Still, we look happy enough in the prom photos—the front row of good-girl friends, and then the back row assortment of random boys tuxed up to squire them for the evening. All dressed up, we thought we looked so old. Now I look at the picture and think how young we really were. We get younger every year, as 1990 gets farther and farther away.

Within five years after we graduated, everything was different. Our high school experience in many ways resembled our parents' time more than it resembles today's. We lived in a time when we had cords on our phones—if not the cord connecting the handset to the base, then definitely the cord connecting the base to the wall. We lived in a time when *chatting* was something that didn't involve typing, and *text* and *page* were words that applied to books, not cell phones. If we wanted to see naked pictures, we had to sneak peeks in magazine stores, or rely upon drawings in *The Joy of Sex*, spreads in *National Geographic*, and carefully paused moments in R-rated videotapes. The only kids we knew in towns outside of our own were the ones we had gone to camp with. The only bands we knew were the ones that were played on the radio or on MTV. For me, it was a time before *Ellen* and a time before the kiss on *Dawson's Creek* and Ricky on *My So-Called Life*, and a time before the Internet and all the other pop cultural things that might have tipped me off to my own identity before I hit college. Because I was happy, I didn't really question who I was.

I don't know whether the good girls were as ignorant as I was to my gayness, or if they had figured it out before I did and were waiting for me to piece it together. One of them had definitely picked up on it—during my freshman year of college, my friend Rebecca sent me a letter saying basically that it was totally cool if I was gay, and that I didn't have to hide it anymore. I was hurt—not that she thought I was gay, but that she thought I was hiding something so important from my friends. I assured her that I would tell people if I were gay—and as of that writing, I was correct. Later on, during college, I'd figure it out. And as soon as I did,

I didn't really hide it. It seemed as natural as anything else, and I didn't go through any of the anxiety, fear, or denial that I would have no doubt experienced had I figured it out in high school. It was a gradual realization that I was completely okay with, and everyone else was completely okay with. The good girls would have been much more shocked if I'd told them I was going premed.

Because I've grown up to have a writing life that brings me into contact with a lot of teens, I see all the possibilities that are open now that weren't open to me then. I see all the fun trouble we could've gotten into. I see how late I bloomed into being gay. I see how being a good girl meant missing out on some things, closing myself off to certain experimentations and risks. It was a sheltered life, but I'm happy that I had the shelter. I needed the shelter. I bloomed late in some things, but I bloomed well in so many others. I know some good things that I missed, but I also know a lot of bad things I missed, too.

Now, most of the good girls—from high school, from college, from after—have found good guys (or good girls) to be with. And I have found the other boys who were once surrounded by good girls. Together, we boys form our own good-girl circles, doing all the things we used to do exclusively with the good girls: confide, support, chatter, have fun. I don't think many of us would have imagined in high school that we would one day have such circles, that we would one day find so many guys we liked, so many guys like us. We still consult with the genuine good-girl articles, but now we can also be our own good girls.

After all, we were trained by the best.

WELCOME TO MY DOLLHOUSE

● ● ● ● ● ● ● ● ● ● ● ● ● ● ●

Michael Musto

I've always liked playing with girls, if not quite in the way Dad was hoping. I feel safer with them, freed from the male constraints of bluster and machismo—*especially* in the gay world. I belong with the lipstick-for-lunch bunch, and miraculously, I've been able to stretch our platonic little gender-blending mix-'em-ups into a lifetime of nonthreatening fun and games.

It's always been as natural a fit as the gown I got to wear in elementary school for an exciting Greek line dance that bordered on a drag show. When I was a kid, men seemed too busy, too pressured, and too distant to deserve—or want—my company. The ladyfolk got not only to wear clothes with more zing and possibility (appliqués! shoulder pads!), they could have the real fun, like sitting around over Entenmann's apple crumble cake and dishing everyone on the block and the TV set, in between bowing their heads and murmuring their rosaries. Thanks to forward women like my mother and my aunt who lived upstairs, I learned the cathartic virtues of down and dirty gossip, something I not only turned into a life-affirming pastime, I've made a living out of it, complete with free meals and health benefits!

At age ten, I spent a lot of time at that gossip table, the only man for miles, while seizing every other free moment to go to the neighbors' backyard and play with two preteen sisters, Teresa and Dawn, who took me in like a stray dog. On balmy summer afternoons, we staged fake tea parties and pseudo-TV tapings, and after braiding our dolls' hair and slathering their heads with glitter, we'd put on even more shows, making the dolls talk and gossip almost as intoxicatingly as *we* did. I had a feeling this wasn't accepted behavior for a boy growing up in testosterone-laden Bensonhurst, Brooklyn—in fact, it was screaming out for an intervention-via-straitjacket—but I didn't have a choice. I could pass for a guy, but not for a straight one, so I knew to avoid the schoolyard across the street, where wry humor got you nowhere unless you also had a mean right hook or a killer kick in the ass. Any extravagant use of my limbs was generally applied to impersonating Diana Ross, not to scoring hoops and tackling people, so I demurred and stayed in the dollhouse where I could get by without anyone looking in and making fun. The girls accepted me, no questions asked, and welcomed my friendly ear and stylish advice. I knew I'd found my place.

Aiming for a little normalcy, I did eventually try to cultivate a straight male friend—Jimmie Boy, a pesky neighborhood squirt who seemed only occasionally scary. We'd lightly bonded a few times on my stoop, so I suggested we go see a movie together (that sounded better to me than stickball), but it turned out we had even less chemistry than my parents. Jimmie Boy was pushing to see the John Wayne Vietnam butchfest, *The Green Berets*, a bloated flag-waver you couldn't have dragged me to with a rifle. Instead, I was begging for the foofy Julie Andrews toe tapper *Thoroughly Modern Millie*, knowing that would be just my cup of period froth—who doesn't love Carol Channing and Beatrice Lillie? Jimmie Boy looked as horrified as if I'd asked him to dine in the back of a sanitation truck. When I offered to pay, he said fine. We sat there in tense silence as the movie unspooled with all of its spangly costumes and campy humor. Jimmie Boy bolted midway, practically vomiting. I stayed till the end, enthralled, then went right back to the girls.

They might not have liked *Millie* either, but at least they would have been nice enough to stick it out. Females were my salvation—once my hormonal years hit, me and the ladies, any ladies, clung to one another with an even fiercer desperation. Without the hint of sex—which can make things so messy and complicated, after all—we were able to explore our friendships with a minimum of game playing and an absence of hidden motives. With another guy, the subtext would always be either, "Why doesn't he want me?" or "I wish he didn't want me," but with the girl-gay combo, that's out of the way and you can just sit down and compare your fingernails. There's no threat of rejection—we simply don't like each other that way—so we're liberated to move on to a more healthy interpersonal ballet without strings attached. Of course, sometimes the girl will develop a friendship-paralyzing crush on the gay, but that's when you simply move on to another, less complicated fag hag. There are plenty out there.

In the 1970s, I went to the then all-male Columbia College, maybe to punish myself, though I did find ways to make the experience more than bearable. I majored in ultragirly English literature and lived in Plimpton Hall, the Barnard dorm filled primarily with girls, girls, girls. On paper, this was a straight guy's dream, but in reality it was even more tailor-made for a gay because I was shacked up with my gal pals, my peers, my kindred playmates. I was back in my dollhouse, far from creatures that liked football and John Wayne (except maybe for a few lesbians). I even wrote for the *Barnard Bulletin*—and would have gladly gone all the way and enrolled in Barnard if the school authorities had allowed it. After all, I still had that lovely Greek gown.

My Ivy League friendships were the archetypal straight woman–gay man ones that are now the stuff of popular culture. I listened, they talked. I lent support and accessories, they returned them. I lived vicariously through their dating stories, they told me to get some of my own. Most importantly, we'd both been hurt or let down by guys and needed one another to fix the damage.

Flash forward to today, when I'm still reliving those same familiar patterns from my childhood. I can't help it: I'll always be quite the ladies' man. Happy, Dad?

DONNY AND MARIE DON'T GET MARRIED

● ● ● ● ● ● ● ● ● ● ● ● ● ● ● ● ● ● ●

Brian Sloan

Whenever my family pretends they were surprised to discover I was gay, I like to remind them of my obsession with *Donny and Marie*. This ABC show from the mid-1970s was a televised wonder with its sparkling sets, ice dancers, and musical medleys. Marie was a glamorous fifteen-year-old who seemed impossibly adult with her hair blown out like Farrah Fawcett and her body draped in Bob Mackie gowns. The real kicker, though, was her charming, sexy brother. Sitting inches from the TV, watching Donny in those oh-so-tight polyester pants, sporting that shiny-perfect hair, and blasting America with his nuclear smile, I was a nine-year-old in love.

Anita Bryant was wrong about the gays recruiting children. The real culprit corrupting America's youth was Donny Osmond.

Fortunately, there was another person in my neighborhood who shared my obsession with all things Osmond. Sarah Forman and I had been friends since her family moved to Rockland Hills, a suburb of Washington, D.C., when we were toddlers. On weekends, we'd stage our own elaborate version of *Donny and Marie* on the Formans' slate terrace, pretending it was an ice stage. We would decorate our set with streamers,

Christmas lights, and potted plants, moving the patio furniture out of the way so there was more room for fake skating.

Once the stage was ready, Sarah would play Marie and I would play Donny. Sarah had a certain star quality, reminding me of Jodie Foster circa the Disney years, with her freckled face, tousled dirty-blonde hair, and tomboyish energy. I was an equally freckled kid and a perfect match for her Marie. We even had a supporting cast of some of the younger neighborhood kids as chorus girls and comic foils for our improvised skits. We'd go "on the air" with a studio audience of three: Mrs. Forman, smoking her Salems in a deck chair, and Coco and Kimball, her Dalmatian and hyperactive poodle.

Sarah was the first person who shared my delusions of fabulosity. She understood that, unlike most boys, I preferred putting on shows rather than racing around in circles after a ball. She got how I was different, enjoyed it thoroughly and took it at face value, unlike my own family. When I got home, I would relate stories of our broadcasts, but these fey-boy fantasies never went over well and the topic would be quickly changed to the Redskins game that week. Given my interest in the Osmonds and a propensity for baking, the joke among my brothers was that I was the sister they never had.

Actually I was the one with a sister. I had Sarah.

In marked contrast to my home life, there was a sort of benign anarchy that reigned at the Formans'. At my house, with four boys and two strict Catholic parents, we had countless rules and regulations about what could and could not be watched on television, the volume of music on the stereo, and the proper way to be seated at the dinner table (that is, actually to be seated). Sarah had no siblings and two younger, hipper parents, so things were more relaxed in the Forman home. You could watch television while eating dinner (on TV trays even!), something my parents considered worse than missing church on Sunday.

I remember noting with awe that the Formans subscribed to both *The Washington Post* and *Playboy*, reflecting a much looser set of social mores. The living room's bookcases were filled with lots of seventies self-help books (*I'm OK–You're OK*) and racy novels (Jacqueline Susann was well represented), as well as a fairly extensive LP collection, heavy on rock and pop. In contrast, my parents had an encyclopedia set and a bunch of 8-tracks by Henry Mancini. Sarah's mom used to play "Mrs. Robinson," that catchy tune about adultery that never quite cracked the top ten on my parents' wood console stereo. Sarah and I loved that song, so Mrs. Forman would blast it endlessly as we danced around the living room. Back at my house, my parents were utterly horrified when I started singing the praises of Mrs. Robinson.

If Sarah had been a boy, this incident alone would surely have been enough to ban me from the Forman household for a few weeks, if not longer. But Sarah was a girl, and I'm guessing my folks thought they'd better cultivate this relationship, as it might be the only way I might not turn out gay. My parents have since confessed to having conversations with Sarah's parents in which they actually discussed the inevitability of our future wedding. Yes, around the tender age of eight, it was clear to everyone that Sarah and I were meant for marriage. Of course, this was not to be.

At the beginning of my junior year, I had a falling out with my best male friend for what, in retrospect, was the gayest reason ever: He had a new friend of whom I was terribly jealous. Charlie, who was a man of all sports, had met this other superjock during football camp and they'd become "tight," as he liked to put it. So for the first time since the start of high school, I was on my own to secure a date for my school's equivalent of the traditional homecoming dance, known as the Regimental Ball. For the first time, I couldn't just take some random girl that Charlie had set up for me. Liberated from that pool of second-hand dates, the field was wide open. In my case, that also meant the field was absolutely empty. I didn't know any girls other than my best friend's girlfriends. I only knew guys.

Except, that is, for Sarah.

By high school, we were no longer the inseparable best friends of the *Donny and Marie* years. We'd see each other around the neighborhood and at the occasional holiday event, but never as often as we had during childhood. Part of this was due to Sarah's switch to public school and our increased academic workloads. But a larger reason, I think, was my increasing discomfort with myself and my budding sexuality. Other boys didn't seem to notice this, whereas girls, generally equipped with a keener emotional radar, tended to pick up on this sort of thing. I was not as eager to hang out with Sarah and be subject to a much higher level of scrutiny than I would at, say, a postfootball kegger with the boys.

A couple of weeks before the dance, I was sitting at the breakfast table when my mom asked me for the one hundredth time who I was taking to "the Reg." For the one hundredth time I mumbled, "I dunno." She suggested that I take Sarah. I looked up from my bowl of cereal and gave her my trademark that-is-the-worst-idea-I've-ever-heard look. She said that I knew Sarah well and that we would probably have "a very nice time." The way she phrased it actually made the idea sound appealing. I had never had "a very nice time" at any high school dance, ever.

Maybe, I thought, *my mother actually had a point.*

So I dialed Sarah's oh-so-familiar number and popped the question: "Do you wanna go to the Reg?" She had no idea what "the Reg" was until I explained that it was like homecoming but a little fancier. Once it hit her that I was asking her on a date to a formal dance, she was thrilled.

I, however, was scared stiff.

After years of family and neighborly gossip about Sarah and me as childhood sweethearts, the day of reckoning had arrived. Though I'd been to countless dances, balls, and cotillions before this one, I had never experienced such anxiety. Those other dance dates were with relatively average girls, most of them now a dim memory. This was Sarah, the once and future love of my life, at least according to Rockland Hills lore. There was a lot of anticipation in our tight-knit neighborhood over the whole affair. We were like a localized version of Charles and Diana, the storybook romance of the era; suddenly the kingdom was filled with excitement over the Big Event.

As the buzz over our imminent romantic coronation grew, I tried to keep the volume at school on low. Unfortunately there was a meeting of moms, mine and Charlie's, at the local Safeway, where the news of the impending royal date was spilled. After that, the word spread quickly around school. I knew that taking someone to the Reg who didn't go to one of the five all-girl private schools in the area would be noticed. But my classmates were abuzz in a way I'd neglected to calculate. Sarah, being a public school girl, was a mystery to them.

I was in the cafeteria when Charlie stopped by our table to drop a gossip bomb: He'd heard from a guy on the public school's football team that Sarah was "a serious nymphomaniac." I found this news particularly shocking, mainly because I didn't even know what that word *nymphomaniac* meant. I was taking biology class at the time and knew that *nympho* had something to do with the neck. Was Sarah into severe necking?

When I got back to my locker to look up *nymphomaniac* in my *Webster's*, I thought I might faint: "a woman with a compulsive desire to have sex with many different men (*often considered offensive*)." My neighborhood sweetheart and future bride-to-be was an offensively insatiable slut? This didn't sound exactly like the Marie that I knew. But then again, what did I know about Sarah's sexuality? It's not like we had talked about either of our sexual or even romantic adolescent adventures—or, on my end, the lack thereof. Suddenly, with this brazen rumor, things were getting complicated: Not only did I have to take her to the dance but apparently I had to perform as well! This was going to be a problem because, at that point in my sexual career, I was only a solo artist. Suddenly I was being called on to duet with the alleged Madonna of the high school set.

I didn't even have to check my Magic 8-Ball to know the forecast for this evening: "Outcome does not look good."

The Reg was always held on the Wednesday before Thanksgiving and that year the weather was particularly wintry. This cold snap, though, didn't chill the excitement around my house that had been building up about the big date. My brothers were all joking and jibing me about the whole affair, while my parents were genuinely sweet in their anticipation, wrapped up in the fairy tale aspects of this potentially major night.

Once I was dressed and ready to go, I got collared by one of my older brothers for some predate coaching. Kevin had always been the most concerned member of the family about my nascent masculinity. He'd provided endless lessons in baseball, careful instruction on the art of weightlifting, and explicit advice on the best pickup lines to use on girls. His helpful hint for the Reg? I needed to get Sarah liquored up. He'd even taken the liberty of procuring a couple bottles of André (the three-dollar champagne that says class) just for this purpose. As much as I appreciated the effort he'd put into buying alcohol for minors, the evening already had enough potential for disaster without adding booze to the mix. Kevin, however, was undeterred when I tried to decline the offer. Completing this illicit exchange, he grabbed my hand for a firm, masculine handshake filled with meaning.

"Good luck, bro," he said.

I just smiled and thought to myself, *Good luck, indeed.*

I arrived at Sarah's exactly on time, seven P.M. Her mom answered the door with a smile that was wide and welcoming. It was the first time I'd been in the Forman house in quite a while and everything looked basically the same, just smaller. The bookshelves seemed shorter now, with fewer records and books in them than I remembered. The staircase that led up to Sarah's room seemed tiny, too, like I might hit my head on the ceiling if I tried to go up. Of course, the house had not shrunk at all; I had just grown a bit. But the feeling of not fitting in the house anymore was disconcerting.

Sarah entered the living room wearing a floor-length, sky blue prairie-style dress with long, lacey sleeves. The outfit was tasteful, yet slightly groovy, too, a far cry from the plastic poofy quality of most formal wear circa 1982. It's what Stevie Nicks would have worn if she'd been invited to the Reg, which I thought was cool. Not sexy, mind you. Just cool. I mean, who wouldn't have wanted to take Stevie Nicks to homecoming?

As we all chatted, there was none of the usual stiffness that I experienced at other dates' houses. I kept thinking I would've loved to stay there in the Forman living room and ditch the dance entirely. I would have much preferred sitting on the floor and singing along to "Mrs. Robinson" than going to a high school formal.

Given the chance, I guess anyone would return to their childhood rather than face the uncertainty of adolescence. It's just not often that the opportunity to do so seems tangible and yet impossible at the same time.

As she snapped photos, Mrs. Forman said we both looked adorable. We did on the surface: two goofy and gangly sixteen-year-olds in formal wear, smiling with a sweet awkwardness for her Kodak Instamatic camera. I'd like to imagine that Mrs. Forman was a little wiser about my impending sexual proclivities. Whether she did or did not intuit that there was a future homosexual taking her daughter to the Reg, there was a real, genuine happiness radiating from her. In retrospect, I believe her joy was likely the effect of seeing Sarah and me together again in her living room after a few years' absence.

We got in my midnight blue Chevette and headed down the hill to my folks' house for more photos. The scene there was slightly less casual. My mom had dressed up for our arrival, as if she might be hosting the Reg in our living room. There was a Henry Mancini 8-track playing on the stereo as we stood in front of the fireplace for an extended photo op. Unlike at the Formans', the photos this time were not just of me and Sarah. There were multiple combinations of Sarah with my parents, and then with my younger brother, and then with all three of my brothers. It felt like a wedding with my parents recording all the permutations of family for the blessed event. In all these photos, I look uniformly terrified, as if I'd been married off at age sixteen and was on my way to a premature honeymoon.

On our arrival at the Woodley Park Sheraton, we made a ridiculously grand entrance. Each couple arriving at the Reg was announced at the top of a grand curving staircase before gracefully descending to the floor of the main ballroom, step by agonizing step. In a weird way, the whole scene was like a real version of our backyard *Donny and Marie* productions, except that now we had on actual costumes, there was a truly classy set, and a huge audience, too. But when they called our names and the spotlight hit us, there was none of our usual jokey banter or the campy musical numbers that lit up the Forman backyard. I just smiled blankly in the glare of the white light as we gingerly made our way down the stairs to scattered applause, quickly walking Sarah to our table.

The rest of the night was filled with endless awkward silences and stares. I didn't know what to do, how to act and, worst of all, what to say. As kids, Sarah and I used to be able to talk a purple streak about anything and everything under the sun. But stuck in formal wear and placed in the uncomfortable context of a date, I froze up, which was not too surprising given the fact that we hadn't really had a serious conversation in a couple years. It's so puzzling to me now, because I could have easily filled hours' worth of conversation with a lively dissection of our productions of *Donny and Marie*. But those seemed like childish things to talk about. The Reg was a big, supposedly adult evening. And I felt like a kid who didn't belong there.

Fortunately silence in a massive ballroom with two hundred other couples was easy to manage. There was a lot of distraction, noise, and general hubbub to provide the illusion that we were having a decent time. There were friends who stopped by to say hi, though most of those greetings were fraught with a wink-wink, nudge-nudge goofiness regarding the nympho rumors. When Charlie stopped by our table, he was a little toasted and proceeded to say, loud enough for everyone to hear, that Sarah was "hot." As Sarah blushed, I was like, *Really?* The fact that I had to be told that Sarah was sexy should have been a major clue as to how clueless I was to my real orientation.

On the long drive back to Rockland Hills, Sarah was very sweet. She kept saying that she'd had a good time, trying to make me feel better for the total lack of good time I'd provided her that night. I'm sure now that she must have sensed my unease and probably mistook it for the awkwardness between two friends on a date. But it was more than that. It was the awkwardness of one friend who no longer knows how to talk to the other about the fact that he wasn't attracted to her, or to any women at all. The fact that Sarah was hot continued to echo in my head as I wondered why that fact was more a curiosity to me than an actual sexual spark. In some ways, this was the beginning of my understanding that I was pretty different from other guys.

It's a shame that I couldn't have talked to her openly and honestly about all that stuff. I'm guessing that, given her liberal upbringing, Sarah would have been a pretty sympathetic listener. But I was too scared at that age, and that stage in my sexual development, to take that risk.

As we got closer to her house, I realized that I still had not utilized the André. If I returned home with those bottles uncorked, I knew I would hear about it from my brother. I tried to figure out the best way to manage this dicey situation. As we made the turn onto Sarah's street, I pulled over to the side of the road three houses down from hers, directly in front of Mrs. Gorman's house, the woman whose lawn I cut. Mrs. Gorman was roughly 102 years old, so I knew she would not be easily roused.

Sarah looked at me, puzzled, and wondered what we were doing stopping short of her place. I explained that my thoughtful brother had procured some bubbly for us. After some struggle, I popped open the two bottles and, as we sipped from our respective bottles, Sarah and I finally had our first meaningful conversation of the night. I kicked things off by saying how sometimes I wished that I was in public school. That was a shock to Sarah.

"Your school has much better teachers," she said, being very practical, "and you'll definitely get into a better college."

"Sure," I said, nodding. "But the guys at St. John's can be pretty obnoxious. Like Charlie tonight."

She laughed at this, but added that everyone was an idiot when it came to high school dances. This was my cue to confess to my own idiocy, but I didn't take the bait. I tried to change the subject to something more genuine.

"If I went to public school, at least we'd be able to hang out more."

I didn't mean this statement flirtatiously—it was just a sweet way of changing the subject as well as an honest admission that I did miss her in my life.

It was then that I started shaking, not from nerves but from the cold. It was freezing outside, and I had turned off the car. Sarah was also shivering and suggested that we go to her house. Uh-oh.

I started the car up and puttered into her driveway. I walked her to the door, hoping that this would be it. But Sarah invited me into the living room.

I started having a nymphomaniac panic attack, as I began trying desperately to leave, saying that Thanksgiving was tomorrow and I had a busy schedule or something ridiculous like that. She laughed at my excuse and, likely feeling emboldened by the champagne, took my hand to lead me into the house that I knew as well as my own.

We sat on the big leathery couch next to the fireplace, Sarah sitting unnaturally close to me. The only time we'd been this close before was on the Apple Turnover at the Kings Dominion theme park, screaming our heads off while we were thrown into each other repeatedly as the ride turned upside down. Now, in this quieter, more adult situation, there was not a sound between us. There was no avoiding some action. With Sarah leading, we tried making out in a way that was very limited and not terribly exciting. It was basically kissing on the lips with some embarrassing attempts at tongue action on my part. I was fully to blame for our lack of success, as I was not the best partner in this romantic enterprise. I was stiff as a board, just not where it counted.

After a few minutes, the whole thing died for lack of momentum as, frankly, I didn't know what else to do besides kissing. In theory, I knew what to do with a girl, but Sarah wasn't a girl. She was my former best friend, my playmate, Marie to my Donny. Sarah was very much like my sister. Not only are you not supposed to marry your sister, but you're not supposed to make out with her, either. It's just bad form.

Looking back, I wish I had been wise and evolved enough to express that sentiment at the time. No matter what our parents or neighbors or friends thought, the idea of Sarah and me being a couple was fundamentally so wrong that it's hard to imagine now that there was a time when people thought it was actually right. Everyone knows that Donny and Marie don't get married.

After our failed date, Sarah and I never hung out again. It was clear to me that Sarah knew something was up. I felt as if my secret interest in guys had been revealed by our utterly unsuccessful homecoming. If I couldn't get it on with a hot sixteen-year-old rumored nymphomaniac, then all hope was lost that I might turn out to be anything other than what I truly was: a brownie-baking, Donny Osmond–obsessed, gay boy in training.

As a teenager, there is a common fear that when you come out, you will lose your friends. I certainly ended up losing Sarah's friendship not because I came out, but because I wouldn't. Sarah probably would have enjoyed this gay boy in training. It was, after all, who I was as a child when we were the closest of friends. It was only when I tried covering up my innate otherness, when I tried pretending at normalcy, that I became a dull and boring dance companion.

In the twenty-plus years since, I've had a number of other female best friends who have shared my big gay life in a way that I never would have imagined as an anxious and closeted teen. It seems preposterous now that I was scared of girls like Sarah. But girls know the score. Given that I barely knew the teams, this was not only intimidating, it was downright terrifying. If I had been a little less scared and a little more open to cultivating our friendship, Sarah and I would not have ended up married, but we would have been left with something even better: We could have been best friends for life.

LIFE BEFORE GAYS

● ● ● ● ● ● ● ● ● ● ● ● ● ● ● ● ● ●

Elizabeth Spiers

Even if you didn't grow up in the Deep South as I did, you're prob-ably still aware of some of the great Southern traditions—among them: frying things, speaking English in a dialect that eliminates a few cumbersome verb tenses, and affixing to your automobile (excuse me, truck: *pickup* truck) stickers depicting your favorite cartoon character urinating onto the logo of your least favorite college football team. In my family, however, the most hallowed Southern observance is periodically listing for the benefit of your descendants and younger family members the various things you were deprived of growing up. The more gruesome the deprivation, the better.

My list: the Internet, parental disdain for corporal punishment, and gays.

I'm quite sure that, statistically speaking, there were some openly gay people in suburban Alabama in the early 1980s, but I never saw or met them and continued to live gayless until the age of eighteen when I shipped myself off to college and away from Wetumpka, population 6,102. Inasmuch as they existed, suspected gay men were spoken about in hushed tones. Christian conservatism run amok was the obvious culprit, and by extension, the local conventional wisdom that homosexuality went hand in hand with child molestation. In the paranoid minds of my neighbors—and let's face it, family members—there were legions of predatory homosexuals just waiting for the right opportunity to touch their children inappropriately, I suppose for lack of better things to do. And as any politician will tell you, there is no more powerful rhetorical device than the threat of child endangerment. Protecting The Children is the only universally accepted bipartisan platform in existence.

But despite being one of the potentially endangered children, I failed in my earliest years to internalize the widespread fear of supposedly hostile gay men. That gay men would be interested in molesting little girls didn't seem plausible for obvious reasons. (Violent predatory lesbians, if you're wondering, were not a concern. The conventional wisdom was that like unicorns or the tooth fairy, lesbians didn't actually exist in real life; they were merely fantasy creatures produced expressly for heterosexual pornography.) But more to point, no one who ever warned me away from gay men seemed to actually know any.

My earliest understanding of what "gay" meant, as best I remember, occurred at an age when I wasn't entirely sure what "sex" meant, and was still driven by the impulses of the average elementary school child—you know, the ones that cause them to throw hard objects at other kids on the playground, burst into tears over the repossession of a plastic figurine, or say the meanest things they can think of to the most helpless kid in the sandbox. We romanticize them because they're cute and they love us, but children are nasty, brutish, and short. I was no exception.

But as kids do, I grew up a bit. And with growing up came limited sex education and moral instruction at the hands of my Southern Baptist church. The former was as nonspecific as possible, mechanically speaking (*the what goes where?*), while pointedly specific about the participants (heterosexual couples, exclusively) and their motivations (marital love and reproduction, exclusively). The latter was as specific as possible about the interpretation of the primary text (literal) while as nonspecific as possible about the rationale for that interpretation (the text, if interpreted literally, states that it should be interpreted literally). So while I wasn't quite sure how homosexuality worked mechanically, I was told repeatedly that it was wrong because the Bible said so, literally. The English version that had already been interpreted, misinterpreted, translated, and reinterpreted countless times, that is.

Swallowing the Bible literally was only slightly more difficult than swallowing the literal Bible and I had problems with it from the beginning. But I made an effort, if only because I feared hell, the existence of which, ever the pessimist, I found slightly more plausible than heaven. Hell was hard to swallow, too, but on the off chance it existed, I wanted to be on the right side of the bet.

Around the same time, I remember hearing the first rumor of an adult I knew being gay; that this rumor came from other adults gave it more credibility. There were the usual ominous insinuations. The subject of the rumor was a local hairdresser, no less. Originality is rarely a prerequisite for gratuitous mockery.

By that time, my classmates—all Christian and culturally conservative—knew enough about homosexuality and how it was perceived locally to turn it into an epithet. Gays, faggots, and queers, while noticeably absent in a literal sense, were all over the middle-school playground, manifesting themselves in anyone who happened to be the object of the day's regularly scheduled bullying. *Queer* was just another word for assorted varieties of "unpopular."

A few of the bullied middle-schoolers at the tiny kindergarten-through-twelfth-grade school I attended were, as it turns out, actually gay. Not one of them came out of the closet before moving out of their respective houses post–high school graduation, and some of them, not before moving out of the state entirely. If they had outed themselves earlier, the environment would not have been welcoming, and sadly, there's a not insignificant possibility that the response could have been violent.

In the years following, I attended college in North Carolina, where I had gay friends who were open about their sexuality in a way that wouldn't have been possible in my hometown. When I moved to New York after graduation, I worked for a few years in finance, almost exclusively with men, all of whom were, as far as I could tell, exclusively straight. Then I met a guy named Nick Denton, who became a close friend. Nick was gay, but I didn't realize it until the second or third time we met. To be fair, I'm not the only one who has made that mistake, though certain of our friends insist that it was obvious—*obvious!*—from the beginning.

Nick and I started a Web site called Gawker.com in late 2002 and it quickly became an extremely popular media gossip blog. As the site's profile grew, there was a bit of speculation online that Nick and I were a couple. And amusing as that was, I had to admit that on some days it felt like it. I was certainly spending more time with Nick than I was with anyone I was dating and we were in each other's space constantly. It was a stimulating (ah, the conversations!) and sometimes tumultuous (oh, the arguments!) relationship and has stayed that way in one form or another since then. We've fought and made up a million times, both publicly and privately, and the third-party commentary is always the same: *God, you two have such a bizarre relationship*. And they're right: We do. And though I'd never admit it when we're fighting, my life would probably be far less interesting without it.

In the course of writing Gawker, I changed careers without fully realizing it and ended up in what is categorically termed "media." I was writing for various publications on top of writing Gawker and almost all of my editors were gay men. As you'd expect in any industry, some work friends invariably become nonwork friends because they're too fun to leave in the office and before you know it, you're at the Tuesday night Beige party at the B Bar picking out future husbands for people who are not your girlfriends.

I haven't made any conscious decision to prefer hanging out with my gay male work pals more than my straight male work pals, but if I actually log the hours spent with whom, it seems to work out that way.

It's an issue, certainly, of how I feel about the individuals, but if there's one common thread, it's that my gay friends are some of the most independent and fearless people I know and I've always been attracted to people with those qualities. Most of them have had to struggle with their sexual identities and, by extension, their identities as adults earlier in their lives and with less support from friends and loved ones. They are where they are now because they made hard, sometimes painful decisions and followed their hearts. I've never had doubts about my sexuality, but I alienated a lot of friends and family by openly admitting to atheism, making career and educational decisions of which my family disapproved, and moving to what certain relatives of mine unironically call the "City of Sin." In both cases, What Didn't Kill Us Made Us Stronger and, at the very least, provided fodder for an endless succession of painful-stories-turned-funny, best retold over drinks within ogling distance of attractive men of both persuasions.

As for my still nearly gayless hometown, I'm slightly heartened to report that it's not as bad as it was when I was growing up. My own parents, who would object to the term "homophobic" on the basis that they're not afraid of gay people, they merely disapprove of them, have seen and enjoyed enough *Will & Grace* (Jack is their favorite character) and *Queer Eye for the Straight Guy* episodes to know that when the malevolent predatory gays *do* come, it won't be for their children. It'll be for their appalling interior decorating, their Dick Cavett–era haircuts, questionable food preparation routines, and pleated Dockers from 1989. That's not, perhaps, the optimal portrayal of gay America's agenda, but it's certainly an improvement. Baby steps, I suppose. And I look forward to the day when kids there can grow up with the Internet (check), no corporal punishment (working on it), *and* openly gay friends and classmates.

After all, every straight girl in high school needs a boyfriend—to ogle the baseball team with.

THE LONG TRIP HOME

● ● ● ● ● ● ● ● ● ● ● ● ● ● ● ● ●

Zakiyyah Alexander

A few months ago, I ran into my friend Jason in the lobby of a theater moments before a play was set to start. We hadn't seen each other in nearly eight years. He looked good: His once wiry boyish curls were now carefully tamed with product; his style was refined. He'd been in a healthy, committed relationship since his early twenties, while I was very single. We stared at each other for several moments. My feet felt rooted to the ground, stuck.

"Wow," he said, planting an uneasy kiss on my cheek. "How have you been?"

"I'm good," I replied, suddenly feeling like the awkward teenager I once was. I wondered what I must look like through his older eyes. Nervously I adjusted my fitted shirt and skinny jeans.

We paused, unsure how to proceed. It had all been said years ago.

I'm not sure why, but I always knew Jason was gay. It wasn't because of his clothes or his attitude; it was more something I knew intuitively. We met in 1992 at New York's High School of Performing Arts during our sophomore year. Our school was filled with teenagers who were more creatively than academically inclined. We embraced nonconformity, using our teenage bodies as a canvas: nipple rings, blue hair, oversized colorful jeans, mohawks, and T-shirts printed with witty slogans like "Fuck You for Staring" or "Phillies Cunt."

As a sophomore, I would hang out in the halls with those who had decided that cutting classes—particularly the ones we didn't excel at—was a much better way to spend our time than actually attending them.

"Mia gave that *Star Trek* freak she's screwing a blow job in the hallway," my friend Jessica would say while twirling a cigarette behind her ear and jonesing for the Special K she secretly snorted in the girls' bathroom. "James saw them. He was so grossed out he wanted to hurl."

"Did you hear about those juniors who drank each other's blood? They think they're vampires cause of that stupid movie. Fucking 'tards," said Tom. He was clad in the motorcycle jacket his brother had run over twice with his car in order to achieve the perfect worn-in look.

"Mario from Aldini's class is dating this really fat vocal-major girl. But, like, everyone but him knows he's gay. What a closet case!" said Benjamin, a self-proclaimed expert at outing the kids who were decidedly in.

We all nodded, because usually Benjamin was right. The bell would ring and we scattered with great reluctance, not necessarily toward class, but away from the security guards who liked to bust us. We were already smart enough to realize that our future success would have nothing to do with passing earth science.

I could have cared less about who was gay or who wasn't. My main extracurricular activity that year was scribbling my boyfriend Omar's name with ink hearts on my three-ring binder. He was a junior, and was also my obsession during most of high school; during our turbulent relationship, we wore matching Columbia jackets and made out whenever possible. None of my friends could understand what I saw in him. My definition of friendship would soon change.

When we first met, Jason and I were immediately drawn to each other.

Both theater majors, we ran into each other one evening while volunteering as ushers for a senior production of *The Crucible*.

"Hey, do you know the choreography for the dance test?" he asked.

"Most of it" was my response. I looked at him with curiosity, not quite sure what to expect from this kid I hardly knew. Drama majors were required to attend dance class once a week, though we never took it seriously until test time approached.

Failing dance was far worse than failing chemistry. It meant you were really stupid.

Five minutes later, Jason and I were grapevining down the hallways, making the most of our jazz hands. We didn't stop talking until another usher shushed us.

"Oh my God," Jason froze. "Did he? Just tell us? To shut up?"

"I know," I said, attitude flaring, arms akimbo. "Who the fuck is he?" Peals of laughter followed, as we dared the dorky volunteer to reprimand us.

After that, we were inseparable. Jason was a fast-talking kid in retro bell-bottoms who was trying to turn his curly kinks into dreadlocks; a frizzy jet black–dyed mop with brown roots were the sad remains of his Jew-fro. I had recently chopped all my hair off and was finally liberated from the hours spent at the Brooklyn black hair salons. I wore red lipstick, baggy carpenter jeans that almost fell off my skinny frame, and plaid shirts bought for fifty cents at second-hand stores.

From the back, I was sometimes mistaken for a boy, but I dug it.

Jason and I were an odd couple; we didn't look like we should be friends, at least not by the way we dressed. Both voyeurs, we liked nothing more than to sit back and watch the mechanics of life and comment on them, loudly.

"Look at her, the one walking with the pea coat and the bleached roots," Jason pointed at a woman walking toward us as we sat on the steps of Lincoln Center. "She's a total elitist in that fucked-up privileged American way."

"Yeah," I agreed, getting into the game. "She's part of the system. She fucking eats it for breakfast. She's . . . bourgeois," I said, tasting the foreign word in my mouth.

Jason paused, an idea forming in his mind. "I dare you to say that to her."

"Like, out loud?"

"Yeah. Bet she won't even notice. I'll do it with you." Jason smiled and nodded.

Three counts later we both called out "Bourgeois!" to the poor woman in the pea coat, who looked back at us confused. For the rest of the afternoon we called out to anyone who fit our loose definition of *bourgeois*, and laughed at their baffled responses.

Jason and I were weird kids, though we thought we were slick adults. Together, arm in arm, we trolled the city. Or we watched the world pass us by. On doorsteps. In diners. Anywhere where life was happening, we'd pause, observe, and talk. We analyzed the relationships we saw happening around us (what people were wearing downtown as opposed to uptown) and discussed the cultural significance of *Reservoir Dogs* (the best cult film ever, in our opinion). We imagined the storylines of the films we would make together when we grew up—he would direct, I would write—and we pondered over where the funding would come from and which stars we'd cast. We'd continue our conversations on the phone late into the night, or at least until Jason's mother told him to go to bed.

"Best friend" was the term he used, and I had to agree.

As close as Jason and I were, we still had boundaries. I was struggling with the lack of connection I felt to my family and used every opportunity to escape my liberal home. My parents had given me freedom at a time when I wanted rules, something I had always equated with love. The two of them were struggling artists; my mother was a talented visual artist masquerading as a housewife while my father was trained in theater but now taught in public schools. Raising three children and living from check to check had not been in their life plans, and their unhappiness was palpable. More than anything I longed to have straight-laced parents like the ones on television shows, parents like the Huxtables. Parents with

two incomes who didn't make their own clothes. Parents who didn't resent the mundane direction in which their lives had gone. Parents who
enjoyed being parents.

At dinnertime, my younger brothers and I would take our food into
different rooms, each with televisions to tune out the silence. We would
eat or (more often than not) not eat the spicy vegetarian meals prepared
by my exhausted mother.

At home, I was filled with a loneliness that I couldn't articulate.

At school, my red lipstick and attitude were all the armor I had to
shield myself from being outed as the flawed, fucked-up kid I was. Jason
understood my discomfort and never minded that our sleepovers were
always at his house in Queens, where there was a well-stocked refrigera-
tor, comfortable furniture, and his nurturing, if overbearing, mother. It
felt like a genuine family experience, and I liked it. It didn't bother him
that I never wanted to talk about my folks. We both had secrets to hide.

Not once did I ever use the words *gay* and *Jason* in a sentence. My friend
lived in an asexual space, though he was perfectly comfortable discussing
sexuality, as long as it wasn't his own. Who needed labels, anyway?

My boyfriend at the time, jealous of my nights spent with Jason, once
said, "You know your friend's a faggot, right?"

Though I quickly hung up on him, it was shocking that he could see
what I thought was hidden.

A few months later, in acting class, a girl boldly said, "Jason, you're
gay, right?"

I stopped breathing, scared of what Jason would say and equally scared
of what he wouldn't say.

Jason replied in the negative, and the moment was over.

It was the first and only time that he blatantly lied about his sexuality,
at least in front of me. But the idea of Jason coming out had started to fill
me with a sense of dread, and I wasn't sure why.

I didn't think I was homophobic. My bohemian parents had changed
their names and religion more than once. They let their children sleep on
stiff futons and perched themselves on throw pillows in the living room

instead of regular furniture. Our house was constantly filled with aging dancers, actors, and musicians who attempted to mask their fear of mediocre careers with the blissful sounds of African drumming and puffs of marijuana, a pungent smell I still associate with my childhood. There was no room for prejudices.

In the last few months of senior year, I finally broke things off with Omar, and was single for the first time. Jason was now the only successful relationship I had maintained with someone of the opposite sex. Because I couldn't rely on my own, he had become my family. Slowly and naturally, Jason and I took up the space in each other's lives that was usually reserved for a lover.

I was scared that if Jason came out, our relationship would have to change.

If he started dating, I didn't know if there would be room for me. I wanted Jason to find love, but a tiny part of me wanted to find it first. And most of me wanted things to stay as they were for as long as possible.

On a sticky, hungover May morning, after the two of us had binged on Bacardi at a lame party in Staten Island, I was forced to confront my fears. The two of us were sprawled out on the orange plastic seats of the Staten Island Ferry. The murky water we were floating on smelled of garbage.

"Zakiyyah," Jason spoke in a voice I had never heard before. "You're one of my best friends. I've been trying to find the right time."

Please, please, please, I thought, *let me get out of this.*

"I'm gay," Jason said. "And I know this doesn't really change anything. I mean, I hope it won't. But I just, I needed you to know. From me."

In his eyes, I saw the need for affirmation. What do you say when your best friend comes out to you? *Congratulations? I'm scared that if we grow up right now we'll never be able to be the kids that we once were? I want everything to stay the same for just a little while longer, at least until graduation?*

Instead, I just mumbled, "Oh, okay."

Jason smiled, relieved.

All the way home, he talked nonstop about how happy he was that I knew, and who he had to tell, and who he wasn't telling and why. With a vague smile plastered to my face, I tried to listen as last night's alcohol soured in my stomach. The ferry docked in Manhattan and we arrived in a much different place than we had started.

I quickly said good-bye and headed home.

In the days and weeks that followed, Jason did change. He was finally free to be a normal horny teenager who could verbalize his desires. It was unsettling (and later hysterical) to hear of his nightly fantasies starring Bruce Willis circa the *Moonlighting* years. The list of the guys he had hooked up with was revealed to me with fanfare. Jason had been living a secret life; finally I was privy to the details. I felt hurt to have been left out for so long. I had naively assumed that if he hadn't been talking about being gay, he couldn't have been doing anything particularly gay. Now, I had to get to know this new guy, someone who walked and talked like Jason but was different.

He was confident, self-assured, and much more experienced than I was. He was out.

That day in the theater, as I looked into Jason's eyes for the first time in nearly a decade, I went back to the time we shared. We met each other somewhere between adolescence and adulthood, and for a short time, we were as close as two friends could be. Jason had needed someone to love him who wouldn't question who he was; I needed the same thing. It was easier for me to receive this attention from a man, and easier for Jason to receive this love from a woman who wanted nothing but his friendship.

It was time to take our seats. I looked at Jason again.

"So," he said, "where do we go from here?"

LAY IT ALL DOWN

. . . .

Edwin John Wintle

As a teenager in the 1970s, I longed for the sixties. My particular adolescent prison was a redneck New York City exurb, the polar opposite, I imagined, of life in The Haight during the Summer of Love. I dutifully went to Madison Square Garden to see Yes and REO Speedwagon, but I pined secretly for the open skies of Woodstock and the sounds of Joan Baez and Crosby, Stills, Nash & Young. I was a featheredback sixteen-year-old in PRO-Keds, a hooded sweatshirt, and ripped Lees who wanted to be barefoot and naked but for a tie-dyed sarong and body paint. Instead, my bleary-eyed friends and I smoked joints in a climate-controlled arena and pumped our fists in unison with thousands like us, all transfixed on the laser show in hopes of being transported along its colored beams, even if only for a second, *somewhere*. Disconnected and lonely, I was sure that sixties kids had been engaged by the world, accepting of one another, and intoxicatingly free. With them I would have danced beneath the stars, read aloud poetry I'd written myself, and fallen in love with another wild-haired, peace-loving boy like myself.

By the time I was thirteen, the counterculture had ended ignominiously with the Tate-LaBianca murders, the Vietnam War was wrapping up, taking the righteous peace movement with it, and Watergate had crushed any naive hopes I'd had that politics and integrity were not antonyms. My fantasy of being a hippy artist had died and I'd morphed into a pseudonihilist who hid out among the 'heads. We smoked bales of pot and ate mushrooms to Led Zeppelin and said nothing of consequence. Ours was not a time of ideas. We were engaged in a passionless rebellion whose only goal was purposeless self-immolation.

It was in the doldrums of my senior year that providence intervened: I met the first in a series of older women who'd all come of age during that singular decade—the decade I'd spent learning to match my clothes, hide my Barbie collection, and accept that no one would ever show up at the "groove-ins" I held under the giant maple in our front yard. One by one, these nonconformists would help me revive the kid who'd loved to spread out an old blanket and dance shoeless to shrieking Motown in front of an entire mystified neighborhood. There was Linda, a former modern dancer with a passion for Nam June Paik; Kitty, a bullfighting *aficionada* whose life was split between waiting tables in New York City and romancing toreadors in Seville; and Susan, a brilliant abstract artist so raw that everything in her path made her either laugh or cry. But the woman who led this procession when she found her way into my stultified seventeen-year-old life was Judy.

The night I met her, Judy was on her way to kill herself. At least that's what she said—she didn't seem to have any concrete plan, except maybe to drive off a bridge or something. My best friend, Katie, and I, bored senseless on a November weeknight, had decided to hitchhike the two miles into town to buy a bag. No sooner had our thumbs hit the cool air than a rusty shit-brown Dodge Dart with a peeling vinyl roof screeched to a halt just feet from where we stood. Inside was a pretty, heart-faced woman with a long mane of frizzy auburn hair and the gigantic, frightened eyes of a child.

After revealing her mission to us, Judy asked me to take the wheel— she was far too distraught to drive—and insisted that Katie ride shotgun while she jumped in the back. Maybe she thought this arrangement would hide her mascara-smeared face, but it was far too late for that. In town, Katie and I scored the "grass" (Judy's word) and we cruised on out to the dirt road that ran alongside the reservoir. With Joni Mitchell's "Help Me" blasting from the car's cassette deck, we sat on giant rocks that overlooked the black glass water and smoked and giggled Judy back to life, convincing her that since we'd just met, it was absolutely the wrong time for her to stage her grand exit. When it dawned on us that we were freezing, she suggested we move the party to her place.

Home for Judy was a cozy two-room cottage on a nearby lake that she'd rented for the off-season with her boyfriend, Bob, a sexy moose of a man with size thirteen feet and a mop of crazy black curls. At twenty-three, he was four years younger than Judy, though their difference in maturity seemed greater. Even to my teenage eyes it was obvious that Bob was hero-ically insecure and hugely threatened by Judy's and my mutual adoration. This would have killed the immediate crush I had on him if it weren't for the fact that he had Judy. That she was fucking him kept Bob sexy to me, and since I'd never get to have him, I enjoyed watching him squirm when she snuggled up against me and purred like a kitten. In return, Bob took every opportunity to remind me in passive-aggressive ways that I was the beta dog who'd crossed his piss line and invaded his territory.

Together, Judy and Bob made music, and to my untrained ear it was beautiful. They wrote folksy pop songs, including one that (much to my embarrassment) questioned whether Katie and I would ever become lov-ers, and they played Beatles covers I'd somehow never heard, like "Hide Your Love Away" and "Rocky Raccoon." They scraped together food and gas money by gigging at little taverns in the area, making them the first struggling artists I'd ever met. I was starved for anything bohemian, anything that bucked the deadening myopia of our small town, and their lives seemed completely authentic and wildly romantic to me.

Katie and I quickly became Judy and Bob's number one groupies. We attended every show—stoned, of course—and laughed when Bob wouldn't let Judy sing any of the songs I requested. He refused to deviate from the crumpled playlist that always dangled from his music stand, unless the request came from Katie or another member of the tiny audience. While Bob kept his black eyes tightly closed as he played guitar, Judy sang as though she were in some nameless pain, her wet eyes staring out over our heads as she searched for the notes and, it seemed, something more.

The extent of the couple's financial straits became clear just before Christmas, when Katie and I found them eating melted brown sugar for dinner one evening. Horrified, we left and returned with care packages cobbled together from our parents' pantries and offered to cook them a feast of canned goods. Judy wept at the gesture, while Bob left the room muttering, only to return when the meal was ready. A full belly, several beers, and a few bong hits softened his mood and he agreed to accompany Judy on a song she'd learned specially for me, as a Christmas present. I'd never heard "Candles in the Rain," the Woodstock-inspired anthem by Melanie (of "Brand New Key" fame) and when Judy sang the words in her plaintive, tremulous voice—". . . *some came to sing, some came to pray, some came to keep the dark away . . .*"—I understood why she had chosen it as my gift.

Afterward, Judy revealed to Katie and me for the first time that she'd actually attended Woodstock—she had been just a year older than me in '69—and that she owned a large collection of handmade Christmas ornaments she'd bought there. I decided that she needed a tree to decorate, especially since the upcoming summer would be the festival's tenth anniversary, and I persuaded Bob and Katie to venture out into the sleeting night with me to find the perfect one.

Dressed in dark winter coats, we stealthily surveyed the yards of the lake community's larger summer homes for the right-size pine while Bob ranted in a loud whisper about the uneven distribution of wealth. A half hour later, Katie and I fought back yelps as we slipped and slid on the ice, nearly dropping our end of the seven-foot blue spruce Bob had sawed down while we kept lookout. Our theft was justified, I told myself, and therefore not a crime at all; since we were stealing from the rich to give to the poor, it was an act of political protest. I'd be Judy's new hero, ranked just behind the Chicago Seven.

Later, after the ornaments were all hung and Judy and I were alone—Katie had left to make her curfew and Bob was passed out on the couch—we went out into the yard to see the Christmas tree through the cottage's picture window. The sleet had turned to a light snow, and the flakes caught the tree's colored lights as they floated softly by.

"It's perfect," Judy said, holding my arm tightly. "You'd never guess that the people who live here are destitute."

"Things will get better," I offered weakly. "The gigs will pick up, I'm sure."

I'd known enough to wait until we were alone to grill her about Woodstock, as it was long before she'd met Bob and I didn't want an edited version. We wiped the snow off an overturned rowboat down at the water's edge and sat on its hull, huddling close for warmth. I implored her to tell me about the music, the sharing, the love, and how it felt to trip on acid with thousands of like-minded people. I wanted to know about The Oneness.

Judy explained that 1969 had been a very sad and difficult year for her because her father had committed suicide that February. He'd been an aspiring musician who worked in radio and even had, for a brief time, his own FM show. He was still Judy's idol. She attended the festival that August despite her father's death because she knew he would have wanted her to. Many of the songs she heard there made her think of him and she cried a great deal. People held and comforted her, giving her a sense that her dad was there with her, too. He'd had a terrible drinking problem so Judy stayed sober in his honor; plus, she didn't want to dilute the intense connection she felt. Buying the ornaments was a way to carry the experience with her through the family's first Christmas without him.

I had no response for what I'd just heard, but I sensed that one wasn't needed. Judy pulled my head to her shoulder and stroked my hair, all the while looking off toward the tree and its psychedelic decorations. When

I looked up at her face I recognized the expression in her eyes; it was the same as when she sang.

"You're so sensitive," she said after a while, "and you have tremendous empathy. You've got to study acting in college. I know you'll be good."

"My parents are paying," I whispered, "so at this point it's prelaw."

"Your heart will dictate" was all she said.

Spring came and Judy and Bob moved away. The following fall I went off to college, where I kept in touch with Judy by letter over the next four years. She dumped Bob in the year after I left but continued writing music on her own; she even recorded a demo tape that she sent off regularly to record executives. Money remained scarce, and she eked out a living by selling freezer plans over the phone. Despite her own struggles, Judy encouraged my creativity in each letter, and I was eventually able to tell her that I'd dropped prelaw in favor of literature and theater. When I came charging out of the closet in my junior year, I wrote to Judy immediately and she responded that she'd always known, that we'd understood each other perfectly the first night we'd met. I wanted to argue the point—was I really that easy to read?—but I realized it was true, and that she wasn't simply referring to my being gay. Judy had taken a scared, wounded teenage boy and shown him that the 1960s had not passed him by.

SHUTTERSPEED

● ● ● ● ● ● ● ● ● ● ● ● ● ● ● ● ●

Bennett Madison

In the summer I am seventeen and naked in James's bed.

It's July and two A.M. in his tiny apartment in Dupont Circle and his chin is scratchy against my chest. The room is lit in flickering yellow and the sheets are gathered around our hip bones, the cat walking across our calves.

"Listen, Bennett: I want to take your picture," he tells me. He reaches up to run his fingers through my hair.

In the summer Anna and I are seventeen in my '88 Honda Civic.

Velocity Girl is buzzing on the broken speakers, a scratchy tape Anna made for me. Doing 75 on the Beltway and her singing along with her bare feet against the windshield. The windows are rolled down and her hair's burning white under street lamps and I am thinking she is like maybe some kind of highway mermaid. A dangerous, stranded thing. Take a picture, quick.

On second thought, maybe you shouldn't.

At seventeen, Anna is tall and gangly and blonde and ridiculous, always wearing some insane outfit that involves things like Spandex biker shorts and shower shoes and cheap, ostentatious jewelry. In the best picture I have of her, she's painted her eyes with liquid eyeliner in elaborate curlicues that stretch to her cheekbones and she's wearing a pair of dangly plastic earrings shaped like pterodactyls with—I swear to God—little hot dogs hanging from their stupid plastic-dinosaur wings. In the photo, Anna is sitting against a brick wall outside the high school, staring at the camera, dead-on but inscrutable. There is something about Anna that's locked away; something about her that she herself is afraid of. We're the same like that.

Anna is beautiful, but she does her best to conceal it. When supermodels talk about how they were ugly ducklings in high school, I never believe them, but if I were to believe them, it would make me think of Anna, whose beauty is awkward and almost repellent, like a wounded bird. Walking through the halls with her, I notice that people keep their distance, and I like it. It feels good to be in the strange dazzle of her shadow.

When we're seventeen, Anna is kind of like my girlfriend except that mostly we just hang out and watch movies and drive around with no destination. We make up pointless, self-aggrandizing stories together and we convince each other that they're the truth. But Anna doesn't know about James or Mike or Sam or any of them. Actually no one knows about them. Sometimes I think I'd like to tell Anna everything, but what's the point of the truth, when the lie is so satisfying? It seems like it would change things to let her in on the secret.

And sometimes I think I'd like to kiss Anna. But that comes later.

I am in love with her. I mean, really in love. I'm not at all in love with James or Mike or Sam or any of them, even though several of them have claimed, at various points, to be in love with me. It would be nice to love one of them back but they're all losers and really should be in love with someone who is out of high school. In my opinion.

*   *   *

Being a teenager is supposed to involve certain things. Things like listening to loud, annoying music, lying in your bedroom popping gum, and talking on the phone forever while twirling the cord around your finger; things like learning to smoke cigarettes and drinking your first forty at a bonfire party on the beach on the last night of the school year. Getting wasted, getting high, making out behind the bleachers with the girl you barely know from geometry class. But I'm sort of afraid of cigarettes and I don't live near the beach. I rarely go to geometry class.

Instead, I am watching myself divide and divide into a series of unmatching pieces. Here is the naif. Here is the schoolboy. The libertine. The prig. The one who does his homework and the one who doesn't. Here is the grownup and the child. And the something in between. The pieces are suspicious of one another and don't get along. The one who does his homework is easily bullied into submission.

And certain nights in the summer, minutes after I go to bed, another unnamed version of myself wakes up and crawls out of my body and takes the car downtown. He stands in corners in dark bars where he is probably drinking beer, maybe even smoking cigarettes, and is almost certainly doing who-knows-what with disreputable older men who may or may not be Republicans, or "in finance," whatever that means. He entertains the idea of falling in love with any or all of them. Eventually he slinks back through my bedroom door and the next morning I wake up with a headache, thinking, *A Republican?* Or, *Was it all a weird dream?* Or maybe I don't remember any of it at all. The next night, repeat. I tell no one.

Here is where it began:

Mike had just dropped out of law school and wanted to be a sportswriter and was the first person I ever kissed. Me a newish fifteen on summer vacation in Chicago. The night I met him, after we had sex, he drove us to the lake, where we sat and looked out over the water. What I remember best from that night is the spiky shock of his stubble there on the rocks and how familiar his arm felt around my shoulders even though it wasn't hard to figure out that he was too old.

That night, I had my parents' camera with me. I'd just finished ninth grade and photography class and I took these pictures of the water, the reflections, stuff like that. It's possible that Mike got a few shots of me—us, even. But early the next day the camera was stolen with the film still in it. My parents never bought another camera. You have to know my family to understand, but this is why there are hardly any photographs of me past fifteen.

A few summers later, I'm seventeen and naked in the apartment of a near-stranger, this guy who wants to take my picture. I'm prickly when I tell him to *wait for me to put my clothes on.* I roll onto my stomach and he reaches over and rubs my shoulder blade, offended.

"That's what I meant. Just a picture of you. Nothing to do with sex," he says. James is twenty-three—a little older, but not too bad, especially considering that he acts like a child. He has lit candles around the room. *Don't think I'm dorky for this,* he'd warned me as he'd done it. Now he is dragging his finger along my chin and staring me down. I realize that I hate his haircut.

"I have this thing about pictures," I tell him. He kisses me.

"The summer is ahead of us," he mumbles into my ear.

"Pictures are bad luck, kind of." I kiss him back. "You can't try to capture it. It fucks things up."

"I just want to remember how this is. Take a picture, so no matter what—you think that's weird?"

"Kind of," I answer, standing up and putting on my pants.

Seventeen and buttoning my jeans in a strange boy's apartment, I am of course thinking of Anna and when I am dressed I flop back on the bed as James snaps a photo of me, then another. Hair messy, half smile, eyes heavy-lidded.

The shutter snaps. And the image is sealed, a splinter of myself that takes off now for its own life. Someday I will wish I had copies of these pictures, to remember what it felt like to exist in this instant. To be this person, in this body. But right now it's summer, I'm seventeen, and I can feel the thing that was here floating away, frightened by the flash. I never talk to James again.

When we are seventeen, Anna and I put some miles on that car of mine, just driving around the Beltway in circles, headed nowhere in particular. Midnight and the Mormon Temple rising above us on the highway's oily coast. Going for coffee, going to the diner. Mini-golf, 7-11, video arcade, buy some comics. Just spin the tires, turn that radio up. We like the sad songs best. Shattered harmonies that scratch deep.

One night, we go to the roller rink. When we skate, we have a rare velocity. Anna shows off, mercilessly lapping all the little kids even though they are eight years old and she is six feet in skates. Grabbing my hand, Anna pulls me to the center of the rink. This whole Rockville crowd, these sixth-grade girls with their cutoffs, their waterfall bangs, I just watch them hypnotized as Anna kaleidoscopes around me, feet flying witchy, arms in the air. Casting a spell. *Whoomp there it is* pulsing and the disco ball, oh yeah, the disco ball. I just stand there. Ridiculous grin.

The next week I'll see James—remember James?—out of the corner of my eye while I'm making out with a stranger in a bar. When James and I glance at each other I close my eyes because it is rude to look at one person while you're kissing someone else.

Later I'm in my car giving head to this guy named Sam when he tells me he sees a cop car. He's in the passenger seat, I'm in the driver's, a parking lot at one in the morning. When I jerk my head up, I see flashing red lights in the rearview mirror, pulling up behind us. The only reason we don't get arrested is because Sam's a firefighter, and there's some kind of fraternal code.

*   *   *

Soon it's fall. At the senior homecoming dance, Anna is sticking her tongue out at the yearbook photographer: her arms thrown around my neck, eyes smeared in green and purple, and her hair towered into a ridiculous tiara. She's sparkly and Las Vegas in voluminous white and the shutter snaps and she slouches into me, eyes closed, and lets her hands fall to my hips. "Even though you're a mean person who doesn't like nice things or Africa," she says, "you are nice when it matters, which is what I know."

Anna prides herself in never saying quite what she means. She believes that a truer version of the truth can most honestly be located in an elegant obfuscation.

The dance is winding down, and I'm the only boy whose date's hands start bleeding spontaneously. This happens to Anna now and then, and no one can decide whether it's because she's a saint or an elaborate faker. I suspect a combination of the two. Maybe she just needs some moisturizer. Either way, that night, while we sit on the bleachers, blood starts to trickle from Anna's fingers. She knows it is supposed to be from her palms but come on, she says, close enough. Under the streamers in the dim, dusty light of the gym she holds out her bleeding hands to me and says, "Jesus fuck, not again." You think I'm making this up, but it's the truth.

Years later I'll look at the picture from that night—me and Anna at the dance—and I'll see something that I missed. The ghost of an image on top of the one I remember. It's nothing much, just the suggestion of a frown laid over her clownish, carefree grimace. A harsh twist of the eyebrow; a hovering suspicion. Double exposure. But has she guessed my secret or her own? And what do the bleeding hands have to do with any of it?

It is pretty early when I drop her off at home after the dance. I watch her run up the lawn in her fucked-up Cinderella gear. "I love you," I call out the window. Or do I forget?

"I love you," she shouts back. I don't question whether she actually means it.

Then I'll go out. It is a Saturday night. Take Piney Branch to Military to Nebraska, then on down Connecticut and into the city, where I'll toss my tie and too-small jacket under the dashboard and unbutton my shirt halfway down my chest.

A long, moping year goes by; it's another summer, and I'm eighteen. Anna and I spend the night at Lisa Roth's house. Lisa's parents are in the Bahamas and she makes us what she calls Long Island iced teas. Really, they're just powdered tea and vodka. It's August. Lisa, Anna, and I will be heading for college within the month, but we pretend that things haven't changed much. Things have changed. Things will change.

That night, Anna, Lisa, and I snap pictures on a disposable camera. We stumble around thinking we're much drunker than we really are, because we're secretly not so used to drinking and we don't know any better. Anna, Lisa, me, music blaring, sunglasses indoors, the two of them biting my ear and making faces for the camera. They try to dress me up like a girl, but I just look like an asshole. Hours later, Anna and I will kiss for the first time on Mr. and Mrs. Roth's bed.

I kiss Lisa first is actually what happens. Her and me and Anna on her parents' bed together. We have collapsed, laughing, and then there is quiet. I am looking at Lisa. She looks at me. This is her fault, I am thinking. This was her intention from the beginning of the night. And then a kiss. It may be a joke. But when it's over, Anna is crying so I kiss her too and here is where it all comes apart. There is no picture of this.

In August, Anna is crying, so I kiss her.

I kiss Anna because the day I met her we were twelve and she shot me with a toy pistol, right in the chest. "Murder," she said before tossing her hair with a smirk and running away. Flip-flops and leg warmers disappearing down an empty hallway. That night I kiss Anna with the knowledge that we will never be finished.

The next morning, I wake up as she's getting dressed, and I watch her. A toss of blonde hair before she pulls her shirt over her head, and when she turns to face me, she's just blazing with this ravenous, limitless brilliance. When our eyes meet, I'm afraid for a second that I might turn to stone. But I don't, and Anna turns again and leaves the room.

Those late nights in the summer, that year, I can feel the city bursting inside of me. Walking alone down 17th Street it's the lights and the pavement and some crappy beat tripping from an apartment window, the peak of the Washington Monument just visible but miles away and I am supercharged. Strolling past the bars, the eyes of those guys are on me. Chlorine sizzles.

"People say fish have really short memories," Anna had told me, one night at the roller rink after we were tired out. "Like, three seconds. People say, 'Who cares if you flush your fish down the toilet, it'll forget all about it after three seconds.' But a starfish remembers where its arm once was. It remembers it so well that it grows back. And let's not even start on jellyfish."

"How can a starfish remember anything?" I asked her. "I'm pretty sure they don't even have brains."

We were sitting on the bench on the edge of the wooden rink; the night was almost over. We rolled our feet back and forth, feeling our wheels catch on years of spilled Pepsi.

"Starfish have photographic memories," said Anna.

The summer I am eighteen, I am all best intentions. Every kiss is spinning with the odds of love. Anna, Lisa, James, Sam, the rest. With every kiss, I think, *This might be it.* And like on *Wheel of Fortune*, "*Big money, big money, big money.*" But Lisa will be sleeping for a while still, and Anna has finally burst into something both more and less real. Like she opened the yearbook, flipped to her page, and was surprised to see no starfish but, instead, a true and distant sun.

James and Sam and all of them I blow off one by one for no offense other than the fact that they take me seriously. It strikes me as pathetic. Luckily, there are plenty of guys on 17th Street who don't have names yet. For now, that's enough.

That summer the beer they buy me is cold and I can feel my heart expanding and expanding. Anna and I will meet again, now and then, in the edges of photographs. Smile, flash, blink; a flicker of infinity. The shutter will snap. This is how we used to look.

V

• • • • • • • • • • • • • • • • •

Fathers and Daughters,
Mothers and Sons

"I hope my sons are gay so that they will bring home lovely young men who will redecorate my kitchen."

—from "Darling, I Like You That Way,"
by Ayelet Waldman

IN PRAISE OF WOMEN

Andrew Solomon

I have always liked girls more than boys for pretty much everything except sex. When I was in elementary school, my best friends were girls, and I always wanted to sit at their table in our tacitly gender-segregated lunchroom, a wish that did not earn me stripes in the heterosexist world to which I was supposed to be getting acclimated. This propensity has never changed. When I was growing up, the person in the world whom I most loved was my mother, and I carried from that relationship the expectation that women would be my comrades. I have very close male friends, but more of my friends are women, and the friends to whom I am closest are women. I like reading novels by women; indeed, I often like novels that are intended for women and wrote my dissertation on Virginia Woolf and George Eliot in part because I loved the company of those two great women. It's not that I don't like men. I'm very close to my father and brother and to various male friends, and I love reading Tolstoy, and I have been deeply in love with men, and have been very happily partnered with a man for many years. But when I am away from female company for a while, I miss the woman's touch, and eye, and self. At a younger time, when my sexual relationships were more transient than I would have liked, my friendships with women were winningly permanent.

There are two ways to be gay. Some gay men separate themselves entirely from women; they choose men not only for the bedroom but also for social enterprise, and live in a male world untouched by any femininity except, perhaps, their own. They find women distasteful or confusing or even hateful. They themselves may not be masculine in the conventional sense of the word; they can be butch or flamingly queeny, tops or bottoms, *Brokeback Mountain* cowboys or faux-finish painters, but they are guy's guys, citizens of a unisex world. Other gay men strongly identify with women, often feeling that their own thought processes are akin to those of the fair sex or simply that the kind of thought that makes them feel seen and whole is the woman's gaze. Such gay men feel most comfortable with women, and women are their best friends. They have an emotional life that has some of a woman's flux and acknowledged melancholy. They may sleep with men, but they also love women deeply and truly. Such men need not be feminine, but they understand women's hearts and follow the complex logic of women's minds. It's Tom of Finland versus Henry James. My allegiance is to category two.

The Cambridge scholar Simon Baron-Cohen has proposed that autism is a form of what he calls "extreme masculinization" of the human brain, and has defined as super-masculine highly developed analytical skills, an interest in patterns and logic, and an insensitivity to unspoken (and often, even to spoken) communication—the later-life version of frogs and snails and puppy dogs' tails, or a scientist's vocabulary as coming from Mars. By implication, a woman's brain is all about intuition, empathy, and picking up on social cues, what was once known as sugar and spice and everything nice, and is sometimes marked as coming from Venus. There is a counter-autistic way of being gay that is about having a more emotional brain, trading on intuition, being awake to psychological nuance and a bit vague about math. Of course many men who are like that are not at all gay, and many of them marry women and live happily ever after. Among gay men of this stripe, however, the gap between erotic and emotional identification can be profound. Perhaps that is why some gay men live so deeply in their friendships, and especially in their friendships with women.

Before I delineated all this, I felt more deeply torn between genders. I would classify myself as mildly bisexual, which means that I have tended to fall in love with women and have sex with men. I didn't mind having sex with women, and I was fond of men's company, but it took many years for me to bring my gender preferences into line and form a fully committed relationship with a single person and, by extension, a single gender. For years I waffled back and forth, torn between the different ways I loved. The gender I finally chose for romantic love was male, and with John, my partner, I have found that blending of emotional and physical intimacy, but it was not easy. It was probably made more difficult because I share the popular bias against too much femininity in men. Those same qualities that so attract me in women often put me off in men. I like my genders to be reasonably distinct, and it was with force and clarity that I chose to spend my life with a man; my imagination failed me when I contemplated neutered compromise. There it is: I didn't go to the trouble of coming out of the closet to be with someone who didn't entirely float my boat. I decided to find the boon of female companionship outside my romantic life, and so my best friends are women.

John and I are contemplating having children, and while I will love any child I have, I have a particular dream of a little girl to balance the maleness of our household. When I think of godparents for this child, I imagine godmothers before I get to godfathers; a child with two fathers might want knowledge we don't provide. For me, the hardest part of planning a gay family is the absence of a mother in our putative child's life. It's not that anyone else would be more loving than John and I, but female softness was the sun and stars to me when I was little, and I am sorry not to be able to deliver it to our children. John feels the same way. One of our sorrows, close as I am, and as John is, to my father is that neither of us ever met the other's mother. It has been a great joy developing friendships with each other's longtime female friends; among the best things we have in common is our love for women, which helps attach us to each other, a deeper mutual interest than travel or architecture. Because it is mutual, neither of us is threatened by it; I have had partners who didn't like the women in my life for the strength of their convictions and their power in my psyche. It was problematic: I loved men enough to give up on according primacy to an individual female, but not enough to give up on women. There is some human equilibrium dictated by social tradition, in which you marry the opposite sex and have friends of the same sex. It seems like a cheat to hook up with your own sex, and make friends only with your own sex, too. It is walking away from half the world.

I have *Orlando* fantasies of slipping back and forth between the genders. I wouldn't mind being a woman every second Wednesday, for example. I used to like to imagine being a woman instead of being a gay man. I never contemplated the surgery simply because the procedure seemed too traumatic and too imperfect. If through some relatively painless process I could have become a woman with a fully functioning reproductive system and fully sensitized sex organs and so on, I would have had seriously to contemplate the possibility in my troubled adolescence. I wouldn't do it now; I've come too far down the road of my life as myself and it would disrupt things to make such a change. I've achieved love, and though a domestic life involves constant adjustments, my particular situation would not be improved by my swapping to another gender. I like being a man and I think I'm good at it. But I might like, might have liked, being a woman, too.

Older now and settled, I wonder sometimes what it is about women that is so touching. It seems impossible to generalize without lapsing into cliché, but the pattern is strong enough that I can't believe that I just happen always to have had female best friends. Is it simply a perpetual re-creation of the mother-son bond? I don't think it is, though the relationship with my mother may have been the necessary precondition of these friendships. Though the friendships with girls go back to childhood, the loss of my mother to cancer when I was in my twenties was one of the spurs to keeping up these alliances with particular vigilance, because at some level they salve an irretrievable loss.

I have built my career on figuring out what makes people tick. I remember the many long afternoons I spent with my mother in contemplation of these mysteries. I would come home from school and say that someone had been mean to me, or nice, and we'd talk about what kind of person that person was, and about why he or she might have acted that way. It seemed to me a fine way of ordering the universe, this delicate appreciation of human nuance, and the more methodical principles with which men seemed to address the chaos of life were always a bit anathema to me. Women help me to look in, always inward, and while I am a fan of outer space and once hoped to be an astronaut, I am more myself when focused on interiority. I prefer for myself seduction as a technique to ravagement. And I prefer people who seduce to people who ravage. I love gentleness. I believe in female advice—about clothes, about other friends, about love itself. Outside of the private world I share only with John, there are no decisions I make in which women do not play a role.

I also find women beautiful—beautiful ones, that is. That too may be the aftershock of having a beautiful mother. While men's hard bodies excite me, there is something to gentle curves and to that attenuated female slenderness and to faces that aren't always threatening to erupt into beardedness that is curiously appealing to me. There is a sensuality in the littleness of women's bones. But this drifts far too easily into moons and menstrual cycles and tides, and from there to hysteria and penis envy, and on into such a vast compendium of neo-Victorian clichés, preferring the kindness of women to the honor of men and so on, that I become queasy. It seems that I, as a man, should remove my intrusive and slightly objectifying gaze from these innocent victims of ingrained social attitude. Sometimes I think that as a gay man I'm exempt; but sometimes I suppose that because I neither have female sexual organs nor spend time exploring those of other people, I should keep my views of women to myself, and simply express generic fondness.

A photo came in the mail today of one of my goddaughters and her mother, who is an old girlfriend of mine, and the image of their two smiles gazing out at me fills me with happiness and calm and a particular sadness, too. I see the passage of time in the faces of women in a way that I don't in the faces of men. I have godsons too, and they have fathers, and I love them just as much, in my own slightly different way, but there is a certain ache that I reserve for the girls.

FAMILY ALBUMS

* * * * * * * * * * * * * * * *

Philip Himberg

"And have you inserted your penis into anyone's mouth or rectum in the last six months?"

"Yes," I replied, riveted to a tiny red ant that crept across the vast expanse of the Formica tabletop.

"Approximately how many times?" the boy asked.

"Well, it's been . . . I don't know. How many weeks since my last visit here? Twenty-five? Twenty-six weeks? Let's say thirty-two times."

"Did you use a condom?"

"No." The ant made a right turn and disappeared into the corner of a pink bakery box filled with Valentine cookies. The boy flipped a page over and inhaled through clenched teeth. "Okay. Has anyone inserted his penis into your mouth or rectum in the last six months?" he asked.

"Oh, probably, who remembers?" I could never manage to get through the whole interview without joking. The boy didn't look at me. "I suppose so. You want to know how many insertions?" I asked pointedly.

"Yes."

"Damn, I just lost the key to my Betty and Veronica diary. I guess now we'll never know for sure." I grinned, but my interviewer, a dark and not

235

altogether unattractive Semitic lad in his midtwenties, never glanced up from the answer sheet.

"Would you say more than twenty times?"

"Yes."

"And was this person your primary partner?"

"Yes."

"And did he use a condom?"

"No, we don't. We're monogamous—six years."

"Okay. On to the next category." The boy flipped the page again, bent it back and ran his thumb down the center to flatten the seam. He poised his number two pencil over the tiny bubbles, ready to smudge in my replies.

Jim and I had been coming to the Men's Study since it had begun five years earlier. At the start, we were two of two thousand supposedly healthy gay men who were being followed as part of the Natural History of AIDS study sponsored by the N.I.H. Every six months we went through a battery of blood tests and interviews, which tried to link behavior to the appearance and progression of the virus. Since 1984, one half of the participants had sero-converted and almost half of those had died.

"In the last six months, did you place your penis in anyone's vagina?"

"Yes."

He glanced up at me. "Perhaps you didn't understand the question. Let me repeat it."

"I heard the question. The answer is yes."

"Let me reread to you the definition." The boy fumbled back to the preceding pages. " 'Placing one's penis into a vagina means' . . ."

"I know what it means. The answer is yes."

"Okay, fine. So, how many times did you place your penis, uh, you know . . ."

"Well, that I can tell you exactly," I said. "Three times in October, three times in November. No insertions, per se, in December. Two in January. Hmm. That makes eight. Eight times."

"Are you sure you don't want me to reread the definition?" the boy asked.

"Yes, I'm sure."

The interviewers were an odd lot—a cadre of unkempt psych students with white lab coats and earrings—all of whom struggled valiantly to contain their curiosities toward the study participants. My lover, Jim, had described them once as "perfectly cute queer robots—with cowlicks." They were well trained to conceal any hint of exuberance, with painted-on poker faces and flattened monotones, and usually they tore through the twenty-minute interrogations without ever glancing up from the computer sheets in front of them. It was as if any eye contact might make them burst out of their professional personas into full-tilt versions of "The Man That Got Away."

This particular boy seemed especially on edge. I had never met him before, so I surmised he had just recently been hired—probably a U.C.L.A. psych major. He had black, thick eyebrows on a ridged forehead that had reminded me, at first glance, of a sexy young Omar Sharif. At present, he had succeeded in furrowing himself into a veritable Neanderthal.

"And did you use a condom?" he asked.

"No."

"No?" he challenged.

"No, it wouldn't have made sense," I said. "See, we were trying to make a baby."

The boy suddenly brightened and looked up. With his features relaxed, he looked like Yuri Zhivago, which made me happy.

"Oh. That's cool," the boy said, dropping all professional protocol. "Whaddayaknow? Well, now I feel better."

"Well, I'm glad you do. I do, too," I responded.

"Can you tell me a little bit more?" the boy asked.

I filled him in on the baby-making trials. We were at the fifth attempt, and Cathy was on her way out to L.A. next week to try again. We had started off doing it the natural way, and when that proved unsuccessful, we moved on to inseminations. I would make deposits into a bank in Westwood and those carefully labeled vials would be sent to Cathy, who lived back East on Cape Cod. The specimens arrived via UPS in giant tanks of frozen nitrogen, and their removal required delicate handling with rubber gloves. Although Cathy proclaimed herself an expert at it, after two expensive experiments, we had determined that shipping frozen spunk back East was a waste of time and money. Apparently, unless you could centrifuge it upon thawing, you were stuck with a lot of useless drowned spermatozoa. Old-fashioned fucking was determined to be the most effective.

"I wish someone at the sperm bank could have filled me in on that one," I had whined to Jim at the time.

"Well, we're learning as we go along," he replied.

"Yeah, well, I waste hours jerking off in some cubicle for nothing."

"Oh, stop complaining. There's no one in the world who loves jerking off more than you do. This is the one time in your life you have a decent excuse."

"So we scheduled real-time inseminations, with fresh sperm, as soon as we could and complemented those with actual lovemaking," I explained to the interviewer boy, who was looking less like Julie Christie's paramour and more like Nicky Arnstein by the minute. "It turns out that the greatest chances of fertilization occur when you do it the old-fashioned way, and after that, on-site inseminations are the best bet. And that's where we're at," I concluded.

The boy nodded his head and stood, gesturing for me to follow him out the door to the blood draw room. "Well, I think it's great. And who is the surrogate?" he asked.

The word stung me. "She's not a surrogate," I told him. "She's the mom. She'll always be the mom."

1968. Suburban Connecticut. The hallways of Hamden High were filled with dark-haired girls in angora the color of gelato who prayed their rosary for admittance to cheerleading club and packs of boys with big white teeth who slapped each other hard, laughed at stupid jokes, and delighted in slamming themselves against metal lockers.

It was a world of black eyeliner and linebackers, of letter sweaters and tiny gold crucifixes, and I was unceremoniously dropped there at the threshold of puberty like a cactus plant at the North Pole. Not that being outside the group was something new for me. I had been banished from the inner circle of boyhood at twelve, when I willingly replaced the burdens of Cub Scout merit badges for my bar mitzvah lessons. Back in elementary school, my best friends had all been girls. I had played "house" with Lisa Diamond up the street and "Broadway musical" with anyone who was kind enough to sit on my mother's couch and pull open the bay window curtain—"Slowly, and in time to the music, please!"—as I danced back and forth to the strains of "The Carousel Waltz." By age fifteen, I had grown about as far from the social inner circle of the neighborhood gang as I could get. Of more urgent concern was not my self-defined spirit of artistic nonconformity, but a dark, peculiar tugging. Sex with myself was focused not on women, but on a long and varied fantasy parade of odd characters: Salvatore, the school bus driver; Monsieur Boisvert, our suave French professor who wore Canoe and sported a perpetual five o'clock shadow; and even certain unlikely boys in the locker room. The cast changed weekly, but the gender did not. In terms of real contact, I had experienced something barely approaching sex with my friend Bobby a couple of years earlier, at our pool club, huddled under towels. But that was short-lived and he was now dating girls.

Swimming against this dark current, I chose to hide out as the high school drama freak, a gawky spire with wire glasses, beret, and London policeman's cape that hung down to my knees. It was in this masquerade that I wandered the cream-and-brown-tiled hallways, half-obscured in yards of wool, waving those bolts of fabric like a signal to like-minded souls. I didn't know my fluttering would catch the unlikely eye of Cathy Smith.

Cathy, with long, thin, sandy-colored hair parted to one side, was as round and solid as I was thin. She told me she had suffered the pain of being the heaviest girl in her class through most of her elementary and junior high school life. But unlike other haunted, heavyset girls who mastered only the art of hiding, Cathy made up for her size by being one of the smartest and best read. Inspired by the voices of Tolstoy and Flaubert, Anne Sexton and James Dickey, she developed an impassioned sense of the theatrical as well as a love of the stage. In junior high she spent many an afternoon constructing lavish collages out of magazine pictures, giving them names like, "My Darling, My Hamburger" and "Butterflies Are Free."

One November night, Cathy kissed me in the front seat of her father's purple Toronado, parked in her driveway. I remember that I got scared when her lips parted because she was soft, too soft, not like the kisses I had imagined with the men in my fantasy life. Their mouths would have been closed, a pressing together of lips, a scraping of beards. When Cathy's tongue left my mouth, I tried placing mine in hers, but she had already pulled away. I looked at her, in the pale green glow of the dashboard lights, touched her on her cheek, and felt a surge of emotion that was decidedly unfamiliar. "I love you," I blurted out. I had never said it before. I felt like a grown-up character from a wide-screen movie, replete with a lush soundtrack.

After our kiss and my declaration, Cathy and I were inseparable—between classes, after school, on weekends, the two of us let loose in whatever vehicle Cathy's father happened to have on loan from the car dealership where he was head salesman. I told her I loved her again and again. We sent poems back and forth. In a yellow Thunderbird we parked alongside autumn fields and discussed Bob Dylan and Dylan Thomas. We sang Simon & Garfunkel and James Taylor and the Fifth Dimension, our blue Coupe de Ville swerving lanes in a frenzy to acknowledge the first few bars of "Up-Up and Away" on the car radio.

Some months later, we both got jobs at the Cinemart, a fancy neighborhood movie theater that still sold assigned seats. I was a true usher, tuxedo and all. Cathy was the candy girl, in a dirndl skirt. We mischievously stole candy and made out in the storeroom behind huge plastic bags of popcorn. Cathy and I foiled our boss's ability to prove inventory shrinkage by removing one solitary Junior Mint from each tiny box, slowly amassing little mountains of the chocolate candy, which we consumed in peals of laughter on our way home.

On two occasions, we told our parents we were shopping at the mall on a Saturday, then drove 180 miles round-trip to New York to see Broadway shows with Lauren Bacall and Katharine Hepburn, lunching at Sardi's, praying no one would think to investigate the odometer.

And so it went, this madcap teen romance, all impulse and indulgence until a voice intervened and my old fear crept up my back like a poison vine. No matter how I tried, I couldn't force a sexual interest in my new best friend. All I was able to write in my journal about it was "I hope something changes soon," as if this predicament I had been in for years was now like a stubborn winter freeze that had held on into May. I blamed my dilemma on the lack of a soundtrack. "If only there was music," I wrote, with a slow pen, darkening the letters over. Cathy was attentive, her kisses ardent, but my eyes unquestionably burned with visions of men.

As winter settled in during my final year of high school, and the anniversary of Cathy's and my first kiss came and went, I panicked and pulled away. The more she sensed a retreat, the more Cathy would accommodate. She showed me her diary, which contained, in tiny, delicate scrawls, a listing of what she had eaten each day, what movie, if any, we had seen, and if I had kissed her. Day after day, the litany ran on: shrimp cocktail, *Butch Cassidy*, baked potato, lobster bisque, *Midnight Cowboy*, kissed behind the school, at my locker, rhubarb pie, *The Royal Hunt of the Sun*, fried chicken, *The Sterile Cuckoo*, in the car, *True Grit*, behind the ear, *Bonnie and Clyde*.

I came to realize that while telling Cathy I loved her and that she and I would always be together was the greatest mistake of all, it had become unavoidable. What choice did I have after the day she bought me tickets to *Hair*, plus seven Streisand albums, including *Simply Streisand* and *Je m'appelle Barbra*, thereby completing my collection? At Christmas she

had presented me with a storybook of our romance, complete with poetry and collages. I knew that I loved Cathy as a friend, but not like in
the movies. Whether it was the absence of a film score or Panavision, I
decided I had to say something.

On Valentine's Day, the air rife with expectation, I took Cathy aside
by the lockers, handed her a bouquet of tiny pink roses and told her
that I couldn't go on bearing the responsibility of a boyfriend-girlfriend
relationship.

"But do you still love me?" she asked.

"Not in that way," I stammered. "Just as a friend, I guess."

Her eyes welled up but not a tear escaped. Though I had never seen
her cry before, I saw now that she wore her grief in fathoms and leagues,
that her eyes had stockpiled years of disappointment, of rejection, but
that she had, until now, refused to let them break. When enough silence
had passed, I couldn't bear it anymore and simply walked away.

We spoke the next day over the telephone while I was on a break from
work on her day off. I imagined her eyes, wet and dark. I saw her room,
the closet packed with lacy floral skirts. I heard Laura Nyro in the background singing "New York Tendaberry." Cathy's voice, normally gentle
and even, was pinched along the edges.

"What did I do?" she asked me.

I looked outside the phone booth where snowflakes as big as quarters
and as wet as her kisses were turning to giant droplets as they hit the glass
wall and struggled for just the right word, as if the wrong one would an-
nihilate us both. Anything not to hurt her, anything to remove from her
more burden, more doubt, to quell my ever-mounting guilt.

"It's me, not you," I replied. "It's all me."

Of course she didn't get it. "But I must have done something!" she insisted, unwilling to let me go. "What can I do?" Her voice became whiny.
"It's because I'm fat, right?"

"You're not fat," I countered quickly. "Don't do this to yourself."

After the matinee that day she appeared, even though I had begged
her not to. She stood in the parking lot, under the glare of orange lights,

a half-sculpted clay figure in a camel coat. By now the sky had darkened and the snow landed on her head and shoulders, staying there in perfect formation. Her long thin hair was parted in the middle and covered with icy frost.

I approached her because there was nothing else I could do, hugged her awkwardly, and she lay her lips against my collar. In our bulky over-coats, we couldn't even feel each other. When we pulled away, I watched her eyes fill. I walked her back to her car. Neither of us spoke.

She drove off, a translucent figure behind fogged windows, and I began to cry, thinking of her, tucked behind the wheel, and about her diary of kisses and films and food. I sat myself down on a concrete parking-lot divider when my sobs choked me, twisted in my cape. From my woolen confines, I made a solemn promise. No matter how I felt, and no matter what I thought, I would never say "I love you" to another girl.

High school ended. We went our separate ways, but remained constant friends through letters and occasional phone calls. I found that life did, in fact, supply a kind of soundtrack. I fell in love with a boy named Mi-chael. And then another named Nick. And later a significantly older man named Bob. I learned that sex and love could be mutually inclusive, and I learned that while love could hurt, it was always worth the experience. I also experimented with a few girls along the way—it was the seventies, after all.

When I told Cathy I was sleeping with boys, I sensed her relief through the telephone wires, as though the one missing chip of a jigsaw puzzle had finally found its home. She passed no judgment. She said she still loved who I was. In this, she was constant.

We saw each other through the revolving door of each other's love lives, confiding back and forth the titillation of new affairs, the tribula-tions as they arose in longer-term relationships, the eventual heartbreaks and oftentimes complicated denouements and disengagements. After college, Cathy lived in England, and years later met Greg, a warm and sweet-natured hippy who stuck around long enough to teach her vegetarian cooking and the joys of tantric sex, but not long enough to help her raise their son, Hanlon.

Labor Day, 1989. A white-hot Los Angeles morning. Even in our Santa Monica apartment five blocks from the Pacific, Jim and I could feel the baking Santa Ana heat battering at the blinds. We were lying back on our bed, after some enjoyable sweaty lovemaking. The phone rang.

"Get it," Jim said, nudging my thigh.

"You get it."

"No."

"Well, then let the machine get it."

"I hate that. Go get it."

"I'm covered with sticky you," I whined.

"So here's a towel."

"No, I like sticky you. I don't want to get up." I rubbed my stomach.

The machine clicked on: *You have reached Philip and Jim. We can't come to the phone right now. Please leave a message after the beep . . .*

The voice at the other end was sweet, quiet. Perhaps a tad breathless and hesitant: *Hi, guys, listen. I don't know how to say this but I've thought and thought about it. I know I couldn't do this for anyone else, but I really think if you want, I mean, I think I would be able to be the biological mother for you guys. I mean, if you really want to raise a kid. One of your own, you know. I know it sounds crazy, but if you are into it, call me. Let's talk.*

We froze, and then in one move, both of us bounded to the phone, but by the time we had disentangled ourselves from the bedclothes, the caller had hung up.

"Who was that?" Jim asked, knowing full well, but seeking confirmation anyhow.

"It was Cathy," I replied, in a half voice. I grabbed for the receiver with a gummy hand and dialed madly. "It was Cathy."

"So . . . whose jism?" Jim asked me as we were brushing our teeth after returning Cathy's phone call. We had been discussing adoption for nearly a year. Now, Cathy's shocking offer was forcing us into an entirely new arena of conversation. Basking in the fantasy of having a biological child, something I had not seriously considered before, I simply assumed Jim would take it for granted we would use my sperm. Cathy was my friend first and since she and I had briefly even been actual lovers, after high school had ended—fleeting though those encounters had been—it made sense that I would supply the requisite X or Y chromosome. I sensed us heading for a Really Serious Talk.

Jim smiled. "What? What did you think? That of course it should be you? Why, Philip? Because you're one of the 'chosen people'?" Toothpaste dripped down his chin.

"Maybe that's the best reason," I countered. "Cathy's Catholic, or I should say, raised Catholic. Now quite horribly fallen. But still, she has the Christian gene. Surely you don't want to quibble over allowing this child a tiny bit of Jewish D.N.A., now do you?" It felt good to lighten the argument.

"Hmm. I might buy that." Then he grew serious. "Does it matter to you if it's mine genetically or yours?"

"Honestly?"

"Of course."

This was hard, and it felt like one of those discussions that could go horribly wrong. I knew it was important to me and yet I knew I would be willing to give it up if it was that important to Jim. I told him so.

"You know what?" Jim replied. "It doesn't really matter to me. It doesn't. And since it seems to matter to you, I don't have any problem with you being bio-dad. I mean that."

Then Jim asked the next question, the one I'd hope he'd wait to ask until at least another day.

"How are you going to make this baby? I have a funny suspicion that Cathy would like it done *au naturel,* if her boyfriend allows it. And David's cool, he just might."

"And what do you think about that?" I asked.

"Honestly?" Jim rubbed the back of his neck and sat quietly on the edge of the bed. "I guess I think that's sort of weird. I'm not saying no, but, honestly it's kind of weird." He went on. "Somehow, I think it's a decision we should all make, not just Cathy." He paused and looked up at me. "It's not like you're going to enjoy it that much, are you? I mean, you're *such* a *fag*!"

I pretended to be taken aback. "From what I remember, it's okay," I said, with a mock nonchalance. Of course, my memory was rather shaky in this regard. There had been scattered episodes of heterosex in my college years, my "D. H. Lawrence period," I called it. Cathy and I had finally consummated our high school romance, albeit clumsily, one summer break from our respective colleges. I had thought of it as a kind of poetic bookend to our childhood together.

"Well," Jim went on, "just don't get too used to it."

"Don't worry. I'll talk to Cathy. I suppose we can always do the syringe method." I pronounced *sy-ringe* in two distinct syllables and winced when I said it, to make it sound really awful. "It's not very special that way. I mean, eventually the kid's going to ask. It would be nicer to say that we made love. Don't you think?"

Jim shrugged. "I guess."

Day twelve of Cathy's cycle, the night of The Deed, was a full moon, which all of us interpreted as a great sign. Jim and I flew to Boston and drove to Cathy's home on Cape Cod. In order to facilitate everything, it was decided that we would take Cathy's eight-year-old son, Hanlon, to a movie first and that Cathy and I would do it afterward, while Jim took Hanlon out for pizza at the video arcade.

While Hanlon and Jim played Donkey Kong in town, Cathy straightened up her room and I nervously peeled off my clothes and climbed under the comforter. I watched Cathy obsessively sweeping around the edges of the rug. In her white cotton nightgown she appeared to be floating and it seemed to me that she was not all that different from how I remembered her nearly twenty years before. Her hair, still chestnut and shiny, hung halfway down her back.

"Come to bed before I lose my courage," I said.

She dropped the broom, removed her nightie, and snuggled in next to me. She had lit a dozen candles. Her smell was the same as it had always been, a mixture of honeysuckle and tea rose. Her skin was like cool chiffon. We hugged for a while and laughed and kissed under the down comforter. Then I stopped and pulled away.

"Why?" I asked.

"Why what?"

"You know 'why what.' You're going to make me ask outright? Okay, why are you doing this amazing thing for us?"

"No," she said quickly, covering my mouth lightly with her hand. "We're not going to talk about that."

"Not ever?"

"Just not tonight. Besides, I think you know why."

Her voice was low and I kissed her again, softly, deeply, for a long time. I forgot then the oddness of being with a woman, and probably because I had purposefully not come for ten days—a lifetime record, I figured—it wasn't difficult for me to get hard. I reached down to feel her wetness and was filled with the memory of the two of us back in a Chicago dorm room one hot summer night, two decades ago. I embraced the thought that we were still there, barely nineteen.

She guided me into her, and I moved with hesitation, wondering what images flashed through her mind. When I was fully inside, she moaned, and I sensed it was not from lust but from a remembered intimacy. We moved against each other for only minutes but I didn't worry about coming too quickly because, after all, it was about getting the stuff in the right place. As it poured out of me and into her, I clenched tight against her so not a drop would leak. It flashed through my mind that it might not be as easy two days later and a day after that, once we had all spent time together in the bright light of day. We moved apart, lying side by side, saying nothing until we heard Jim's rental car pull into the driveway. I was relieved that this gave us a reason to get up. I pulled on pajama bottoms and went to the hallway. Something told me it was not a good idea for Jim to find us in bed together.

He walked in carrying a sleeping Hanlon: "Pac-Man did him in." The three of us walked together to Hanlon's room and put the boy to sleep.

"So," Jim asked in the hallway, with a grin as wide as could be, "was he good, Cathy?"

I rolled my eyes, more for effect, grateful that there would seemingly be no serious talk.

"He was great."

"I bet." Jim laughed.

"What's so funny?" I asked.

"Nothing. I didn't say anything."

I pushed aside the discomfort of worrying what Jim really felt.

We slept in one bed and spooned each other, with me, of course, in the middle.

"Bob and Carol and Ted," Jim muttered.

I couldn't sleep. Even after I was sure Cathy and Jim had drifted off, I lay awake wanting something more, bugged by the informality of it all. I knew the significance of what was happening overshadowed our inability to discuss it then and there. I pictured a hundred different conversations we might have but then I must have dozed off, for I saw Cathy sweeping all of them under the Oriental rug that covered her bedroom floor.

We had invested a magical quality in that night, yet it took us nearly a year to get pregnant. A year of flying back and forth between Los Angeles and Boston. A year of lovemaking, inseminations, testing. A year of worry and disappointment, of huge frustration. A year of withholding ejaculatory sex from Jim so that I'd have enough of a sperm count to matter, and a year of Cathy's boyfriend trying to understand why she was devoting herself to sleeping with her ex-, now gay, boyfriend. A year of therapy and obsession on everyone's part.

Eleven months from that first try, sperm met ovum. The phone rang one morning, as I was frying another kind of egg, trying hard not to think that exactly two weeks had passed since our last lovemaking episode. I was trying hard not to expect a call, trying hard not to allow myself the depression of another letdown. In any case, Jim had laid down the law for us: "No more. That was the last time. It just wasn't meant to be, Philip. We'll tell Cathy soon."

I answered the phone. "Hello?"

No *hello* back. Just a young boy's voice. It was Hanlon: "Hey guys, you're going to be dads. Mama said it worked."

The day has come when Jim and I are to return to Los Angeles with our infant daughter. Cathy, Jim, and I have had a substantial amount of counseling around this moment, but as the morning arrives, the air feels thick and uncomfortable. I am queasy. We agreed that Fanny—lovingly named after the spirited title character in the Bergman film, *Fanny and Alexander*, that Jim and I saw on our first date—should be with her mom for the first five weeks of her life, that taking her away any earlier would be detrimental to both mother and child. "An amputation," our therapist had called it. Jim, Cathy, Fanny, Hanlon (who is now nine), and I have lived together as a kind of family on Cape Cod since a week before Fanny's birth. It hasn't been easy.

The birth itself was quick, almost too quick. We arrived at the tiny hospital in Wareham, Massachusetts, just forty-five minutes before she popped out and went home a few hours later with our newborn daughter.

The hormones raging through Cathy's body made each subsequent day a sort of obstacle course. After one week, we felt it better to allow Cathy alone time with the baby, so she and Fanny moved back to her own house, about seven miles from the farmhouse we had recently bought as a vacation home.

Jim and I spent most days walking around perplexed and scared. There were no rules for this. Some days Cathy would bring Fanny by or encourage us to take her for hours; other days, she guarded her closely and complained about the physical pain of being separated from her because of her nursing.

We had always assured her that when the time came to leave, the risk would be ours; that if she could not, in fact, relinquish this baby, there would be no argument. We would simply have a child who lived three thousand miles away.

Day thirty-five has arrived. Cathy has carefully packed up every newly washed cloth diaper, piece of clothing, and attendant bit of paraphernalia. As we pull our car up to her house, we see her through the living room bay window, speaking to the baby in her arms.

"What do you suppose she's saying?" I ask Jim.

He doesn't reply, but takes my hand.

A half hour later, Fanny is safely buckled into the rear seat of our rented Pontiac, and I'm standing beside the car door. Jim is at the wheel. Cathy is beside me in a white T-shirt and denim jumper, clutching Fanny's brother's hand.

"I'll be okay," she says, as she hugs me awkwardly with her other arm. "Call me when you arrive so I know you're safe and sound." I kiss her lightly on the cheek. I don't have any words. I expect her to burst into tears but her eyes remain calm, waterless, just as they were the day I handed her that bouquet of consolation nearly two decades earlier. I climb into the backseat beside our already sleeping infant. The car backs up slowly over the leaves strewn on the driveway. I look back once more at mother and child side by side and notice that two huge wet spots have sprung up on Cathy's chest where her breasts are leaking, weeping milk for her departing child.

Fanny is now fifteen, the same age her mother was when I met her back in the high school drama club. Jim and I are taking her to New York to celebrate Cathy's fiftieth birthday. Our unusual family has come together four or five times each year since Fanny was born—in the summers, at Christmas, over school holidays.

When Fanny was nine months old, Cathy ceded her parental rights as planned so that Jim could be the other legal dad. Since then, Cathy has been "Mama" but really more of a fairy godmother. Jim and I agreed that she should not be burdened with the task of disciplining a child she sees only every four to five months.

It has not all been a fairy tale. Jim and I broke up when Fanny was six years old. I have stopped trying to analyze whether this was the old cliché of pouring our love into our child rather than into each other or simply a predictable growing apart. My guilt over it has certainly cemented itself into my being. Luckily what has remained central to both our lives has been Fanny. We are laughingly referred to as the "poster couple for gay divorce." No fights, no recriminations, little tension. We live near each other and Fan goes back and forth week by week. Sometimes we even vacation together. Mama's visits over fifteen years have amassed a surfeit of etched memories, free-floating in our minds and hearts. They are catalogued in duplicate photographs that sit, like those of most families, in huge frantic stacks of shoe boxes in our respective hall closets, in a scattering of mismatched picture frames on pianos, bureaus, and mantels, and in wallets and albums.

When she was not quite four years old, Fanny asked me if I knew I was gay. I was driving at the time and nearly crashed my new Infiniti into the gatehouse of Bel-Air. I recovered with aplomb, telling her I did know I was gay and asking her what gay meant. "Papa," she replied, as if to a nitwit, "gay means handsome." That was as good a definition as we needed at that stage.

At her bat mitzvah, her three weepy parents watched her lay into the Torah, lashing out with great charm, intelligence, and wit at its homophobic and misogynist portions. At the end, Fanny turned directly to us and said, "From my mother, I learned the definition of unconditional love, from my dad, Jim, I learned love of the outdoors and nature, and from my papa, Philip," and here she paused for effect, "I learned which Barbra Streisand album showed her at her peak."

Despite us or because of us or a combination of both, Fanny has grown to be a confident young woman who is proud and eager to tell the world about the two dads who have raised her and the mom she adores, who lives five hours away by plane.

"Is it weird having two gay dads?" she is often asked.

"No, why would it be? It's what I know," she replies.

"Why didn't you just move out to California to be near your daughter?" people ask Cathy.

"That wasn't the intention," she explains to them. "The idea was for Jim and Philip to have a child of their own to raise." She often sees the bewilderment—or is it judgment?—behind kind eyes.

On this, our sixth or seventh New York sojourn as a family, Cathy is with Hanlon, now twenty-three, and her long-term companion, a sweet, slightly older man named Gary who has been devoted to her for more than a decade now. We go see *The Light in the Piazza*, a new musical at Lincoln Center. The lush, romantic story begins in Florence when Clara, a young American girl, loses her hat to a gust of wind. The hat is rescued by a handsome young Italian named Fabrizio. Their eyes lock, and they fall immediately in love.

After the play, Cathy and Gary walk hand in hand, and Jim walks with Hanlon. I ask Fanny what she thought of the play. "I don't buy that opening," she says. "No one falls in love at first sight. It's overly romantic." She rolls her eyes.

Her words alarm me and I look to Cathy for her reaction. How can Fanny, at fifteen, so adamantly disdain this notion, the basis of so much literature and art and music? "Surely you don't really believe that it's impossible to recognize one's soul mate across a crowded room?" I ask her.

"Papa," she says very seriously, as if she's the parent speaking to a child, "to really love someone, you need to *know* them. You can't truly love someone you don't know. You can feel sexual attraction for them, of course. But not love. That comes later." I'm annoyed that she's telling me something I cannot logically argue.

At Café Fiorello, we order profiteroles with hot fudge sauce. Fanny goes to the ladies' room. Jim, Hanlon, and Gary are discussing Hanlon's life at college. Cathy takes both my hands from across the table.

"Did you ever figure it out?" she asks me.

"Figure out what?"

She looks surprised. "The answer to your question."

I'm puzzled, but I know she isn't being coy. There was, there is a question, but it is so wedged into my life, so much a part of me, that I have to unearth it, gently, slowly, from its resting place. The question begs at me from a candlelit room, nearly sixteen years back, and then the CD shuffle that is my mind flips back further still—to two figures awkwardly embracing in the parking lot of a suburban mall, to the reflected green glow of a dashboard. The question endures. It's a question that has been asked of me about Cathy time and time again: Why did she do it? How could she give up her daughter?

"I think I know that you loved me," I tell her.

"And I loved that you loved Jim. Giving you Fanny, giving you parenthood, I just knew it was the right thing."

"What about you?" I ask her.

"I have a daughter," she says. "A beautiful, amazing daughter."

"But I hurt you so much, back then," I say.

"And you also loved me so much. In your way. Before anyone else did. You were the first. That changed everything for me."

I let this sink in.

There is another, a bigger question, of course, one that I ask only of myself and cannot share out loud. What part of me could have allowed Cathy to do this? What kind of man allows a friend to make that kind of sacrifice?

This thought is interrupted by Fanny's return from the washroom. She sits beside her mother, amidst our silence. She digs into the gooey ice cream in front of her. Perhaps the answer to my question takes me to a place where I cannot linger. Or maybe it's a lot simpler. How could I have missed the opportunity to be this child's father?

To distract myself, I decide to ask Fanny a question. "So, honey, you never really said which Streisand album does show her at her peak. I've always meant to ask you. Ever since your bat mitzvah."

She looks at me blankly. "Oh, that. I don't remember. It's bad enough that people think you named me for her. I mean, for her character in that movie. I always have to tell them that even though I have gay dads, they weren't queer enough to name me after some gay icon's Oscar-winning role. And then when I tell them that my name is actually from the title of some Ingmar Bergman movie, they just look really confused."

I pretend to be crestfallen.

Cathy pipes up and takes Fanny's hand. "Well, didn't Papa always say it was *The First Barbra Streisand Album*?"

Fanny looks very serious. "No, I think it was *The Second Barbra Streisand Album*."

"No," Cathy says adamantly. "Definitely it was *The Third Barbra Streisand Album*."

And then at the same moment, they both crack up.

Cathy spoons some melted ice cream to her lips, in near hysterics. Fanny joins her, practically snorting ice cream from her nose. I watch the two women I love most in my life, my heart full to bursting, and I begin to laugh, too. I laugh so hard that I feel tears streaming down my face.

LIKE FATHER, LIKE DAUGHTER

· · · · · · · · · · · · · · · · · · ·

Abigail Garner

The producer retrieved me from the greenroom at 6:14 A.M. and told me I'd be on after the next commercial break. After a week of non-stop interviews on my book tour for *Families Like Mine: Children of Gay Parents Tell It Like It Is* in 2004, I knew the routine, so I headed to the main set. I assumed that like all the other morning shows, they would want me sitting with the hosts on the comfy couches. The hosts would sip from their call-lettered mugs as we all tried to act casual while they asked me questions for three to five minutes about growing up with gay parents. This time, however, the producer stopped me just a few steps out of the greenroom and redirected me to where she wanted me to sit: at a news desk in the back of the studio, set up for a split-screen interview.

I waited for the punch line, but when she didn't offer one, I summarized her plan to make sure I wasn't missing something: "Even though I'm physically here in San Francisco, just yards away from the main set, you want it to look like I'm somewhere else, beamed in via satellite?"

She nodded. "That's our format for hard news."

My book? Hard news? *Heterosexual female raised by homosexuals. Story at eleven.*

255

She wasn't kidding and I didn't have time to argue. I climbed onto the swivel stool and waited for my cue. Getting interviewed by media in the Bay Area, home of a comparatively large number of queer-parented families, I secretly wished for some new and insightful questions, especially since seconds earlier I had been upgraded from opinionated author to hard-news correspondent. But the questions they chose were ones I had heard before verbatim, because I had written them myself for the press kit distributed by HarperCollins.

When the segment ended and the show cut to commercial, I slid off the swivel stool and began untangling myself from the earpiece and clip-on microphone. I heard quick, determined footsteps coming my way. When I looked up, I saw one of the on-air hosts heading right toward me. I had not seen his face before, but the suit and the thick fake tan makeup were big tip-offs. "Okay," he started, trying to catch his breath, "I've got less than two minutes, but I have to know: Was it weird?"

"Was *what* weird?" I asked, giving him and his intrusive question the benefit of the doubt. Maybe he wasn't asking if it was weird having gay parents. Maybe he was asking if it was weird having to be wide awake at six in the morning. Maybe he was asking if it was weird hearing a producer call my life "hard news."

"Your . . . *family*," he emphasized, as in, *what else could I be talking about?* "My wife," he continued breathlessly, "she's very conservative. Very religious. Not like me. So when I saw your story on the news last night I said, 'please honey, you have to watch this.'"

He was referring to a report that aired the previous evening on ABC's *World News Tonight* covering my book and my advocacy on behalf of people with gay parents. The footage included me giving a college lecture, speaking at a rally, signing books, and having dinner with my father and his partner.

The morning-show host continued, "I wanted my wife to watch because I thought it would open her mind, you know? So we were watching you last night and I was thinking, this is normal, I can handle this, but then I saw you at the dinner table and . . ." He gave his best faux-shocked expression: jaw dropped, eyes widened, and he stepped back with his hands behind him to catch his fall against the wall. "Two dads at the dinner table! It looked weird. It did! Was it weird for you? Because it looked weird."

Realizing my time was limited—he had less than sixty seconds before he had to return to the set—I made a point to touch him on the arm as I told him, "It didn't seem weird to me because it is what I have always known. What mattered most was that I felt loved."

What I really wanted to say was *Don't start with me about what looks weird. You're the one in a business suit and full makeup.*

Variations on the question "Was it weird?" have saturated my life to the point that I don't know what it's like to *not* be asked such questions.

"What was it like?"

"How did you find out?"

"How did it affect your sexuality?"

Personal questions like these started when I was so young, I lack perspective about what questions are inappropriate for people to ask. Interrogations about my sexual orientation started when I was in fourth grade: "Your dad is gay? That must mean you are gay, too!"

I heard it enough to wonder if everybody else saw something in me that I did not. Was I gay? I didn't think so. Then again, I knew men who came out when they were thirty, forty, and fifty years old. What if I really were gay, but in deep, deep denial? The constant questions forced me to scrutinize my own sexuality and build a level of self-awareness that most nine-year-olds don't have.

I'm in my thirties now, but the presumption remains that my own sexuality is fair game for anyone to ask about, and that everyone is entitled to judge my father based on how I turned out.

Having a father come out as gay certainly did influence my sexuality, but not in the way most people assume. I grew up in a community that included my father's family of choice: a circle of gay men who expanded my me-centered universe with creativity, warmth, and vibrancy. Although many of them did not survive the AIDS epidemic, their influence has followed me into my adult life. Most notably, as my attraction to men began to emerge, I gained my first subconscious lessons of how to respect, appreciate, and love men by observing how gay men respect, appreciate, and love one another. Nowadays I regularly find myself smiling at a man in his twenties or thirties and enjoying the distinct gay male energy he emanates, even if he doesn't notice me. Sometimes a gay man's eyes will meet mine when I'm checking him out and he will give me a look of pity or annoyance, as if to say, "Oh, you clueless girl, get your gaydar fixed."

Little does he know, my gaydar is finely tuned. I am not pining over him with my heterosexual desire; I am admiring him with my queer sensibility.

Unlike most blossoming straight girls, I had easy access to the *International Male* catalog—my coming-of-age lust material. I could regularly find the latest edition of *International Male* on a side table in my father's living room of white carpeting and track lighting. It didn't really occur to me that the magazine was for gay men. I thought it was for men who cared about their appearance. It would be another decade or so before I figured out that those things are usually assumed to be the same thing.

In the late seventies jogging had caught on as the next big exercise fad, and clothes were being designed to keep up with the trend. The shorts for men were light and very, very short. *International Male* models showed off short-shorts with slits up the side that went nearly up to the waistband. Instead of a seam, the fabric from the front panel and back panel simply overlapped at the hip. The magic was in the overlap, the hint of a peekaboo. With every stride, the slit on the side opened and closed, opened and closed. The models posed both ways in fake frozen running positions. A man's hip, skin exposed. More than leg, but not quite ass. This tease is where my lust began.

Recently I discovered an unsolicited copy of *International Male* in my mailbox, addressed specifically to Abigail Garner. I laughed out loud thinking about how the catalog found me again. I suspect that as companies and nonprofits traded or sold their mailing lists, my consumer pro-file convinced a computer somewhere that I had promise as a future *IM* customer. I donate to LGBT and AIDS organizations and I subscribe to *Out* and *The Advocate*. I have been sent sample issues of *Instinct*, *Genre*, *Details*, and *Playgirl*. Each complimentary copy addressed to me comes with a mass-produced "special invitation" from the editor in chief who points out that we both know I'm not your average man.

Well, no, I'm not.

My first realization that my family was going to be different from other families was the morning after Christmas when I was in kindergarten. My eight-year-old brother and I were settled into an overstuffed chair, sitting side by side to watch our cartoons. Our father came into the room and kneeled down, blocking our view to the TV. He put one hand on one of my knees and his other hand on my brother's knee. "Kids," he said, "I'm leaving. I don't know how long I'll be gone or if I'm going to come back. Just know that I love you and nothing will change that."

Sure, okay, I said to myself, *but right now, you're interrupting our cartoon.*

When he lived with my mother, my father, a perpetual ticking time bomb, would get angry with me for reasons I couldn't anticipate or con-trol. Some people might have described him as strict. The word implies that discipline is based on rules being followed or broken. In my dad's case, his anger would come out even when I thought I was following all of his rules. If you took the standard concept of strict and combined it with emotional distance and unpredictability, you got my dad.

In my eyes, at that age, the more time he was away from the house, the better.

After we heard the front door close, my brother waited for the next commercial break to find Mom, and I followed. She was crying over the kitchen sink. That's when it hit me that when Dad said he was leaving, he didn't mean he would be out running errands all day or gone for a week's vacation. He meant *moving out*. Despite my mother's grief, the house instantly felt lighter.

*   *   *

In first grade, I was pulled out of class weekly to go to "Family Change" group. We met in one of those small windowless rooms at the end of a hallway that no one ever has to walk down unless adults are referring to them as "special." In this group, there was a girl whose house had burned down. Another girl's dad had just died. A boy's grandma was moving to a nursing home. I couldn't figure out my place in this group. Sure, my dad had moved out of the house, but that was good news for me. He was happily living with his partner, Russ, and as a result he was much kinder to me. This new version of my dad was so different; he kept surprising me when he didn't seem bothered by things that used to make him blow up. When I handed him a note from school that I was certain would make him explode, my newly mellow father read it and stunned me by responding in his most soothing voice, "We'll take care of this. Don't feel bad. Lots of children get lice."

Finally, I knew what a fun, supportive dad was supposed to be. So why did they put me in a support group with kids who were dealing with bad things that were happening to them?

I was there, I learned, to talk about the divorce. A lot of help that would be, considering that the reason why my parents had split up was "private."

"We can talk about it with each other and with some of our close friends who know and understand," my mother told me.

From that point forward, I divided my world into two parts: safe and unsafe, gay and not gay. Family Change group was definitely not a safe place where I would be speaking up.

From the day my dad moved out until the day I left for college, every "coming out" about my family was a monumental event. Each time, I would prepare myself, certain that I could be casual and calm about it. But my thoughts ran through every reaction I had ever witnessed, plus a few reactions that only existed in my mind. The ever-present imaginary faces of ridicule came at me like a 3-D nightmare: *What?! Your dad is a fag?*

Every report of gay bashing terrified me, wondering when it would be our turn. I worried that I might accidentally put my dad in harm's way, innocently disclosing too much information to a well-disguised nutcase with an axe to grind and a tire iron behind his back.

Even when I was almost certain someone was safe to tell, my eyes would start to well up and I'd tremble uncontrollably before I could finish my first sentence. My worries about how my tears and trembling would be judged set off a spiral of irrational internal dialogue, only accelerating my panic: *They are going to think I have "issues." They will think: What do you expect, really . . . she's so ashamed of what her father is subjecting her to, she can't even speak coherently. . . .*

My tears were not of shame, but of fear and anger. My tears told the story: *I hate that it took me so much energy to hide something I should not have to hide. I hate that I don't trust you until you will go out of your way to prove to me otherwise. I hate that I can't explain to my parents that not wanting to talk about this is not because I am embarrassed. I hate that when my tears flow, the people who see those tears have no inkling of the meaning behind them, and that instead all they see is a girl with issues. A girl who is messed up because her dad is gay.*

It was only the anonymity of college in another part of the country that allowed me to practice talking about my family in the same casual way other people talked about theirs.

The summer after college graduation was the first time I attended a Gay Pride event. I had just started dating a man who was staffing one of the vendor booths at the Twin Cities Pride Festival, and I wandered into the park to say hello and to see for myself this legendary gathering I had only heard about. Later, when I told Dad and Russ I had been to Pride, Dad crinkled his nose and said, "That's not what we're about." It would be another three years before I chose to join PFLAG in the Pride Parade. Dad and Russ came to check out Pride for themselves the year after that.

Sometimes I forget how much our perspectives have deviated as I have plunged into queer activism and my father and his partner now move within a circle of mostly straight friends. Our differences clash on issues of identity politics, how "out" we are, and how we use language and humor to express ourselves. When I cross that line between our differences, I recoil and vow to rein in my too-queer ways.

That is, until I forget and slip up again.

Recently Russ was unwrapping a large box that had just been delivered. As he hunted for a knife to open it, he told me he had ordered a lawn sprinkler.

When he pulled it out of the bubble wrap, I saw this wasn't just any sprinkler. It was a copper pipe bent into the outline of a swan. When you attached it to the garden hose, it spun around and made a fancy watering display. When you turned it off, you could simply leave it outside as a decorative lawn sculpture.

Russ held it up and asked me what I thought. I envisioned it in their front yard, a yard that is really more of an all-out landscaping-palooza, complete with specially delivered boulders, a meandering walkway, and after sunset, flattering mood lighting for the shrubs. It's a front lawn that gets everybody's attention, particularly older women strolling by who "simply must know what kind of hostas those are."

Rather than putting so much effort into creating a front lawn that announces to every passerby that they are gay, it would have been a lot cheaper to put up a lawn sign with the words: "Homosexuals live here."

Staring at the copper swan, I said, more to myself than to Russ, "Wow. That's pretty gay."

"It's *not gay*," he grumbled.

Dad called me into the kitchen and a few minutes later he looked into the living room where Russ was still rearranging bubble wrap.

"Russ, what are you doing?" Dad asked.

"Packing it up and sending it back," Russ replied. "Abigail says it's faggy."

"I did not say it's faggy. I said it was *gay*."

The swan never made it to the yard.

* * *

In 2003, when ABC launched *It's All Relative*, a comedy about a college-aged daughter with two gay dads, *The Advocate* called it "groundbreaking."

Russ declared, "It's just a sitcom."

Despite Russ's preshow judgment, he and Dad had me over for the series premiere. For this special event, the TV joined us at the dinner table. Finally: We were allowed to laugh. Together, and at ourselves.

For once, a couple on TV really was gay, and I didn't have to rewrite supposed platonic relationships between characters in my head. As a teen watching sitcoms like *My Two Dads* and *Kate and Allie*, I pretended the parents on those shows were using *roommate* as a code word with a wink.

After the show Dad brought out a dessert that, like most culinary treats he creates, appeared out of thin air: halved pears baked in butter and cream, sprinkled with cinnamon and sugar. I don't think it's a stretch to say that more gay dads than straight dads have mastered the art of cooking with fruit.

We sat around the table dreaming up potential directions for the show that we thought the writers might take. We agreed that it would be a disaster if it leaned too much on stereotypes or if it went the opposite direction and became a weekly public service announcement.

We wondered if, as the show progressed, the portrayal of this gay-dad family would feel authentic, or if it would only come off as stereotypical. The baked glazed fruit dessert in front of me reminded me that in my family, that line between authentic and stereotype is sometimes blurrier than we would like to believe.

Of all the questions I am asked about my family, the one that makes me the most weary is "Don't you resent the fact that your father is gay?" This question does not even make sense to me. Being gay is inherent to who my father is; to suggest that he should not be gay is to suggest that I should have a different father. Furthermore, if I didn't have a gay dad, I would not have Russ—another possibility I am unable to entertain.

What I do resent is the expectation that I *should* resent my father. I resent the rhetoric that denounces him. I resent the people who judge him for coming out, and people who think that my life could have been "easier" if my father "hadn't been so selfish." I remember my father when he was in the closet, and being raised by that persona would have been anything but easy.

My mother and father, now divorced for twice as long as they were married to each other, remain in close contact. Unless someone points out their remarkable ability to get along, I take it for granted. When my mother retired from teaching, I brought a boyfriend I had been dating only a few months to her retirement party at an outdoor pavilion in one of Minneapolis's many beautiful parks. On the car ride over, I mentioned that my father would also be at the party. My boyfriend thought I was joking until we actually saw Dad at the park, mingling seamlessly with all of Mom's other guests.

As the party wrapped up, Dad left with my boyfriend and me. As we walked back to our cars, two buff men ran by on the path in front of us, wearing nothing more than athletic shoes and shorts. They passed us, apparently oblivious to how stunning their tight pecs and abs looked to me, even better than the ones I first admired in the pages of *International Male*. When I returned to reality, I fumbled my words, trying futilely to remember what I was talking about before the joggers halted my thoughts midsentence. I wanted to recover before my boyfriend noticed my wandering eye, but when I glanced over, he was stifling a laugh.

"You should see yourselves," he said to Dad and me. "It was like synchronized whiplash, the two of you with your eyes glued on those guys!"

Dad and I looked at each other sheepishly, unable to deny that we had been caught.

My boyfriend just shook his head and smiled: "Now I see where you get it from."

SITTING IN THE DARK
WITH MY MOTHER

● ● ● ● ● ● ● ● ● ● ● ● ● ● ● ● ●

Zach Udko

I'm on my dorm-room bed, drenched in sweat, shivering, and trying to figure out if I have swollen glands.

"Where are my glands?" I ask my mother.

She feels the front of my neck.

"Are they swollen?"

"A little. Why?"

"What do you mean, a little? Are they swollen or are they not?"

It's the night of my college graduation, and I'm having a nervous breakdown. A few days earlier, I had my first sexual encounter with a guy, a buff, blond econ major from Orange County whom I'd been eyeing for several weeks in my wine tasting class.

Now I'm convinced I'm sero-converting, and I haven't yet told my mother that I'm gay. This, for some reason, feels like the perfect time to do so.

My roommate is Googling my symptoms and reporting back to us various diagnoses, as I pace back and forth. "Are you experiencing minor flulike symptoms? Are you feverish? Tired? Weak?" he asks.

"Yes! Yes! Yes!"

I can't decide if I should take off my shirt and show my mother the bruises all over my chest—odd yellow blotches of various shapes and sizes. This is probably some strange skin rash associated with the disease, I am telling myself, not marks left behind from the bites of an aggressive lover of Pinot Noir.

I remove my "Congrats Class of '02!" T-shirt. I'm standing in my boxer briefs, shaking.

"What the hell happened to you?" She's trying to stay calm.

"I don't know."

"What do you mean, you don't know?"

"I slept with a guy."

"You did what?! What do you mean? Why would you do such a thing?"

"Because I think I'm gay . . . but more importantly, I think I have AIDS."

With the most bewildered look I've ever seen on her face, she turns to my roommate, pleading, as if to ask, *Did you know about this?*

And then she utters the only sound a devastated Jewish mother can make at a time like this: "Oy."

Earlier that evening, my roommate and I had rehearsed this scene. For some reason, I felt that if my mother was fearful for my life, she would indulge me with sympathy, throw her arms around me, and say that my sexual orientation didn't matter. I would distract her from my homosexuality with my hypochondria. I would scare her into acceptance. My roommate cautiously obliged.

"We must focus on the AIDS," I remember telling him in earnest, fearing that I'd contracted the disease. "This isn't about my lifestyle. This is a matter of life and death."

The next morning my mother insisted that I get tested, so we packed up the car with all of my college belongings and drove from Palo Alto to Los Angeles. Six hours later, we arrived at my pediatrician's office, where I sat pale and shivering among hyperactive toddlers, anxiously waiting to give a blood sample.

The doctor who has taken care of me since I was a baby gave my mother a hug and told her, "He's engaged in a very low-risk activity. He's fine. I promise."

Three months later, we returned to be sure that I was still negative. I was perfectly healthy. Suddenly, however, my relationship with my mother wasn't.

"Did you see that man's bulge?" my mother whispered to me in the dark. "I mean, he's enormous. Just look at him strut around in those tights!"

We were sitting in the audience of the Winter Garden Theatre. This was my first trip to Manhattan and my first Broadway show. My mother was referring to the rather impressive package of the Rum Tum Tugger in *Cats*, played by Terrence Mann. I was three years old.

After the show, my mother persuaded the house manager to let us backstage and introduce me to the cat with the huge thing between his legs. He signed my program and I told him, "I'm your biggest fan."

While a three-year-old doesn't necessarily know if he's gay, looking back at that moment, I am certain of two things: First, I knew that the Rum Tum Tugger was indeed a curious cat, and second, I knew I wanted to spend as much time as possible in the theatre (an institution so glorious, my mother always told me, it deserves to be spelled the British way).

A lot of gay men fall in love with Auntie Mame, but very few have mothers who plop them in front of the television, put in the video, and proclaim, "This is my alter ego. Pay attention." My mother prided herself on being a carefree liberal-minded thinker, an aesthete, a wacky citizen of the world, full of vitality and a sense of adventure. When I was two years old, in a fit of extravagance for her friend's birthday party, she donated Ajax, a chimpanzee, to the Los Angeles Zoo and threw a lavish affair complete with a pâté replica of the chimp. Just for kicks, she decided to stage a mock circumcision. My mother trimmed the pâté chimp's foreskin off, and the guests spread the rest on sourdough toast points.

Life is a banquet and most poor suckers are starving to death.

Born in New York and raised in Los Angeles, my mother spent much of her childhood learning about fashion, grace, and style in her parents' dress shop. In the sixties, she was a wild child at the University of Wisconsin at Madison—a drop-dead beauty with long hair that danced around her little waist, big brown eyes, and a guffaw that could contagiously fill a room with delight. In college, when she decided she had to meet Billy Wilder, her favorite filmmaker, she created the Wisconsin Film Society Award and made the arrangements to present the honor to him at his office. It took two hours of conversation for a very flattered Wilder to realize that she was just a gutsy fan who had faked her way in.

During senior year, her friends staged an all-nude production of *Peter Pan* that was shut down by the police; I'm told she was one of the dancing Tinkerbells.

After marrying my father, she decided to channel all of her creative energy into me and my older brother. While my brother showed signs of turning into a business-minded jock, I became the sole inheritor of my mother's lust for performance.

When I was five, my mother gave me a Carmen Miranda headdress. For the next several years, I would samba around the house, singing "I, Yi, Yi, Yi, Yi, I Like You Very Much," gyrating my hips with a fruit bowl on my head.

My mother would ask, "How much do you like me?"

And I'd answer in a Brazilian accent, "Very Much! I, Yi, Yi, Yi, Yi, I think you're grand!"

"Who do you love *most in the whole world*?" she'd ask.

"You, Mommy, of course." Then I'd direct the question back at her. "Who do *you* love most in the whole world?"

Sometimes she would say me. Other times she would say that she couldn't pick between my father, my brother, and me. But I was clearly my mother's child. I was the only one interested in discussing aesthetics, the only one who noticed that she changed nail polish and told her the new shade looked divine, the only one who shared a passion for eyebrow plucking and moustache bleaching. While some boys pretend to shave with their dads, I would look forward to sitting in her bathroom once a month for a treatment of burning foam on our upper lips.

We watched *The Sound of Music* and *Mary Poppins* until the tapes stretched out and we had to buy new ones.

"Who would you like to marry when you grow up?" she'd playfully ask.

"Only Julie Andrews. Only Julie," I would say.

"Someday, you're going to find a woman who you'll love even more than me. And you're going to love *her* most in the whole world."

"No, I won't," I insisted. "I'll always love you most in the whole world."

"You'll see."

"No, you'll see!"

I started writing plays when I was nine years old. During the long nights when my parents went out for social dates, I'd slave into the night with my babysitter Lydia, a U.C.L.A. student. I would dictate scenes, and she would type them up beautifully on my family's word processor. *Yitzak and the Rabbi*, my first play, explored a young man's frustrations with Judaism; with the help of a bunny rabbit friend, he embarks on a journey to find an alternative source of spiritual fulfillment.

As far as my mother was concerned, the play was brilliant. Determined to help me find my own voice as an artist, my mother persuaded our temple to produce the show for their Youth Enrichment Program.

It was decided that she would direct. Ben Savage (pre–*Boy Meets World*) got the starring role, and my mother cast me in a smaller part.

"It's best for the show," she said. "Trust me."

She took her job very seriously: storyboards, scenic design, lighting, and music. Ben Savage complained about the brevity of our lunch breaks. My mother told him he wasn't in a union yet and we had to push to get the finale right.

I remember sitting down with her during the postmortem. "I want you to give me a musical to direct," she said. "Something that will speak to your generation."

That summer, I wrote a show featuring summer camp kids, a mystical voodoo cleaning lady, singing anti-Semites, and a single mother infatuated with Ralph Nader. The production was a clunky success, but I think my mother ached for something more ambitious.

"You're funny, Zach," she told me, "but ultimately a piece of work for the stage needs to say something. You need to give your work some dramatic heft."

She was right. I was ten, but I wasn't pushing myself far enough as an artist. For my third show, I decided I wanted to save the planet by writing an eco-friendly musical. Again, my mother directed—meticulously, obsessively, passionately. In her mind, she was preparing *Save Our Planet* for a national tour; we ended up performing at a handful of junior high schools.

Together, we were giving each other a life in the theatre.

My parents had always exposed me to the most interesting and thought-provoking art of the day, never shying away from mature content. When I was twelve, we returned to New York for five days of theatre. *Angels in America* was the hottest ticket in town, and my mother was determined to get us seats. A friend of a friend pulled some strings, and we sat in the back row of the balcony. I remember loving the play. My father, exhausted from a long business meeting, slept through the first act.

At intermission, my mother wanted to leave. "We don't need to stay for the rest, do we?" she said.

This was the first time I ever remember my mother wanting to walk out of a show. No matter how bad it was, we always stayed until the curtain call.

I didn't want to let on that I was wildly intrigued by the show. I kept my mouth shut.

As my mother guided us out of the theatre, a large African American usherette blocked our path at the top of the balcony.

"Honey, you can't leave now, you're gonna miss the best part."

"I want to see the best part, Mom."

We went back to our seats to watch the second act, and for the first time in my life, my ultrapermissive, liberal mother covered my eyes twice: once when Prior strips down naked for his medical exam, once when Louis gets buggered in the Rambles.

Watching Tony Kushner's play, my mother was confronted for the first time with real gay men struggling through the early nineties—as fully developed characters, not as AIDS statistics in *The New York Times*. But why did she cover my eyes, the same eyes that she didn't shield from such spectacles as Malcolm McDowell's ultraviolent rapes in *A Clockwork Orange*? Did she know she was sitting next to an emerging homosexual? Was she horrified that such a nightmarish fate lurked in the wings? To this day, she claims she had no idea I would grow up to be gay.

"We thought we had a little David Mamet running around the house. Who knew we had a little Tony Kushner?"

I wish.

Though my mother behaved like an ultrapermissive gal pal on the surface, she didn't have a single gay friend in her social circle. In the cab after *Angels*, she continued to voice her discomfort. "I just can't relate to any of these characters and their attitudes," she told me.

"But don't you think it's well-written?" I pleaded. I wasn't ready to commit to being gay at age twelve, but I was definitely interested in everything Mr. Kushner had to say. "Wasn't it a good story? Weren't you affected emotionally?"

"It was disgusting. The way those men talk, the way they live. What a shame."

That night, it became clear to me that in spite of our shared cultural preferences, my mother would be less than thrilled about having a gay son.

In the coming years, it didn't help that I repeatedly refused to shake my mother of her denial. A mother can choose to ignore the warning signs, and a son can simultaneously give mixed signals.

I want to marry Julie Andrews. (You're a boy who likes girls.)

I only want to marry Julie Andrews. (You have a particular taste.)

If I can't marry Julie Andrews, I want nothing to do with women! (What a poetic, romantic, lady-killer!)

I never dated girls, but I let my mother believe that I was interested in them. At my private high school in Los Angeles, there was not a single out student. When a young man came out after he graduated, he wrote an anonymous letter to the school paper. He urged the student body to adopt a more accepting attitude toward homosexuals, but he still didn't even feel comfortable signing his name. Driving me home from school, my mother mentioned the article and said, "Isn't that just terrible?"

"What's terrible? That he didn't sign his name?" My mother always told me: *Never do or say anything that you wouldn't want printed on the front page of* The New York Times.

"No," she said. "That he's gay."

"Why is that so terrible?"

"Life is tough enough as it is without having to worry about all the horrible things gay men have to worry about. Right?" I chose to stay silent—and I started spending more time in the theatre.

My high school drama teacher was the first gay man I got to know well. During rehearsals for William Hoffman's *As Is*, one of the first AIDS plays ever written, we sat, rather awkwardly, in our hospital gown costumes and he offered the cast a Q & A about "Being Gay."

I raised my hand immediately. "Does your mother know?"

"No, she doesn't." He was approaching forty.

"How could your mother not know?" I pressed.

"I don't want to rob her of her denial," he said.

Stepping into the role of Saul, a gay Jewish man losing his lover to AIDS, I remember experiencing the same sensations that charged through my body when I saw *Angels*: a rush of liberation and self-hatred. I knew I was gay and I was terrified that my life would one day become its very own stylized tearjerker. I didn't want my mother to see the show, but keeping her away from one of my school plays was unthinkable. I told her it was a small role, no big deal. She came; she saw; she said I gave a good performance; we didn't buy the video.

When I was sixteen, we went to London and sat in the front row of Mark Ravenhill's *Shopping and Fucking*. My mother braved her way through several blow job scenes, but the play's climax, featuring an anal knife rape, was too much for her to handle. It did not help redefine my mother's already rather limited view of gay people.

After the show, I wanted to tell her that I was gay and nothing at all like the characters portrayed in the play. But I continued to suppress my feelings, so the two of us sat in a London tea shop, sharing finger sandwiches and neutered conversation.

When I got to college, I hid behind a supersexual facade, always talking about straight sex and never having it. I kept an arm's-length distance from the few out campus homosexuals.

I wrote a passionate column about the legs of our provost Condoleezza Rice in the school paper. (Your taste is evolving.)

In my spare time, I worked on composing a musical adaptation of *Showgirls*. (You're still a very horny lover of women.)

At two hundred pounds, I was the chunky campus prankster, and the chub factor safely prevented me from being a viable sexual commodity. My mother and I spoke on the phone nearly every day, but sex never entered the conversation. When she wanted to talk about Love, I skillfully changed the topic to Art.

Then came the summer before senior year: While studying documentary film at N.Y.U., I starved myself on a strict diet of tofu hot dogs and Tasti D-Lite and lost forty pounds in five months. I felt attractive and ready for sex.

During senior year, I enrolled in Wine Tasting for two consecutive semesters in the French department, by far the best class I ever took in college. For our final exam we had to offer insightful commentary on more than twenty different varietals and blends. After ten or so, I turned to my friend Kristy and said, "I'd like to entertain other options with Evan."

She suggested that we take a few bottles back to my room and host a private after-party.

A most excellent idea, I thought.

Who knew that three days later I would be telling my mother all about it?

If I were given the opportunity to rewrite a single scene from my life, I would without question choose that night.

A year after coming out to my mom, I returned home for a vacation and found a book on her shelf called *A Catholic Mother Looks At the Gay Child*. The cover features a silhouette drawing of a mother holding hands with her son, walking toward a towering cross. The sun is setting, and the little boy looks light on his feet. On the back cover, the book's author tells us, "Ten percent of the population is homosexual. These people are not just numbers on a graph. They go to school, play, and grow up just like everybody else. But when they get to adulthood they are in no-man's land. . . . Here is a book that gives hope to these lonely, perplexed kids—and their parents." While the book seemed to be well intentioned, I had not realized just how difficult my coming-out process had been for my mother.

Turning to the first page, I found a note addressed to my mother:

> *I thought this might help your friend*
> *(the one with the gay son).*

My mother had been so terrified to share my sexuality with the world that she created a fictional friend with her situation.

I asked her if the wisdom for Catholics had helped my Jewish mother.

"It validated my concerns," she said.

Still, she wouldn't tell any of her friends that I was gay.

Finally, three years later, she told one girlfriend.

This friend didn't live in Los Angeles, knew none of her other friends, and was dying of cancer.

"It's not a big deal," she said, when I asked her why she hadn't told more people. "I don't run around telling the world that I'm straight! You want me to protect you from all the prejudices of the world. You want me to be like that waitress mother from *Queer as Folk* with all the buttons on her vest."

"You watch *Queer as Folk*, Mom?"

"I know," she said. "It's terrible. I much prefer *The L Word*."

Three years after I came out, my mother visited New York for a reading of a play I had written. As she entered the theatre, my mother told me that she was afraid of being assaulted by my "New York army of gay supporters."

"Everyone in this theatre knows more about you these days than I do," she said. "I feel like I'm walking into a place with no idea of what to expect. I feel like an intruder." For a mother who directed all my childhood work, she wasn't fully prepared for the downtown playwright who was emerging before her eyes.

After the reading, my advisor, Janet, who had become a close friend of mine, invited my parents to her apartment for a drink.

As she opened a bottle of pinot grigio, Janet told my mother, "I have a gay child, too. You know how I found out? It was on the front page of *The New York Times*. A picture of her in the middle of an ACT UP protest. Could you imagine?"

"Not *The New York Times*! That's terrible," my mother said.

"You're frustrated," said Janet. "But your son is gay. What can you do about it?"

My mother took a deep breath, a gulp of wine, and let this question sink in. "Nothing."

Not long after, she began asking questions:

"Do you go to those bars with the naked men dancing on platforms like in *Sex and the City*?"

"Who leads when you slow dance?

"Don't you find Alan Cumming attractive? He's adorable!"

"Why don't you date an interior designer? Your apartment is such a mess. Have you seen the one on *Queer Eye*? He's a little short and pudgy, but he's hot!"

Last December, my mother returned to the city for a reading of a new play of mine, one that dealt with explicit gay themes. Janet brought her friend Mark Ravenhill. I dragged my mother across the theatre to introduce her to him.

"This is my mother. She took me to see your play *Shopping and Fucking* when I was sixteen. We sat together in the front row."

I realized how this must sound to Mr. Ravenhill, as if I had the most permissive liberal mother in the world. My mother threw up her arms and let out an embarrassed laugh: "How was I supposed to know it was so graphic?"

Did she know that she was fueling the imagination of a gay teen with aspirations of becoming a writer? How was she supposed to know that she was providing me with a dream education?

Two years ago, I sat in New York's Royale Theatre next to a gay friend who had not spoken to his mother in years, watching a revival of Marsha Norman's *'night, Mother*. In the middle of the performance, I began for the first time to feel like my mother's torturer. In this play, a full-grown woman, Jessie, tells her mother that she has decided to commit suicide that evening. As she quietly makes final arrangements, she insists that her mother has no say in the matter.

"I have to go in the bedroom and lock the door behind me so they won't arrest you for killing me," she tells her mother. "They'll probably test your hands for gunpowder anyway, but you'll pass."

I found myself hating Jessie and experiencing a new sensation at the theatre: guilt. I wanted to call up my mother to apologize for being a difficult gay son who ridiculed her repeatedly for refusing to tell her friends about my sexual identity, who called her homophobic, who played her hysterical voice mails for friends, who forced her to inextricably connect a life-threatening illness with my sexuality, an association that didn't need further reinforcement.

But when she picked up the phone, all I could say was that I just saw the most incredible play, and she agreed that it was a very powerful piece and began to describe in vivid detail the film version with Sissy Spacek and Anne Bancroft.

I believe my mother has always known, deep in her heart, that I am gay. Taking a gay son to *Angels in America, Falsettos, The Dying Gaul, Take Me Out, Shopping and Fucking, The Paris Letter,* and drag versions of *The Bad Seed* and *Christmas with the Crawfords* are acts of unconditional love. In the quiet moments we shared side by side in those red velvet seats—no matter what was said before or after the lights came up—my mother and I were able to escape into a world of tolerance and mutual understanding.

Recently, she called to tell me about a wonderful documentary she just saw on Logo, the gay network.

"You're watching Logo now?" I said. "I don't even watch Logo."

"Sure, it has wonderful programs. This documentary explained that parents and children are on two different time lines when it comes to the coming-out process. You've been dealing with these issues for ten, fifteen years. I've only had five years to process all this. And five to seven years is a perfectly normal adjustment period for parents. That's what they said in the documentary."

"Well, if that's what Logo says, then it must be true," I teased.

As she continued to describe the program, I heard my mother telling me: *I'll come around. Be patient.*

We all imagine that fantasy moment when we are finally able to see eye to eye with our parents—when we feel like we are all watching the same show.

We hope this will happen before they die.

I'd like to think that my mother and I are moving toward the beginning of a new act.

Perhaps the cast will be expanded: A boyfriend? A husband? A child?

The house lights will dim.

The curtain will rise.

And a passionate, inspiring, larger-than-life mother will sit onstage discussing Art and Love with her son—a man she has fully prepared for life's banquet.

DARLING, I LIKE YOU THAT WAY

Ayelet Waldman

The readers of Salon.com are very worried about my nine-year-old son. They worry that he's been "betrayed and humiliated" and they worry that in order to please his selfish mother, the poor boy will have to be gay. The source of their collective anxiety is an essay I wrote in 2005 about gay marriage in which I recounted my son's comment, "I think I might be gay." Lest you dismiss the hue and cry as more homophobic red-state vitriol, let me assure you that only liberals and the odd libertarian read Salon. The only reason the state legislatures of Alabama and Mississippi don't ban the site altogether is that, aside from one or two New York English professors forced by the sad state of Ph.D. hiring to relocate to Tuscaloosa or Jackson, no one in the land of Dixie has ever bothered to log on.

No, the worry, the rage, the horror comes from my brethren on the left.

The essay is about my young son's (seven years old at the time) attitude toward homosexuality. I begin with a story about his best friend, a fifty-nine-year-old lesbian with whom he shares "a passion for the San Francisco Giants, dark chocolate truffles, and New York frankfurters . . .

Other than his dad, Zeke would rather be with Laura than pretty much anybody else, including me." Zeke has always known about Laura's sexual orientation, and her loving relationship with her partner is one of the many reasons he was able to speak so un-self-consciously about his own sexual orientation.

In the essay, I talk about the moment when I first introduced the subject of homophobia to my kids, ironically at a moment of joy for all of us who care about the civil rights of gay people. We had always referred to Laura's partner as her wife, because, as I wrote in the essay, "There seemed no other way to describe that relationship in terms the kids could understand, in a way that would align this romance with the other long-term commitments the children knew—our marriage, those of their grandparents—and distinguish it from more transient ones." When the mayor of San Francisco began issuing marriage licenses, we celebrated, but we also had to explain that this was the first time gay people were allowed to be legally married in the United States of America. That shocked my son. Zeke believes that you're supposed to marry the person you love, whoever and whatever that person happens to be.

But what really freaked people out was that I wrote that not only does the prospect of my son being gay not bother me, but I actually hope he might be. The reason I give for wanting a gay son is light-hearted. "How many straight men maintain inappropriately intimate relationships with their mothers? How many *shop* with them?"

I was taken to task for my biases. One gay reader chided me: "Shopping? Inappropriate relationships with your mother? This is not the 1950s and this type of stereotyping is insulting and one of the reasons it's still hard to be gay in Bush's America." And: "As a gay man, I found these comments to be condescending, out of touch, and quite a bit insulting. Either support gay rights or don't; but please don't equate them with some deep desire on the part of gays and lesbians to trash sex-role stereotypes."

Good points, and ones with which I agree. That's why I described my stereotypes as "shopworn and musty clichés."

However, at the risk of incurring yet more wrath, I'm going to go ahead and dive headfirst into the roiling lava pit of bias. While I know and love a few straight men, by and large, the gay men I know are simply more fun. For every straight male friend I have, there are three or four or more gay men with whom I'd rather spend my time. My gay friends dish with more relish and verve. They have a better design sense and are far more willing to discuss the proper placement of a piece of furniture than any straight men I know. For a long time, being part of the gay community mandated a familiarity with a certain kind of culture. You listened to opera, you went to the theater, you wore something fabulous to a Madonna concert. This may be a function of my generation—do nineteen-year-old gay men even know who Barbra Streisand or Maria Callas is?—but I have never met a straight man, other than my husband, who would comb the antique shops of Venice with me, searching tirelessly for the perfect tasseled pillow. As far as my joke about close relationships with mothers, I'm terrified at the prospect of daughters-in-law. With good reason: I am one myself. I hope my sons are gay so that they will bring home lovely young men who will redecorate my kitchen (another wretched stereotype!), rather than nubile young girls who will cast a disparaging and dismissive eye on my crow's feet and thick waist. Zeke, his lover, and I would be a giggling and gossiping threesome, shopping for Jimmy Choos and beaded Victorian lamps (and another!) before the boys head off to a circuit party. (Now *that's* just real life.) In the other, more likely but far less appealing scenario, Zeke and some young woman named Hannah or Emma will screen their calls and roll their eyes as I leave increasingly frantic voice mail messages. She will perfect an impression of me, complete with nasal whine and pinched lips, and he will wince at the droll accuracy and drag her off to the bedroom while my forlorn voice begs to the empty air, "Please, darling, give your mother a call, just so that I know you're all right."

Enough of the stereotypes. I do know some gay men whose ears aren't pierced and who've never evinced much interest in the Divine Miss M. They wear conservative suits (Brooks Brothers and J. Press rather than

Paul Smith and Zegna); they are soccer dads and computer executives who take their partners to auto shows. But even these men have a little something extra, if only the sensitivity wrought by dealing with oppression and discrimination throughout their lives.

From the time I was a teenager, and probably before, I've been drawn to men like that. I was a geeky, unpopular girl. I lived in a wealthy town but my family didn't have much money; still, much of my unpopularity may have had less to do with my parents' inability to buy me rainbow-colored Izod shirts and Fair Isle sweaters and more to do with my moods. I wasn't necessarily a happy kid; in retrospect, I probably showed some symptoms of the bipolar disorder with which I was ultimately diagnosed. Outsiders flock together, perhaps because no one else will have them, perhaps because they know each other's pain. For whatever reason, among the few friends I had were scrawny boys I met in drama class and on the gym bleachers holding excuse notes as elaborate as mine. I always felt most comfortable in the company of these boys with uneasy smiles who spent most of their days scrambling after the books the cool boys dumped from their arms or running away from games of "smear the queer." Not all of those boys were gay, of course. Some turned into sensitive men, like my husband. But many were.

Soon enough, I had a better reason to like those boys. Like a lot of girls who feel insecure and unattractive, I ended up with a reputation as a slut. My behavior came to justify the initially unearned slur. But with my fellow theater rats, I never had to worry. They wouldn't flirt with me, fuck me, and then tell their friends. It went without saying that I wouldn't end up splayed out in the backseat of a car. We could be affectionate, even physically, without the specter of sex and its humiliating ramifications.

As an adult, these relationships continue. A number of years ago, my husband and I met a gay man who had written a brilliant memoir. After a few hours of enchanting conversation over delicious food, we invited our new friend to join us on a trip to Italy. For two weeks. I cannot imagine a universe in which we'd have dinner with a straight guy and immediately invite him to share our vacation rental. Our friend was every bit the marvelous companion we knew he'd be (note prior reference to shopping for tasseled pillows).

I have a remarkably patient gay friend who once accompanied me on a research expedition to one of San Francisco's most notorious strip clubs (for a scene in one of my novels, I swear to God). I was shy about going alone, but I was also embarrassed at the prospect of looking up some woman's vagina in the company of a straight man—these women are so naked that if I'd had a Q-tip and a speculum I could have given a dozen Pap smears. I wanted to see what the women did to the men in these kinds of places, but I didn't want to be distracted by my companion popping a massive boner. Unfortunately it turns out that friction knows no sexual orientation. I had to cut my friend off after three lap dances.

My affinity for gay men is probably one of the reasons I fell so hard for my husband. My husband wrote a book that can be considered a gay coming-out novel, in part inspired by experience. Though he's straight, he, like me, loves gay men and enjoys their company, and he is a tiny bit of a sissy himself. For example, he was the one who decided to see *The Devil Wears Prada*, even though it was the opening weekend of *Superman*. He loves to shop; most of my nicest clothes and all of my jewelry were gifts from him. He appreciates music and art, more, in fact, than I do.

I want my sons to be like their father. They may be straight and unusual, like he is, but if they're gay there's a hell of a lot better chance they'll turn out like their dad.

My own prejudice was on full view when I wrote in Salon about the idea of my daughters being lesbians. "Would a lesbian daughter give me grief about shaving my legs? Would her girlfriend the Gestalt therapist bring bulgur salad to family potlucks?" What that stereotype and the others are about, obviously, is prejudice and insecurity. "The stereotypical gay woman makes me insecure, conscious of my failings as a feminist. I make less money than my husband; I rely on him for simple home repairs; I care too much about what I look like; I once got a Brazilian bikini wax."

But the critique of these admitted biases wasn't the real issue people, even gay people, had with the essay. Underlying all this outrage, I'm convinced, is a lonely and sad self-hatred.

Those people who are aghast that I have exposed my son to ridicule believe that being gay or just musing on your sexuality will necessarily make you the butt of other children's bullying. That is probably true in much of what someone described as "Bush Country." But my family lives in Berkeley. There are many gay families in my children's school. The school shows movies like *Daddy and Papa* and the high schools all have Gay-Straight Alliances. My children's world, thank God, is nearly devoid of homophobia. Sounds bucolic, doesn't it? It is, and it's one of the main reasons we live here when we could live so much less expensively somewhere else. Bullying may have been the sad experience of many gay men, but I think things are changing for kids nowadays. At least two-thirds of high school students support gay marriage, according to the Hamilton College National Youth Opinion Poll. This generational shift in favor of gay rights has been consistent over the years, and it explains why the religious right is desperately trying to amend the Constitution: They only have so much time before our more open-minded children are old enough to vote.

The people who are horrified that I have imposed expectations on my son are guilty of hypocrisy on the grandest scale. Would you prefer that your son were straight? Do you joke about your son marrying the little daughter of your college roommate? You, too, are imposing an expectation on your child. My son's sexual orientation will develop on its own, no matter my hopes and idle fantasies. How many studies on twins have to be done before people understand that homosexuality is innate? It has nothing to do with choice or a mother's smothering nature. People are gay because of genetics or fetal hormonal exposure or some other random physical and chemical spin of the wheel. Bless mutation and complication and all that gives us such magnificent diversity.

When I was an undergraduate, I went to a concert given by a not particularly talented lesbian folk singer. I have a perfect recollection of her hoarse voice warbling off-key the song she wished her mother had sung to her when she first came out: *Honey, I'm glad that you're gay; darling, I like you that way.*

That's the response my sons and daughters will receive if ever they make a similar announcement. As a grizzly protects her cubs, I will do everything in my power to make sure that none of them ever wishes away their homosexuality on the letters page of an online magazine.

ACKNOWLEDGMENTS

We are deeply grateful to all the wonderful authors who contributed to this book. We asked for your stories, and you didn't hold back.

Many thanks to Trena Keating and Lily Kosner at Dutton; Richard Abate, Kate Lee, and Colin Graham at ICM; and Jorge Valencia, Joel Wyatt, James Lecesne, and everyone at The Trevor Project for all their support, enthusiasm, and effort on behalf of this book.

We would also like to thank our families and friends for all their love and support.

Melissa would especially like to thank "The Gang:" Tristan, Tyler, Andy, and Peter for their steadfast and loyal friendship that inspired this book. Big kisses and big love from their own "Melvina."

And Tom sends love and thanks to the main girls in his life—Antonia, Katie, Marissa, Mary Clare, Sarah, and Tina—who are always there for him, in good times and bad.

ABOUT THE
CONTRIBUTORS

Melissa de la Cruz is the author of many books for teens and adults, including the bestselling *Au Pairs* series, which has been published in ten countries and was sold to Warner Bros. Studios as a major motion picture to be produced by Flower Films and Alloy Entertainment. Her other books include the *Blue Bloods* series, the trilogy *Angels on Sunset Boulevard,* and the novels *Cat's Meow* and *Fresh Off the Boat*. She coauthored the tongue-in-chic handbooks *The Fashionista Files* and *How to Become Famous in Two Weeks or Less*. She has appeared as an expert on style, trends, and fame for CNN, Fox, and E! and has written for many publications including *Glamour*, *Marie Claire*, *Harper's Bazaar*, *Allure*, *Cosmopolitan*, *The New York Times*, the *San Francisco Chronicle*, and *McSweeney's*. She is a graduate of Columbia University. Melissa divides her time between New York City and Los Angeles, where she lives with her husband. She is currently working on two new young adult series: *The Ashleys* (debuting in 2007) and *Social Life* (coming in 2008). Visit her online at www.melissa-delacruz.com.

Tom Dolby is the author of the bestselling novel *The Trouble Boy*. His second novel, *The Sixth Form*, set at a Massachusetts boarding school, will be published in January 2008. His writing has appeared in *The New York*

Times, *The Village Voice*, the *San Francisco Chronicle*, and *Out*, where he is a contributing writer. A personal essay of his appears in the recent anthology *From Boys to Men: Gay Men Write About Growing Up*. He was a 2005 Library Laureate for the San Francisco Public Library, and was one of *Instinct* magazine's Leading Men of 2004, both honors that make his mother very proud. Tom was born in London and raised in San Francisco, and is a graduate of Yale University. He currently lives in Manhattan, where he is working on his third novel, though he also enjoys visiting his many girlfriends in Los Angeles and San Francisco. You can find him online at www.tomdolby.com.

Foreword

Armistead Maupin is the world-renowned bestselling author of the *Tales of the City* series, which has been the basis for three highly acclaimed television miniseries. His ninth novel, *Michael Tolliver Lives*, was recently published. He lives in San Francisco.

Authors

Mike Albo is the author of the novel *Hornito: My Lie Life* and the critically acclaimed comic novel *The Underminer: The Best Friend Who Casually Destroys Your Life*, which was cowritten with his longtime friend, *New York Times* television critic Virginia Heffernan. As a monologist and performer, Mike has completed four critically acclaimed sold-out solo shows: *Mike Albo*, *Spray*, *Please Everything Burst*, and *My Price Point*, all cowritten with Heffernan, as well as many solo performances and tours across the United States and Europe. Mike has written for *The New York Times*, *Paper*, *Surface*, *The New York Observer*, *New York*, *The Village Voice*, *Newsweek*, *Nerve*, and *Out*. Check out www.mikealbo.com and click on his chakras for upcoming shows, vidcasts, writing, an effusive blog, and more.

Zakiyyah Alexander is a playwright, performer, educator, and friend to many a gay man. Her plays have been produced and developed in theaters around the world, from New York City to Johannesburg. Honors include The Theodore Ward Prize, the Jackson/Phelan Award, the Drama League New Directors/New Works, the New Professional Theatre Playwriting Award, the Young Playwrights Inc., and more. Her work is included in the latest edition of *New Monologues for Women by Women*. She is a resident member of New Dramatists and a past participant in too many writers' groups to mention. Currently she is working on a short commissioned piece for Hartford Stage, adapting the short story "The People Could Fly" into a children's musical, as well as developing a new play, *Clean*, with the 24/7 Company. Zakiyyah received her M.F.A. in playwriting from the Yale School of Drama.

Stacey Ballis is the author of four novels: *Inappropriate Men*, *Sleeping Over*, *Room for Improvement*, and *The Spinster Sisters* and is a contributing author to the anthology *Everything I Needed to Know About Being a Girl I Learned from Judy Blume*. Her Web site is www.staceyballis.com.

Cecil Castellucci has published three novels for teens: *Boy Proof*, *The Queen of Cool*, and the upcoming *Beige*. Aside from writing books, she writes plays and makes films. She has lived in New York City, Paris, and Montreal, and now resides in Los Angeles. She's planning on taking a freight ship to China and thinks that taking the train (sleeper car only, please!) is a divine way to travel. She has had many fairy godfathers and is always happy for the new ones she meets on her voyages. She still plans on buying a château. For more information, go to www.misscecil.com.

Cindy Chupack has won three Golden Globes and an Emmy for her work as a writer and executive producer on HBO's *Sex and the City*. She joined the show in the second season, and six of the episodes she penned were individually nominated for Writer's Guild and Emmy awards. She is also the author of *The Between Boyfriends Book: A Collection of Cau-*

tiously Hopeful Essays, which was a *New York Times* bestseller and has been translated into nine languages. For more information, visit www .betweenboyfriends.com. Cindy has also written humorous essays about dating and relationships for *Glamour*, *Harper's Bazaar*, *Allure*, *Slate*, and *The New York Times Book Review*. She lives in Los Angeles with her husband, Ian, whom, she is happy to report, did not know what a White Party was.

Anna David has been on staff at *Premiere* and *Parenting* and wrote a sex and relationship column for *Razor Magazine*. She's done celebrity cover stories, first-person essays, and reportage for the *Los Angeles Times*, *Vanity Fair*, *Cosmopolitan*, *Details*, *Self*, *Redbook*, *The Saturday Telegraph*, *Esquire UK*, *Variety*, and the *New York Post*, among many others. A first-person sex story she wrote for *Playboy* was made into a reality show pilot for TBS. She's the sex expert on G4's *Attack of the Show*, regularly appears on *Today*, and has also been on *The Best Damn Sports Show Period*, *The Other Half*, *Cold Pizza*, *The Modern Girl's Guide to Life*, CNN, E!, and VH1. Her first novel, *Party Girl*, is coming out in July 2007 from Regan Books. Her Web site is www.annadavid.com.

Simon Doonan is the bestselling author of *Wacky Chicks: Life Lessons from Fearlessly Inappropriate and Fabulously Eccentric Women* and *Nasty: My Family and Other Glamorous Varmints*. In addition to his role as creative director of Barneys New York, Simon writes the "Simon Says" column for *The New York Observer*. He frequently contributes observations and opinions to a myriad of other publications and television shows, and is a regular commentator on VH1 and *Full Frontal Fashion*. He lives in New York City with his partner, Jonathan Adler, and his Norwich terrier, Liberace.

David Ebershoff is the author of two bestselling novels, *Pasadena* and *The Danish Girl*, and the short story collection, *The Rose City*. He has won a number of awards, including the Rosenthal Foundation Award from the American Academy of Arts and Letters and the Lambda Literary Award. His fiction has been published in more than a dozen countries to critical acclaim. He is currently an editor at large at Random House and teaches in the M.F.A. program at Columbia University. His new novel, *The 19th Wife*, will be released next year. You can reach David at www .ebershoff.com.

Abigail Garner is the author of *Families Like Mine: Children of Gay Parents Tell It Like It Is*, which was a finalist for the Lambda Literary Award in GLBT Studies. She is a recipient of the Excellence in Journalism Award from the National Lesbian & Gay Journalists Association, as well as the winner of two Best Column awards from the Minnesota Magazine and Publications Association. She is a graduate of the Minneapolis public schools and Wellesley College. Her blog, "Damn Straight," is online at www.abigailgarner.net.

Gigi Levangie Grazer has never won anything nor does she anticipate winning anything in the near future. Moreover, Gigi has never been a finalist for anything. Gigi is fond of vanilla lattes and bin candy. Gigi lies about her age—upward. Gigi is married and has quite a few children. Gigi hopes to meet you someday. Gigi does not believe it is a party unless someone is fighting. Gigi wrote the original screenplay for the film *Stepmom*, after which she turned to the relative coziness of writing novels. Her first two novels, *Rescue Me* and *Maneater*, have been optioned for movies or miniseries, and her third novel, *The Starter Wife*, will air as a miniseries starring Debra Messing on the USA network in summer 2007. Gigi's next novel, set in New York, focuses on a power couple's marriage. Gigi also has several drawers full of unproduced, hilarious, and touching screenplays. Her Web site is www.gigigrazer.com.

Philip Himberg was born in the Bronx and reared in suburban Connecticut. He attended Oberlin College, where he majored in theater arts. He was on staff at Playwrights Horizons in New York and at the Mark

Taper Forum in Los Angeles before running off to study alternative medicine. Since 1985, he has been licensed as a doctor of Chinese medicine. In 1996, he returned to the world of theater and for the past eleven years has headed the Sundance Institute Theatre Program, overseeing its developmental play labs. He has most recently directed plays by Terrence McNally, Tony Kushner, and William Finn. He lives in Santa Monica with his fifteen-year-old daughter, Fanny Rose, and their cat, Mildred Pierce, and owns a ramshackle farmhouse in Cape Cod. He is hard at work on what he hopes will become a novel or a memoir, depending on how brave he is to confront the truth.

Alexandra Jacobs is an editor at *The New York Observer* and a contributing writer for *Elle* who has also written for *The New York Times*, *The Washington Post*, *Harper's Bazaar*, and other publications. Her article "Girls Allowed" for London's *Sunday Telegraph Magazine* was optioned by Columbia Pictures. She lives in Los Angeles with her husband and daughter.

James Lecesne created the critically acclaimed solo performance *Word of Mouth*, directed by Eve Ensler and produced by Mike Nichols. His live-action short film *Trevor* won an Academy Award in 1994 and inspired The Trevor Project, a nonprofit organization that operates the only twenty-four-hour suicide prevention helpline for GLBT and questioning teens. Working with young people in Cambodia, Tibet, and Bosnia, he created *The Road Home: Stories of Children of War*, which premiered at The Asia Society in New York City and was presented at the International Peace Initiative at The Hague. He also adapted Armistead Maupin's *Further Tales of the City* as a miniseries for Showtime, which received an Emmy nomination. James also recently wrote one of the final episodes of *Will & Grace*. His upcoming young adult novel, *Absolute Brightness*, will be published by HarperCollins in fall 2007.

David Levithan is the author of *Boy Meets Boy*, *The Realm of Possibility*, *Are We There Yet?*, *Marly's Ghost*, and *Wide Awake*, as well as *Nick and*

Norah's Infinite Playlist, written with his pal Rachel Cohn. He is also the
coeditor, with Billy Merrell, of *The Full Spectrum*, an anthology of young
LGBTQ writers. David is an editor at Scholastic and the founding editor
of the PUSH imprint, which is devoted to finding new voices in young
adult literature. Except for a brief spell in Rhode Island, he's always lived
in New Jersey. His Web site is www.davidlevithan.com.

Sarah Kate Levy has been a production assistant for an Off-Off-Broadway
theater and film company, a development assistant for reality program-
ming at the USA network, and the Southern California scout for the
Lowenstein-Yost and Lowenstein-Morel literary agencies. She attended
the M.F.A. Creative Writing Program at Columbia, but completed her
degree while teaching freshman composition at U.S.C. Sarah holds a
B.A. in English Literature from Yale. Her fiction has been published by
The Paumanok Review and has received Notable Mention by the Story
South Million Writers Award. She has also cowritten a screenplay that is
repped by Jon Klane in L.A., and a play that has received several public
readings. Sarah is working on a novel, a collection of short stories, and a
handful of travel essays. She lives in Los Angeles with her husband. Her
Web site is www.sklevy.com.

Bennett Madison grew up in (you could be my) Silver Spring, Maryland,
attended Sarah Lawrence College, and now lives in Brooklyn, New York.
He is the author of the *Lulu Dark* mysteries and is currently a staff writer
for an as-yet-untitled cartoon scheduled to air on Nickelodeon sometime
next year. His next book for young people, *The Blonde of the Joke*, the first
in a three-book cycle, will be released in fall 2008 by HarperCollins. His
Web site is www.bennettmadison.com.

Wendy Mass is the author of five young adult novels: *A Mango-Shaped
Space*, which won the Schneider Family Book Award from the American
Library Association; *Leap Day*, a Junior Library Guild selection and In-
ternational Reading Association Top Choice; *Jeremy Fink and the Mean-*

ing of Life, a Junior Library Guild Premier Selection; and the two-part fairy-tale series *Twice Upon a Time*. She has a B.A. from Tufts University and a Doctor of Letters from Drew University. She lives in New Jersey with her husband and their new twins. She tells people her hobbies are hiking, biking, and photography, although they really are searching for buried treasure with her metal detector, collecting candy bar wrappers, and trying to have out-of-body experiences. Her Web site is www.wen dymass.com.

Michael Musto writes the long-running, popular "La Dolce Musto" column about entertainment and nightlife in *The Village Voice*. *La Dolce Musto* is also the title of his book compilation of his liveliest and most outrageous columns, ranging from celebrity interviews to blind items to gay political screeds to controversial self-reflections, published by Carroll & Graf. A regular contributor to *Out*, Michael has also written the books *Downtown* (a nonfiction guide to the underground) and *Manhattan on the Rocks* (a catty yet glamour-drenched roman à clef), as well as appearing on many shows as a pop cultural commentator.

Karen Robinovitz is a prolific journalist whose features on luxury lifestyle, celebrities, fashion, and all things fabulous have been in *Elle*, *Marie Claire*, *Harper's Bazaar*, and *The New York Times*. She has coauthored three books: *Fête Accompli! The Ultimate Guide to Creative Entertaining*, *The Fashionista Files: Adventures in Four-Inch Heels and Faux Pas*, and *How to Become Famous in Two Weeks or Less*, which was optioned for a major motion picture by The Walt Disney Studio. A regular on pop culture–oriented shows on VH1, E!, and the Style network, she is a television personality who also often appears on morning shows across the country. She recently filmed a pilot for her own reality show on Bravo. Karen lives in New York City with her husband, Todd, who appreciates all the gay men in her life without a hint of homophobia or jealousy.

Brian Sloan is a writer, director, novelist, and all-around creative type guy. His second feature, *WTC View*, and his second book, *Tale of Two Summers*, both came out in 2006. His next film, *Prom Queens*, is due out in 2008 and his next book will be done when he finishes it. He lives in New York City, where there are many distractions. Before he knew any better, Brian went to lots of dances while attending St. John's High School in Washington, D.C. Some of those experiences influenced his first novel, *A Really Nice Prom Mess*. You can check out his Web site at www.bri ansloan.com. Or visit him at www.myspace.com/bmsloan and put him in your Top Whatever.

K. M. Soehnlein is the author of the novels *You Can Say You Knew Me When* and the Lambda Award–winning *The World of Normal Boys*, both published by Kensington. His journalism and essays have appeared in *The Village Voice*, *Elle Decor*, *Out*, and the anthologies *Bookmark Now: Writing in Unreaderly Times* and *From Boys to Men: Gay Men Write About Growing Up*. He lives with his partner, Kevin Clarke, in San Francisco, and teaches creative writing at the University of San Francisco. Most of the names used in "The Collectors" are pseudonyms. (A bit of advice: Don't ask your muse if she likes the pseudonym you've chosen for her; she never does.) Visit him at www.kmsoehnlein.com.

Andrew Solomon is the author of *The Noonday Demon: An Atlas of Depression*, which won the 2001 National Book Award, was a finalist for the Pulitzer Prize, and has been published in twenty-two languages; it also won the Lammy and fourteen other national awards. He has lectured on depression around the world, including recent stints at Princeton, Yale, Stanford, Harvard, M.I.T., Cambridge, and the Library of Congress. He is the author of *The Irony Tower: Soviet Artists in a Time of Glasnost*, and the novel *A Stone Boat*; he is a regular contributor to *The New Yorker*, *The New York Times*, and various other publications. He is currently working toward a Ph.D. at Cambridge in psychology, and is writing a book, *A Dozen Kinds of Love*, about how families deal with children of trauma—those with autism, deafness, or dwarfism; those who commit crimes or were conceived in rape; those who are prodigies; and so on. He lives in New York and London. His Web site is www .awsolomon.com.

Elizabeth Spiers is the founder and publisher of Dead Horse Media, which produces DealBreaker.com, a Wall Street tabloid, and AboveTheLaw .com, a legal tabloid. She was previously the editor in chief of Mediabistro .com, a contributing writer and editor at *New York*, and the founding editor of Gawker.com, a media gossip site. She has also written for *The New York Times*, the *New York Post*, *Black Book*, and *Jane*, among others. Her debut novel, *And They All Die in the End*, will be published by Riverhead in 2007. She lives in New York. Her Web site is www.elizabethspiers.com.

Zach Udko studied at Stanford University (B.A. and M.A. in English) and New York University (M.F.A. in Dramatic Writing). He has had his plays read or produced in Los Angeles, the Bay Area, London, Edinburgh, Kentucky, and New York, and they have won national awards from the Kennedy Center A.C.T. Festival. He was a 2006 Dramatists Guild Playwriting Fellow, and currently teaches writing courses at New York University, Tisch School of the Arts. For more information, go to his Web site at www.zachudko.com. If you think Zach's mother would like you, feel free to contact him.

Ayelet Waldman is the bestselling author of the novels *Love and Other Impossible Pursuits* and *Daughter's Keeper*. Her nonfiction has appeared in *The New York Times*, *Elle*, and the *Guardian*, among other places. She lives in Berkeley, California, with her husband and their four children. Her Web site is www.ayeletwaldman.com.

Edwin John Wintle is the author of *Breakfast with Tiffany: An Uncle's Memoir*, a chronicle of his first year as guardian to his precocious, talented, and wildly rebellious thirteen-year-old niece. Ed's professional life has been just as unpredictable as his personal one: He was an actor in the eighties, a lawyer in the nineties, and is currently a part-time film agent. Despite all of this excitement—or maybe because of it—Ed's favorite thing to do is sleep. When he's not negotiating book-to-film deals, he can be found napping in New York City's Writers Room, where he's supposed to be working on his next book, *Wide Awake*, a dystopian novel featuring, of all things, a couple of insomniacs. Ed can be contacted through his Web site at www.edwinjohnwintle.com. Answering e-mails is his second favorite way to procrastinate.

SAVING YOUNG LIVES

FOUNDED BY THREE FILMMAKERS WHO IN 1994 RECEIVED AN ACADEMY AWARD FOR THEIR
SHORT FILM, **TREVOR**—ABOUT A TEEN WHO ATTEMPTS SUICIDE AFTER REALIZING THAT HE
MIGHT BE HOMOSEXUAL—**THE TREVOR PROJECT** HAS COME TO SYMBOLIZE HOPE FOR
THOUSANDS OF YOUNG PEOPLE WHEN THEY HAVE NOWHERE ELSE TO TURN.

ACCORDING TO THE WORLD HEALTH ORGANIZATION, SUICIDE IS ONE OF THE TOP THREE
CAUSES OF DEATH AMONG 15- TO 24-YEAR-OLDS. CURRENT STATISTICS INDICATE THAT
GAY TEENS ARE THREE TIMES MORE LIKELY TO ATTEMPT SUICIDE
THAN THEIR HETEROSEXUAL PEERS. OFTEN THESE YOUNG PEOPLE HAVE NO ONE TO TALK
TO ABOUT THEIR FEELINGS AND TURN TO SUICIDE.

THE MOST VITAL WORK OF THE TREVOR PROJECT IS CONDUCTED THROUGH **THE TREVOR
HELPLINE, 866.4.U.TREVOR,** THE NATION'S ONLY 24-HOUR, 365-DAY-A-YEAR,
TOLL-FREE HELPLINE DEDICATED TO SUICIDE PREVENTION AMONG GAY AND QUESTIONING
YOUTH. THE HELPLINE FIELDS THOUSANDS OF CALLS FROM ALL OVER THE COUNTRY
EACH YEAR.

IN ADDITION, **WWW.THETREVORPROJECT.ORG** HAS IMPORTANT INFORMATION
ON IDENTIFYING SUICIDAL SIGNS, HOW TO ASSIST SOMEONE WITH SUICIDAL TENDENCIES,
AS WELL AS RESOURCES FOR MORE DETAILED INFORMATION. THE TREVOR PROJECT ALSO
CREATED THE **TREVOR SURVIVAL KIT,** AVAILABLE TO EDUCATORS FREE OF CHARGE
ON THE WEB SITE.

THE TREVOR PROJECT IS RELIANT ON THE GENEROUS SUPPORT OF ITS DONORS AND
VOLUNTEERS WHOSE INVOLVEMENT ENSURE THE ONGOING STABILITY OF THE ORGANIZATION.

THE TREVOR PROJECT THANKS THE EDITORS AND CONTRIBUTORS OF **GIRLS WHO LIKE
BOYS WHO LIKE BOYS** FOR THEIR GENEROSITY AND VOTE OF CONFIDENCE IN OUR
LIFE-SAVING SERVICES. YOUR SUPPORT IN PURCHASING THIS BOOK WILL ALLOW US TO
CONTINUE IN OUR MISSION.

FOR MORE INFORMATION, PLEASE GO TO **WWW.THETREVORPROJECT.ORG.**

8581 SANTA MONICA BOULEVARD, SUITE 558, WEST HOLLYWOOD, CALIFORNIA 90069
310.271.8845 T   310.271.8846 F